SAMURAI
WISDOM

Thomas Cleary

SAMURAI WISDOM

Lessons From Japan's Warrior Culture

Five Classic Texts on Bushido

TUTTLE PUBLISHING
Tokyo • Rutland, Vermont • Singapore

"Books to Span the East and West"

Tuttle Publishing was founded in 1832 in the small New England town of Rutland, Vermont [USA]. Our core values remain as strong today as they were then—to publish best-in-class books which bring people together one page at a time. In 1948, we established a publishing office in Japan—and Tuttle is now a leader in publishing English-language books about the arts, languages and cultures of Asia. The world has become a much smaller place today and Asia's economic and cultural influence has grown. Yet the need for meaningful dialogue and information about this diverse region has never been greater. Over the past seven decades, Tuttle has published thousands of books on subjects ranging from martial arts and paper crafts to language learning and literature—and our talented authors, illustrators, designers and photographers have won many prestigious awards. We welcome you to explore the wealth of information available on Asia at **www.tuttlepublishing.com**.

Published by Tuttle Publishing, an imprint of Periplus Editions (HK) Ltd.

www.tuttlepublishing.com

Copyright © 2009 by Thomas Cleary

Library of Congress Cataloging-in-Publication Data

Samurai wisdom : lessons from Japan's warrior culture / translated by Thomas Cleary. -- 1st ed.
    p. cm.
  Includes bibliographical references (p. [249]-250) and index.
  ISBN 978-0-8048-4008-8 (hardcover)
1. Bushido--Early works to 1800. 2. Military art and science--Japan--Early works to 1800. 3. Martial arts--Japan--Early works to 1800. I. Cleary, Thomas F., 1949- II. Tsugaru, Kodo, 1682-1729. Buji teiyo. English. III. Yamaga, Takatsune, 1650-1713. Budo teiyo. English. IV. Yamaga, Soko, 1622-1685. Selections. English. 2009.
  BJ971.B8S24 2009
  170'.440952--dc22

2008036913

ISBN 978-4-8053-1293-3

Distributed by

North America, Latin America & Europe
Tuttle Publishing
364 Innovation Drive
North Clarendon, VT 05759-9436 U.S.A.
Tel: 1 (802) 773-8930
Fax: 1 (802) 773-6993
info@tuttlepublishing.com
www.tuttlepublishing.com

Japan
Tuttle Publishing
Yaekari Building, 3rd Floor
5-4-12 Osaki, Shinagawa-ku
Tokyo 141 0032
Tel: (81) 3 5437-0171
Fax: (81) 3 5437-0755
sales@tuttle.co.jp
www.tuttle.co.jp

Asia Pacific
Berkeley Books Pte. Ltd.
3 Kallang Sector #04-01
Singapore 349278
Tel: (65) 6741-2178
Fax: (65) 6741-2179
inquiries@periplus.com.sg
www.tuttlepublishing.com

First edition
25 24 23 22   8 7 6 5 4

Printed in Malaysia   2206VP

TUTTLE PUBLISHING® is a registered trademark of Tuttle Publishing, a division of Periplus Editions (HK) Ltd.

Contents

BOOK TWO: **The Warrior's Rule**

By Tsugaru Kodo-shi

BOOK THREE: **Essentials of Military Matters**
Compiled by Yamaga Takatsune

BOOK FOUR: **The Education of Warriors**
By Yamaga Soko

BOOK FIVE: **Primer of Martial Education**
By Yamaga Soko

INTRODUCTION

Bushido: The Way of the Samurai Warrior

The warrior culture of the Japanese samurai caste, emerging from centuries of civil war and martial law, produced a complex blend of philosophy and self-discipline now called *Bushido*, the Way of the Warrior. This name is a combination of terms for samurai training systems coined in the 17th century, when the third dynasty of warlords completed military control over Japan and Bushido was articulated as an elite way of life.

An essential purpose of Bushido was to balance the civil and martial aspects of personal, social, and political organization of the samurai regime. The need for this balance was articulated in terms of restraining martial prowess from degenerating into aggression while preventing civil deference from deteriorating into weakness. In between the poles of war and peace, however, lay unavoidable uncertainties in the warrior's way, giving rise to divergent paths in practice. The philosophical spectrum of Bushido therefore represents a diverse range of attempts to confront contradictions generated by disparities between civil and military experience and outlook.

When Bushido was developed as a distinct domain of discipline, a critical concern for the leaders of the dominant warrior class was to preserve their authority within a civil state while maintaining terms of truce among themselves. This implied honing their secular skills while maintaining their martial discipline and military preparedness.

The civil authority of the samurai caste required attention to public opinion, imagery and appearance, as well as to social organization and legal structures. Redefining the role of the samurai in society, Bushido came to emphasize conceptions of moral and intellectual leadership along with martial supremacy. Its literature abounds in prescriptions for the education of the warrior class, to prepare samurai technically for advisory, administrative, and judicial roles in governing bodies, and to prepare them ethically for leadership and social service by instilling personal and professional values of civility, dignity, integrity, and nobility of character and conduct. In this manner the samurai developed new syntheses of the traditional doctrines of Confucianism, Buddhism, and Shinto.

Confucianism and Bushido

The civil side of Bushido, both personal and professional, was steeped in the world view and social outlook of Confucianism, which had been a standard source of political discourse for centuries before samurai took over the reins of government.

Confucianism originated in pre-imperial China during a time of accelerating civil and political disintegration, as an educational endeavor aiming for cultural renaissance and moral reform. Subsequently systematized to train bureaucrats in imperial China, state-sponsored Confucianism became a powerful conservative force in its allegiance to political authority and social order.

As a doctrine for samurai in their capacity as civil servants, Bushido draws on the Confucian belief that leaders should cultivate personal character, conduct, and capacities emotionally, intellectually, and morally so as to be able to perform their public duties ably and impartially, order their peer relations peacefully, and earn the admiration, allegiance, and obedience of their people.

One of the central concerns of Confucianism is the preparation of people for public service. This orientation stimulated and guided the development of education throughout East Asia, creating a cultural foundation for secular humanism with an underlying ideology of social responsibility. The purpose of education, in this view, was not to encourage abstract intellectual endeavor for its own sake, but to mold the character of political leaders, civil servants, and socially responsible citizens. Government was not merely an administrative exercise, but an extension of personal character and conduct.

The basic Confucian construction of the individual as an intrinsically social being underlies a species of secular humanism as well as an acceptance of hierarchical authoritarianism. This sense of organic connection between the person and the state, and the responsibility structure conceived to flow from that relationship, are fundamental to the Confucian outlook. Confucian doctrine was commonly typified as the practice of specific civic virtues in the context of certain central social and political relationships. The system is essentially hierarchical, ranking people by status, age, and gender, all of which made it seem suitable for the samurai structure.

The original Confucian concept of government envisions the individual and collective internalization of moral values as the key element of social order, without which, according to Confucius, the external imposition of law would foster cynicism and hypocrisy. This was to change with time, however, as later Confucians declared human beings intrinsically unruly and adopted an approach to order based on punishment and reward, similar in this respect to the Chinese doctrine of Legalism, which emphasized the absolute rule of law.

Study of history, literature, and ritual formed an important part of Confucian practice, whether of the old ethical model or the imperial authoritarian type, as education was believed to develop capacity and conscience in the individual as a member of society. The idea that government should be based on character and ability inspired the establishment of state schools and official examination systems to recruit scholars into civil service. In Japan, before the rise of the samurai warlords, this concept was originally applied to developing a sector of the ancient theocratic clan aristocracy into a cadre of educated officials to administer a secular bureaucratic state.

For the Japanese warrior caste, Confucianism would provide a principal source of concepts of civic virtue, critical to the development of Bushido as code of conduct for samurai. As the dominant intellectual tradition of state ideology and social science in China, Confucianism was formally introduced to official Japanese political discourse by the 7th century, in the process of developing a central-ized bureaucratic state on the Chinese model.

After the reunification of long-divided China under the Sui dy-nasty in the late sixth century, the Japanese regent Prince Shotoku (574-622) inaugurated the practice of sending missions to absorb Chinese culture, law, and organizational methods. One of the most revered figures in Japanese legend and history, Prince Shotoku is credited with composing the first constitution of Japan. Promul-gated in 604, this document extols typical Confucian virtues of harmony, obedience, cooperation, courtesy, and consultation, while decrying factionalism, fractiousness, and anti-social self-interest.

To inculcate these values, a state university was founded by the end of the century to train scions of the ruling class for civil ser-vice. Confucian ideology can soon be seen in the announcements of Japanese emperors themselves. A declaration by Emperor Tenchi (r. 661-671), in whose reign the college system is believed to have begun, reflects a classical Confucian contract model of authority, in which the devotion of the ruler to the welfare of the people is asserted to legitimate the demand of the ruler for the obedience of the people:

> Those who wish to help myriad people punish one person, while those who wish to kill myriad people pardon one person. We con-stantly belabor Our mind for the sake of myriad people; even in minor matters such as the poetry We recite, there is nothing but concern for the suffering multitudes. As the parents of the nation, how can We not be concerned for the children of the country? As children, do not disobey your parents' instructions!

The concept of societal responsibility of rulership is even more pro-nounced in a declaration by Emperor Saga (r. 809-823), in terms reminiscent of the humanist Confucian sage Mencius,[1] a central source of Bushido philosophy:

---

[1] Mencius: Meng He, one of the most important of the early Confucian philosophers, very commonly cited in Taoist, Zen, and Bushido texts. Mencius lived from about 372 to 289 BCE, in the latter days of China's turbulent Warring States era. He is particularly known for the doctrine of the goodness of human nature.

> We indicate to rulers of men after Us, that rather than punish the country's deviants, instead consider the poverty of the multitudes and relieve their misery, and then criminals will disappear. The reason why ordinary people act badly comes from widespread inability to survive day to day. There is no source of criminality in the country but waste of natural resources. There is a reason why ignorant underclasses are not honest; it's because the rulers, who should be honest, are not.

The imperial college burned down in 1177 and was never rebuilt. In 1180, a widespread civil war erupted, consuming nearly a decade. In the midst of this turbulence, a separate military government was set up between 1182 and 1185 by a dominant faction of warriors, lead by the Minamoto clan. This organization never dismantled the imperial system, and couldn't command all the samurai in Japan, but the general pattern of domination by military rule that it confirmed would continue for centuries, under three successive dynasties of warlords: the Kamakura Era (1185-1333) under the Minamoto and Hojo clans; the Muromachi Era (1338-1573) under the Ashikaga clan, and the Edo or Tokugawa Era (1603-1867) under the Tokugawa clan.

After the ascendancy of the warriors was established, emperors still declared their own rank in terms redolent of Chinese myths of ancient sage kings of Confucian ideal. A proclamation by Emperor Hanazono (r. 1308-18) asserts,

> We always reproach Ourselves rather than Our subjects, so We do know the Divine Order. As We think of close retainers and the multitudes of the people with the same attitude with which We think of Ourselves, there is no deviation; what is regrettable is for someone who is a leader to spend a whole lifetime insincerely. For one who is a mirror to others, to become a warning to others is a truly lamentable matter. Let Our posterity understand this well and clarify the path of the Emperor, and you will last as long as sky and earth.

Emperor Komatsu the Latter (r. 1382-1412) also preached the same principle of ruler-subject solidarity, espousing the classical Confucian policy of meritocracy and the neo-Confucian emphasis on austerity as means of executing this sovereign responsibility to the citizenry:

> When the masters of the earth experience happiness and suffering along with the people, make an ally of the sincerity of the deities, and regard extraordinary amusements as enemies, then there will be no sorrowing people in the nation. When there are no idle lords in the country, and they heed and employ the wise even from among the lower classes, while rejecting the dishonest even among the upper classes, they will endure as long as heaven and earth.

Like the emperors of Japan, as masters of the military governments the Shoguns patronized Confucian learning for civil service training. The samurai leaders favored a new genre of Confucianism, however, introduced to Japan in the 12th and 13th centuries by Zen Buddhist pilgrims and Chinese refugees. Girding the Confucian ethical structure with elements of Taoist metaphysics and Zen meditation, this neo-Confucianism elevated the ideological status of the social order to that of natural law, and cemented its views in the individual by the practice of sustained mental concentration.

While this neo-Confucian philosophy is very prominent in the writings of Bushido, Japanese political thinkers also echoed a harder line of Confucianism incorporating elements of Legalism. Legalism was the ideology of the first Chinese empire, emphasizing primary production, military power, and rule of law. Legalistic Confucianism, historically considered more pragmatic, is woven into the political science of the warriors' rule in Japan.

Emerging in a time of pandemic civil war in pre-imperial China, legalistic Confucianism bases its belief in the need for education, authority, and the rule of law on the premise that human nature is not basically good but bad. Like pure Legalism, this genre of Confucianism also emphasizes the need for practical adaptation to the times rather than idealization of ancient models.

Legalistic Confucianism was never abandoned by Shoguns in their capacity as lawgivers and their outlook as warriors. After the termination of the second military government through a series of civil wars, however, the early humanistic idealism of classical Confucianism was again memorialized in the laws promulgated by the warlord Oda Nobunaga, who virtually unified Japan in the late 16th century.

Stressing the importance of Confucianism for warriors in particular, Oda's legal code *Kanto Hatto*, or *Laws for Eastern Japan* cites the popular Confucian philosopher Mencius to announce a new social order:

> *Widowers, widows, the alone and the orphaned, are the most destitute people in the nation, having no resort.* Their condition is most pitiful. It is my deepest wish to be able to be compassionate to them. If any such people have public concerns, they should be able to have them considered, but in latter days lords and ministers have been unprincipled, indulging in aggressive exercise of power, devouring the weak. If there are complaints from any of those destitute people, relatives and friends will also be held responsible. For it is said that the government of sages extends its benefits even to insects—how could it not include human beings?

In this code, promulgated in 1583, Oda officially designated Confucianism the tradition to civilize the warrior class, asserting its emphasis on education essential to the civil side of Bushido:

> Men with the natural capacity to be prime ministers and generals are most important. If there are men like this, they should study Confucianism. The latter-day focus on military science alone is due to failure to evaluate profit and loss in learning. Since we use the expression Bun-Bu, Civil and Military, whose business is this if not those who rule countries and keep peace in the world?
>
> So it was that Confucius, to curb the forcefulness of a disciple in government service, defined six corruptions:
>
> *If you like benevolence but not learning, the corruption from that is folly.*
> *If you like wit but not learning, the corruption from that is license.*
> *If you like trust but not learning, the corruption from that is theft.*
> *If you like straightforwardness but not learning, the corruption from that is strangulation.*
> *If you like bravery without learning, the corruption from that is disorder.*
> *If you like strength without learning, the corruption from that is wildness.*
>
> Furthermore, the idea that only Buddhists pursue scholarship is arbitrary. To have even one scholar among warriors is most important.

Oda's military and political achievements were to be brought to a conclusion by Tokugawa Ieyasu (1542-1616), who founded the third

Shogunate in the early 17th century. Following Oda's lead in espousing Confucianism, Ieyasu built a college for the neo-Confucian scholar Hayashi Razan (1583-1657). Hayashi also served as a secretary of state and advisor to the first three Shoguns of the Tokugawa regime.

A general conception of the contemplated Confucian contribution to the melding of civil and military concepts in Bushido, extending even to the point of virtual identification of civic and martial virtues, is set forth by the famous scholar Kaibara Ekken (1630-1714), couched in Confucian terms addressed to warriors:

> Warriorhood has roots and branches. Loyalty, filial piety, duty, and courage are the roots of military science; these are martial virtues. Discipline and strategy are military sciences. Discipline refers to the disposition of troops and the way to carry out a military campaign, or what is referred to as martial law. The techniques of weaponry, such as sword, archery, spear, and so on, are the branches of military science; these are martial arts.
>
> It is best to include both roots and branches. Martial arts are rooted in military science, military science is rooted in humanity and justice. It is imperative to know these three elements, understand their order, and know their relative importance.
>
> If you cannot include these three things, then you should strive for the martial virtues of loyalty, filial piety, duty, and principle. If they have the courage of loyalty, filial piety, duty, and principle, even people who do not know martial arts often perform feats in war that earn them a warrior's reputation. And even those who do know martial arts can hardly achieve anything in war or win the repute of a warrior if they are cowardly.
>
> Superior people work on the roots. Hence the saying, when the roots are established, the Way grows. While martial arts are indeed to be learned and not to be abandoned, their practice has to be rooted in martial virtues. It is imperative to realize that there are differences in comparative importance.
>
> Loyalty and righteousness, and strength and courage, also have roots and branches. Master Cheng said, "People have to have a humane and just mind before they can have the spirit of humanity and justice." A humane and just mind is the root; strength and courage are the spirit of humanity and justice, the branches. If you have a heart of humanity and justice, courage will come of itself. If they are inclined to martial bravery without humanity or justice, powerful people will start rebellions, while little people will become bandits. Samurai who have no aspiration to loyalty, filial piety, or duty are

negligent of martial courage and lack morality, so they are incompetent for public service. Also, those who are born in samurai families but don't know military methods or martial arts, are not armed, and are lacking in military preparedness, will be negligent in striving for martial bravery.

Confucian doctrines were woven into samurai education and culture at various levels, from professors and advisers and tutors of lords to local schoolteachers and physicians, in an attempt to guide the pacification of society and reformation of culture through the support of the moral, ideological, and intellectual underpinnings of Bushido. The civilizing purpose, central implementation, and social impact of this policy on the Tokugawa period is summarized in retrospect at the end of the era by Saito Totsudo (1797-1865), an outstanding activist in civil and military education:

> When the late Tokugawa Ieyasu began to govern the country, he thought it a wretched thing that people's hearts had been so violent since the Muromachi regime, with even retainers assassinating their lords and sons murdering their fathers in many cases; so in order that people might know the Way, he recruited Confucians and promoted learning, having many classics and histories printed and widely circulated. Thus famous scholars emerged, beginning with people from the imperial house and the great ministers, as well as lords and barons outside, eventually bringing about the present state of peace. This is as different from the illiterate era of the Muromachi regime as day is from night. The fact that this peace has never been disrupted since it was established, compared to the chronic disorder of the Muromachi regime, is like the difference between sky and earth. The excellence of cultured qualities is evident.

While this emphasis on culture and civility among the samurai was considered essential to establish the peace and order of the Tokugawa regime, the concern that this could also contribute to softness and slackness in military matters is strongly marked in later Bushido, as illustrated by this same author, writing as the world of the Shoguns was confronted by the West after more than two hundred years of isolation:

Once the manner of a knight is correct, it is essential to cultivate the spirit of a knight. While maintaining the manner of a knight is for the purpose of cultivating the spirit of a knight, since manner is external, however magnificent it may be it can hardly be relied upon to any serious extent. A spirit that fills the body like blazing fire is somewhat more reliable. So the manner of a knight can only be truly strong when the spirit of the knight is flourishing. Even if your physical strength is more than average, if your spirit is weak you can't act in face of enemies; no matter how skillful you may be at martial arts, if your spirit is weak you cannot employ them against enemies.

An elementary tension between the martial and civil cultures upon which Bushido drew created a contradiction without a definite resolution, a fork in the road that could appear at any time.

While the civil culture of Confucianism emphasized in the ethical heritage of Bushido values honesty and transparency, the strategic science embedded in the martial culture of Bushido can call for deception and inscrutability. This internal tension amplified the potential for contradictory behavior deriving from the difference between the two main strains within Bushido, one emphasizing loyalty to the person of the leader and the other emphasizing loyalty to public or transpersonal ethical principles. Attempts to approach this problem in a systematic manner produced the seeds of rational and scientific study of human psychology and behavior, society and civilization.

Buddhism and Bushido

For samurai in their capacity as military men, Buddhism was of particular interest in relation to self-transcendence and acceptance of death, professional requirements of warriors. Buddhism also provided principles of personal and political morality, and had a long history of cultural contribution in Japan before the rise of the samurai caste.

While advocating the civic virtues of Confucianism, elevating the state over the clan, Prince Shotoku's constitution promoted Buddhism as a universal source of social uplift and a species of state religion. The first major Buddhist monastic establishment in Japan was completed in 607, shortly after the promulgation of the constitution, and the state sponsored several scholastic schools of Buddhism, welcoming learned monks from Korea and China.

Conceived of in the available Shinto and Confucian terms, Buddhism was patronized in hopes of both magical and intellectual support of the state. In this capacity, as much a political tool as a cultural or religious instrument, the early Buddhist orders in Japan formed an elite institution, a parallel aristocracy, which would ultimately acquire immense authority, both within and without the secular state structure.

In 794 a new capital was built in Japan on the model of the capital city of Tang dynasty China, the fabled metropolis of Chang-an, whose name means Eternal Peace. This new imperial capital of Japan [modern Kyoto] was called Heian-jo, or City of Peace, and was to remain the capital city and center of a wealthy and colorful aristocratic culture for nearly four centuries.

Two dynamic new schools of Buddhism centered in the surrounding mountains were also founded around this time, the Tendai school in 788 and the Shingon school in 816. These schools were to become extremely prosperous and powerful, providing a subsidiary system of ownership, rank, and privilege for aristocrats who were not in line for higher appointments in the imperial bureaucracy.

Buddhist ordination also became a refuge for emperors who formally retired into a religious order to maneuver behind the scenes through a system of shadow government referred to as the *Insei* or Cloister Administration. As stakeholders in the secular world, major Buddhist monasteries came to maintain their own militias, the so-called *sohei*, "soldiers of the sangha," armies of monks, to support their territorial and political interests.

The syncretic Shingon school, which contributed greatly to the development of Japanese culture, including literature, music, and art, also fortified the arsenals of warriors and would-be assassins with magical weaponry. The name of the school, Shingon, means True Word, a translation of the Sanskrit word Mantra, meaning a mystic spell. Addressed to every conceivable purpose, mystic spells include items of special interest to warriors, formulas for destruction of enemies, incantations alleged to produce madness, incapacitation, alienation, illness, and death.

Given the symbiotic relationship of politics and religion in Japan, the complexity of the clan structure, and the preexisting Shinto practice of *noroi* or curse-casting, the esoteric slaying spells of Shingon held a particular allure for the Japanese aristocracy. This interest intensified with the rise of the martial caste and the increasing militarization of Shingon Buddhism, so much so that concern with this dark side of Buddhism began to emerge in the literature of exoteric schools.

Eventually the question of magical murder was addressed by one of the greatest of Japanese Zen masters in a dialogue with a famous warrior and administrator in a vernacular classic of Japanese Buddhism, called *Muchu Mondo*, or *Dream Conversations*. First published in 1344, during the lifetime of the author, this book represents replies of Zen master Muso Soseki (1275-1351), to the inquiries of Ashikaga Tadayoshi (1306-1352), a distinguished war commander and civil administrator who was a younger brother, erstwhile ally, and ultimately victim of Ashikaga Takauji (1305-1358), founder and first Shogun of the second military dynasty. The Zen master explains esoteric killing to the warrior in these terms:

> In the esoteric sect, the method called *subduing* means using secret arts to subdue the minds of malevolent and misguided people, to introduce them to the true principles of Buddhism. Sometimes, when people who interfere with Buddhism cannot be converted from their evil designs no matter what, first they are deprived of their lives to enable the true religion to remain in the world, then expedients are used to introduce even those evil people into Buddhism.
>
> Sometimes someone is seen to be prevented from entering Buddhism by the aggravation of others' enmity, so his enemies are subdued to enable him to enter into Buddhism. When bodhisattvas practice this sort of antisocial action, it is always for the sake of promoting religion and helping people. It is not for worldly fame or profit.
>
> The *Nirvana Scripture* says, "When Shakyamuni Buddha was a king in a past state, there were a large number of evil monks who did all sorts of bad things to a monk who practiced true religion and excited their jealousy. At that time the king himself fought those

evil monks, defeated them, and rescued the monk who practiced true religion. He incurred no sin in doing so, because his intention was only to spread true religion." This was also the reason why Prince Shotoku of our country attacked Mononobu Moriya, who opposed Buddhism.

If you have no intention of spreading true religion, but just pray in order to assassinate your enemies to flourish in the world yourself, as a result of your action you won't be able to keep the world for long. There will also be ill consequences to come in the future. The *Nirvana Scripture* says, "To requite enmity with enmity is like using oil to put out a fire."

Some people say it is a sin to kill with weapons but a virtue to kill with the power of esoteric spells. This is a major heresy. Even killing with weapons is indeed virtuous if it is done with an intention, like that of Shakyamuni Buddha in the past, of destroying evil monks for the spread of true religion, and Prince Shotoku's attack on Moriya. But even if esoteric methods of religion are employed, if your interest is in worldly name and gain, it is all sinful. This is what is meant by the statement of the *Brahmajala Scripture* forbidding murder, "even killing by spells."

Since Buddhist establishments were themselves worldly powers, and different sects disputed and disagreed about which version of Buddhism was true, legitimizing magical murder by the intention to protect Buddhism did not necessarily add moral clarity to the matter in the eyes of all alike. A similar doctrine of the end justifying the means had already been articulated nearly a century earlier to rationalize violence in Buddhism by the Tendai monk Nichiren (1222-1282), who founded the sect now bearing his name. Nichiren made a parallel argument regarding material weaponry in his seminal work *Rissho Ankoku Ron*, or *Treatise on Establishing Orthodoxy and Securing the State:*

> The *Nirvana Sutra* says, "Those who would preserve true religion should not be subject to the five precepts [forbidding murder, theft, adultery, lying, and drinking alcohol] and not cultivate their conduct, but carry weapons." It also says, "Those who keep the five precepts cannot be called members of the Great Vehicle. Protecting true religion, even without keeping the five precepts, is called the Great Vehicle. Protectors of the religion should carry arms. Even though they carry arms, I call this keeping the precepts."

The *Nirvana Scripture* these passages cite was composed after the destruction of the magnificent Kushan empire, wherein Buddhism had reached a peak of sophistication emanating throughout Asia. While the Japanese Buddhists of the middle ages were not likely aware of its original context, the scripture's emphasis on the imminent extinction of the religion seemed to resonate with them in terms of their own turbulent times. Nichiren had a particularly keen sense of national and international crisis, accurately predicting that the Mongolian warlords who were taking over China would try to invade Japan.

While destructive spells were supposedly esoteric, their existence was evidently well known by the middle ages, when the samurai were the masters of the land and their outlook as warriors became a dominant paradigm. A popular aspect of this magical lore and the society that embraced it is illustrated in a story in *Shaseki-shu,* or *Collection of Stone and Sand,* an anthology compiled by Zen master Muju (1226-1312):

> A woman came to a Shingon master she'd believed in for years and said, "Are there any spells in Shingon to kill people? Please teach me."
> He asked, "What for?"
> She said, "My husband always cared deeply for me, but now he's infatuated with a young thing and has abandoned me, much to my dismay. I'm even the mother of his children! I couldn't be more betrayed! So tell me."
> This is something that is difficult to deal with. The methods of subduing are for subduing and slaying enemies of the whole world, out of compassion. To kill simply out of spite is not right.
> Thinking it would be very sinful to abet her by teaching her how to kill, instead he taught her a life-prolonging spell and told her it was a slaying spell.
> Delighted, she believed him and did the incantation for the required period. Afterwards she came back and said, "Even if it's the Last Age of the religion, the efficacy of Shingon spells is still there! I recited it for a full seven days, and killed him!"
> He was appalled, but there was nothing he could do about it.
> According to a certain Shingon master, this actually happened. How much more useful the effect would be if one believed and acted upon the truth! Indeed, since there's a way of imbuing a single spell with a plethora of powers, there can be no doubt that one can both prolong life and kill as well.

This story suggests a certain understanding of the psychological foundation of the curse, yet it is not invoked to dismiss the phenomenon as unreal, but rather as reason enough for conscious concern with the practice and its employment. The justification of defeating enemies of the whole world seems to be more universal in principle than Muso's appeal to protection of Buddhism, but in practice, given the warlike world-view of the samurai era, the expression "enemies of the whole world" is no more self-defining than "enemies of Buddhism," and as such could likewise be subjected to different interpretations by competing interests.

While monastic armies of the middle ages were maintained by major institutions, popular Buddhist militias also developed among the lower classes, including local samurai, fortified by community faith. Followers of devotional Nichiren and Pure Land sects successfully established autonomous areas in these war-torn times, some for as long as a hundred years or more. While very different in outlook, Nichiren and Pure Land sects both employed methods of concentration that could produce auto-hypnosis and obliterate fear of pain and death. The fortitude of Nichiren bonzes under torture is legendary, while Pure Land devotees fought warlords with an unearthly abandon enabled by ecstatic faith in the reward of paradise after death.

Given the difference in manpower and morale between community-based militias and mercenary coalitions of professional warriors, in the end only treachery proved powerful enough to destroy the popular Buddhist uprisings and the autonomous areas they established in the middle ages. The 16th century overlord Oda Nobunaga fought to break the power of organized Buddhism at all levels of society. The Tokugawa Shogunate subsequently legislated strict secular controls on Buddhist institutions, with dictates extending even to doctrine and practice, in order to neutralize any residual independence, and convert the monastic system into an administrative organ of state.

While most of the military action associated with Buddhism thus emanated from other schools, Zen Buddhism has traditionally been associated with Bushido through the patronage of Zen sects by the military class. In one sense this patronage provided the samurai regimes with a cultural and intellectual base distinct from the aristocrats they supplanted, who had largely been devotees of the Tendai and Shingon schools. Zen was also more austere and less philosophical than the older schools, suiting the temperament, times, and training of the warriors in these ways.

The Rinzai sect of Zen in particular typically used strong and violent language in its manner of presentation, including frequent references to techniques of psychological disengagement in terms of "killing" and "dying." This rhetoric conformed to the robust impression that warriors wished to cultivate and convey, and provided a conceptual framework within which to convert the inherent hazards of their profession into means of mental training.

Zen Buddhism was also the original source of neo-Confucian education for warriors in Japan. Neo-Confucianism contains an element of Zen in itself, as every one of the Chinese founders of neo-Confucianism studied Chan, the Chinese precursor of Zen. Adapted to active lay life, rejecting monasticism and celibacy, nihilism and quietism, neo-Confucianism integrated Zen-type techniques of everyday mindfulness into the fabric of Bushido discipline.

Shinto and Bushido

While hearkening back to the origins of Japanese civilization, the special Shinto element in Bushido is a comparatively late development in the history of samurai culture. Representing an emerging sense of national identity in the isolation imposed on Japan by the Shogun in the seventeenth century, revival of interest in ancient Shinto lore aimed to slough off an ingrained inferiority complex associated with the age-old influence of Chinese culture. In terms of samurai political philosophy, this insistence on distinguishing Japanese tradition was critical to the promulgation of an orthodox rationale for permanent military rule, in contrast to the classical Chinese Confucian ideal of a secular state.

The background and atmosphere of this intellectual evolution is illustrated by one of the early expositors of the new nativism, Yamaga Soko (1622-1685):

> All along I've been fond of foreign [i.e. Chinese] books. Though I know nothing of books that have newly arrived in recent times, by laboring day and night I've read most of the books that came from abroad up until ten years ago. Because of this, unawares I thought all foreign things were good. I thought that since Japan is a small country, it cannot match up to China in anything; and that it was in China that sages emerged.
>
> I was not the only one like this; all scholars past and present have thought this way, admiring China and studying China. Recently I have come to realize this way of thinking is very mistaken, trusting our ears but not our eyes, abandoning the nearby and taking to the remote. It is hopeless, truly an academic epidemic, an affliction common to scholars.
>
> Although I've recorded this in *Facts of the Central Court*, I'll set down a summary here. This court [of Japan] is descended from the Goddess Who Lights the Sky; its direct lineage has never deviated, even for one generation, from the divine age up to the present day. Even the assisting ministers from the Fujiwara clan have continued in unbroken succession, generation after generation, and administrators in charge of government have been continuous, because there have been no rebellious subjects or usurping sons. Is this not due to great richness of virtues of humaneness and justness?
>
> Next, from the divine age up to the seventeenth generation human sovereign was a succession of rulers who all had the virtues of sages. Wise and talented ministers assisted them, establishing the Way of heaven and earth. The administrative business of the court, the establishment of the system of provinces and prefectures, the manners of the four classes of people, daily activities, clothing, food, housing, even ceremonies of capping, marriage, mourning, and celebration, each attained balance. With the people at ease and the nation at peace, a model for myriad ages was established, the roles of superior and subordinate defined—is this not attainment of the celestial virtue of the brilliant knowledge of sages?

Yamaga initiated the practice of calling Japan the Central Civilization or the Central Nation while referring to China as a "foreign country," yet his work remains saturated with Confucianism, and his ethical values derive from that background, even in his elevated judgment of the imperial dynasty of Japan. From the standpoint of a military man, however, the decline and fall of the massive and once mighty Ming China in his own time must have suggested an alarming failure of the Chinese system.

The Shoguns continued to support Confucianism as orthodox state philosophy, nonetheless, and later Japanese thinkers also invoked Confucian values to affirm the significance of native Japanese tradition. While exalting the native martial spirit, for example, Rikimaru Tozan, writing in 1802, still refers to Chinese tradition to substantiate his position:

> When it comes to military science and martial achievement, over the long run, ever since ancient times when the celestial deities descended to rule, this was the Country Full of Slender Lances; the uncanny awe inspired by the superiority of the path of bow and arrow over all nations has never come to an end, even after thousands of generations. ....
>
> This country has never had any dynastic change, fortunately, so like the transmission of such things as divination methods that have disappeared in China, in the antiques of the divine age and the principles of bow and arrow there are many things that can be studied in our country that only exist in name in the classical Chinese canons and rites and cannot be concretely defined.
>
> In particular, even at the end of a millennium there exists a traditional practice of referring to the vocation of attacking criminals and rebels as the rank of the archer. In the ancient imperial administration there are memorials for official arrest. Moreover, there are rites of bow and arrow for nobles and lords.
>
> As a class, military clans are called *mononou*, which is construed to mean archers. This is what is meant in historical records when it says that the very name of *archer* is prized.
>
> From such an extensive array of references it can be seen that there are indeed connections.
>
> In recent times literati tend to dismiss our national heritage, but this is not appropriate. Even Chinese characters derive a lot of meanings from bow and arrow. In particular, even if it has been forgotten that the lord of a country is referred to by a character originally meaning an arrow target, to disregard one's own native country is like abandoning one's own parents and loving strangers, like abandoning one's own leader and giving allegiance to another country. It is already a violation of the principles of the *Classic of Filial Piety*.
>
> To emulate the virtues of other people, and learn from the excellence of foreign countries, is indeed the work of *daily renewal* and *abundant possession*, and our ancient kings already synthesized them. In spite of this, while being in a country with a splendid system, to

demean ourselves as *barbarians* and disregard our national heritage is an insult to the nation.

The Shinto vision of the unique unbroken continuity of the imperial lineage in Japan represents a reaction to the sense of political instability and weakness compelled by their perception of popular revolution, foreign subjugation, and dynastic change in China. Under the rule of the samurai of earlier times, Japan had suffered similar symptoms of fragmentation, revolt, and usurpation, even while embracing Confucian ideology. The 15th and 16th centuries were particularly violent and unstable, and by the end of the 16th century European powers were also complicating Japanese warfare and power politics.

Thinkers of 17th century Japan were therefore particularly concerned with establishing social stability, even at the cost of isolation and stasis, while maintaining a constant state of vigilance and discipline. These were among the conditions that stimulated the articulation of Bushido in the 17th and 18th centuries, after the pacification and stabilization of Japanese society and politics under the Tokugawa Shoguns. While the emergence of nativism among intellectuals would ultimately serve the interests of imperial restoration in the mid 19th century, disenfranchising the samurai, the original thrust of the argument made by nativist samurai scholars asserted the primal unity of civil and military government in Japan, proclaiming on this ground that Japan should properly be ruled by warriors in perpetuity. This position is summarized by Nakamura Mototsune (1778-1851) in his *Treatise on Honoring the Military*:

> Our nation is a martial state, whereas China is a literary state. A literary state honors literature, a martial state honors arms.
>
> For centuries in high antiquity, we had no usurpation by rebellious ministers, and no incursion of foreign invaders. Those above were secure, those below were at peace. With no problems in the four quarters, how did that government compare to the ancient Chinese sage rulers Yao and Shun? In those times, Confucianism had not yet been imported, Buddhism had not yet arisen—how could it have been as it was? Just because of the government of warriors. For our nation to have warriors is the natural course for our nation, and should be respected!

Even in China, the present is different from the past, as indeed it must be; how much the more is our country different from that country. Separated by hundreds of miles, the customs are completely different, and the psychologies of the peoples are not the same—how can they follow the same path? "Noble men cultivate the education without changing the customs; they make their government equal, without changing specific adaptations." So our country's military caste cannot be abandoned. Had Confucius rode a coracle over the sea, once he was in our country he would surely have considered the military noble, and would not necessarily have preferred literature. If we get mired in Chinese literature and don't follow our native ways, even if we call that studying the way of sages, how can it be called *knowing* the way of sages?

The great peace in our country in high antiquity was not due to Confucianism and Buddhism. The reason lies elsewhere. Our country has always been a martial state; so it flourishes with warriors and declines without warriors. The changing fortunes of our country are only a matter of the flourishing or decline of the warriors.

The Way of the Knight

Confucianism, Buddhism, and Shinto were each represented by a variety of schools, and elements of all three were commonly combined in Japanese culture and customs. This synthesis took many forms, intellectual and artistic, religious and political, ritual and literary. As the embodiment of samurai culture, Bushido is correspondingly diverse, drawing selectively on elements of all these traditions to articulate the ethos and discipline of the warrior.

One of the most influential of the early schools of Bushido was the knightly way of Yamaga Soko, who attempted to interpret and adapt the diverse threads of the Japanese heritage over a lifetime of study and teaching. A classical Confucian scholar as well as a military scientist and martial artist, Yamaga was also a student of Zen, Taoism, and Shinto. "There are many lines of learning, ancient and modern," he wrote, "so Buddhism, Confucianism, and Shinto each have some truth to them." In his teaching and writing he inculcated traditional social graces and spiritual disciplines while emphasizing martial virtues such as organization, vigilance, and self-mastery in the conduct of everyday life.

Above all, Yamaga Soko was a pragmatist, insisting on the need for practical adaptation of ideas and information rather than idealistic advocacy of ancient doctrines. A critical thinker, he rejected the school of neo-Confucianism patronized by the Shogun, and was banished from the capital city as a result. Though he eventually resumed residence and teaching in the capital, after his death an interdict was put on the printing of his writings, and his school began to go underground in the early 1700's after it was suggested that the famous vendetta of the Forty-Seven Ronin was inspired by his teaching.

Interest in Yamaga's immense body of work was renewed with a Bushido revival at the end of the 19th century, as Japan inaugurated its modern imperial age. Because of his emphasis on empirical knowledge and rational adaptation of tradition, while naturally rooted in the social structure and intellectual outlook of his era, Yamaga's work explicitly invokes and invites the same critical approach to study that he himself applied to the received classics as well as the particular problems of his time.

Both the mystique and the methods of martial rule in Yamaga's school are vividly transmitted in the manual *The Warrior's Rule* by Tsugaru Kodo-shi, one of Yamaga's grandsons, who studied the master's work for thirty years. Kodo-shi's father, Tsugaru Kenmotsu (1658-1682), had been a councilor to the lord of the Tsugaru domain, his older brother Tsugaru Nobumasa (1646-1710), who had first made the acquaintance of Yamaga Soko in 1660, when he was fifteen and Yamaga thirty-nine. Kenmotsu, married to one of Yamaga's daughters, died before Kodo-shi was born, and Yamaga, himself near the end of his life, took interest in the fatherless grandson's welfare.

For his part, Kodo-shi claimed to have conceived his lifelong interest in his grandfather's work on the day of his grandfather's funeral, which he attended as a small child, when he saw the emissaries of lords and grandees paying their respects. He eventually went into civil service himself, after which he wrote his compendium of martial philosophy and practice, outlining the principles of warrior rule. It is concise but deals with a wide range of subjects, providing an excellent introduction to this school of Bushido.

A parallel treatise focusing on military science, entitled *Essentials of Military Matters*, was compiled by Yamaga Takatsune, thought to have been a son-in-law of the master, based on Soko's own notes. This lineage connects Yamaga with some of the most famous names of samurai history, including the warlord Takeda Shingen and the swordsman Miyamoto Musashi. In military terms, the cardinal principle of this school was certain victory, and indeed Takeda Shingen is famed for having been undefeated in warfare, while Miyamoto Musashi is famed for having been undefeated in dueling. In this treatise, the school is referred to as the Kansuke School, after the legendary Yamamoto Kansuke (1493?-1561?), an infantry commander and teacher of military science for Takeda Shingen.

The political and military dimensions of samurai rule represented by *The Warrior's Rule* and *Essentials of Military Matters* are integrated in *The Education of Warriors*, a manual on samurai education by Yamaga Soko. Here the role of the samurai is introduced by a brief discourse on natural law, typically represented as the source of the system. This emphasis on natural law, derived from Taoism and incorporated into neo-Confucianism, was traditionally invoked to rationalize government, social structure, and warfare; in Yamaga's work natural law plays an important role as a perpetual point of reference and source of knowledge beyond ideology. On this basis, *The Education of Warriors* outlines the samurai's essential concerns of leadership, organization, and military strategy, while making the strongest possible statement against militarism per se.

As warriors first and last, the masters of this school of certain victory produced an enormous amount of writing on military science, but the question of morality emerges even in the wartime work of Yamamoto Kansuke, who invokes Shinto, Confucianism, Buddhism, and even medicine to rationalize the role of military science in a civilized society. With the advent of peace under the Tokugawa regime, the character and conduct of samurai were of central concern in respect to their civil roles as political leaders, administrators, and educators, while their origin as men of arms was never to be forgotten.

In developing his school of Bushido, Yamaga Soko wrestled with this peculiar problem of cultivating the capacities of war and peace in an integrated personality. Pursuing this theme in the context of individual responsibility, his brief *Primer of Martial Education* outlines samurai training as the fabric of the warrior's daily life, while his extensive *The Way of the Knight* expands on this comprehensive concept of the samurai way constituting a model of all-around personal development. He summarizes this inspiration himself, providing perhaps the best theoretical introduction to his own work, in his *Relic Writings from Exile*:

> As for lines of scholarship, there is elevation of character and cultivation of humaneness; there is concentration on meditation and quiet sitting; there is cultivating oneself and correcting others, bringing order and peace to society, achieving success and attaining fame; there is concentration on reading and writing. These are divided into higher, middling and lower, and develop into various kinds of knowledge.
>
> But what I think is that to move people by virtue of character so that the world corrects itself without anything being said, all within the four seas at peace with no effort made, cultivating cultural virtues so as to induce enemies to submit spontaneously, is a doctrine of the eras of the [ancient sages of China] the Yellow Emperor,[1] Yao,[2] and Shun, and something that cannot be emulated in latter days. Even if it is imitated in appearance, it has no effect.
>
> Due to this, scholars who entertain this idea have lofty aspirations, eventually turn their backs on society, go into mountain forests and become companions of birds and beasts.
>
> The logic of study of sages as I think of it is the aspiration to cultivate myself and correct others, bring order and peace to society, attain success and honor. The reason is that I have been born in a family of warriors, and while I personally have social relations, along with social relations there are matters pertaining to warriorhood, there are duties, beyond my own understanding and my own ways of doing things. The additional tasks associated with the warrior caste are of many kinds, great and small.

---

[1] The Yellow Emperor was a legendary sage ruler of prehistoric China, associated with the transmission of strategic arts as well as teachings on health, sex, and longevity. The Yellow Emperor is hero of Taoism. There is a very famous ancient text of strategy attributed to him, called *the Book of Hidden Correspondences*.

[2] Yao was a predynastic nonhereditary sage king of ancient China, traditionally said to have acceded to the throne in 2356 BCE. The three ancient kings Yao, Shun, and Yu constitute one of the most important images in Chinese political science.

Speaking in terms of small things, there are manners proper to warriors, including dress, diet, house construction, and the uses of equipment. In particular, there is practice of martial arts, and the design and use of weaponry, armor, and riding gear.

In terms of great things, there is the government of the land, including the varieties of rites and music; the system of provinces and prefectures; mountains and forests, seas and rivers, fields and gardens; disposition of public business and lawsuits of temples, shrines, and the four classes of citizens; political science, military science, rules of organization, battle formations, encampment, castle building, and combat methods. These are all everyday tasks of military leaders and warriors.

So when it comes to scholarship for the military caste, even if you cultivate yourself personally, unless you deal with these things effectively this is not the logic of the study of the sages. For this reason there is meditation on the foregoing matters, and there is contemplation of old records and ancient practices, and in addition there should be no relaxation of meditation practices such as silent recognition and quiet sitting.

Even so, this is not to say one is to develop exhaustive knowledge of every single one of this endless variety of tasks. As I have said before, when you know the ruler and mold of the study of sages, and fit into the standards and guidelines, you can understand what you see and comprehend what you hear, so whatever task comes up the way to consider what's involved is clear, so you don't get stumped when you face things.

This is the backbone of a man of mettle. It could indeed be called breadth of mind and relaxation of the body. When this study is continuous, wisdom is new every day, character spontaneously improves, humaneness is naturally enriched, and courage stands on its own. Eventually you reach the mystic realm where there is no contrivance, where there is neither success nor fame. So you enter from success and fame into where there is no success or fame, only fulfilling the path of being human.

BOOK ONE

The Way of the Knight

By Yamaga Soko

1. Establishing the Basis

Between sky and earth, humans and other beings are produced by the union of two energies. Humans are the most intelligent of all beings; humans are the most advanced of all beings.

Here, ever-reproducing humans may produce food by agriculture, or produce tools and goods by industry, or meet the needs of the world by commerce. So agriculture, industry, and commerce invariably arise together.

The samurai, however, eats without tilling, uses what he doesn't make, and earns without engaging in trade. Why is that?

As I reflect on my present status, I was born in a house of hereditary archers and cavaliers, and I am a public servant for the imperial court. I am one of those samurai, who do not till, manufacture, or trade. There must be a job for a samurai. Someone who eats without having a job should be called an idler.

We should turn our attention to ourselves and examine ourselves thoroughly. Who fulfills their nature by idleness, even be it plants and trees, lowly fish and insects, or birds and beasts, to say nothing of humans?

Birds and beasts fly and run to get food, fish and insects swim and swarm seeking food, plants and trees send their roots deep into the earth. Every one of them is preoccupied by the search for food, all the time, every day, all year long.

All beings are like this. In the human realm, farmers, artisans, and merchants are also like this. If it were possible to live out one's life without working, one should be called a thief of nature.

So why should knights have no occupation? Asking yourself this question, only by examining the work of a knight will the role of knights become evident. As long as you haven't given this any thought, as long as you just go by what people say or what is written in books, since you haven't realized it in your gut and heart, your aspiration is established on an extremely weak basis.

To say that aspiration is established on an extremely weak basis implies being indecisive and inwardly obscured by bad habits of longstanding. So how can the will for the Way be developed, slight as it is?

It should therefore be considered of primary importance to establish the basis of knighthood. To follow others' instructions according to your state of mind at the moment is like when you do something for a while but really can't get it done. Now if you concentrate on what I've said and seek to understand your role yourself, then the role of knighthood should become clear.

Generally speaking, the role of knights is in being personally conscientious, completely loyal in public service for a ruler, faithful in association with friends, and individually circumspect, concentrating on duty. Moreover, one inevitably has personal, family, and marital relations. Even if they are universal social norms, nevertheless farmers, artisans, and merchants cannot always follow that path to fulfillment because they are preoccupied by their work.

Knights focus on this path to the exclusion of agriculture, craft, and commerce, promptly penalizing anyone among the three civilian classes who disrupt social norms, so that natural norms will be upright everywhere. This means that knights have to have both cultural and martial virtues and expertise.

Thus, fulfilling the functions of sword and spear and bow and horse in punitive actions, practicing political, professional, social, familial, and spousal norms in the domestic sphere, with culture filling the heart while being prepared as a warrior for the outside world, they provide for knowledge of the fundamentals and the particulars, as the three civilian classes spontaneously take them for exemplars, respect them, and follow their instructions. With this the path of knighthood is fulfilled; you earn your food, clothing and housing, and so you can be easy in mind, for this can requite the benevolence of the ruler and the generosity of your parents in the meantime.

Without this effort, it's as if you are stealing the generosity of your parents, devouring a salary from your lord, spending your whole life as a thief. Those who do not understand this ought to become civilians at once, either tilling to eat, or making a living by crafts, or supporting themselves by trade. This way there will be less blame from heaven. If you insist on being a knight, hoping for public office, you should work at slavish common jobs with low salaries and little official reward, spending your whole life at easy jobs like guard duty and night watch. This is your role.

2. Aspiring to the Way

When people come to clarify their own role, there must be a way to perform that role, so here aspiration for the "way" should emerge. For example, when you want to go to Kyoto, you can't go without knowing the way there. If you insist on going without knowing the way, you'll inevitably take the wrong route. To know how to cultivate yourself as a knight, serve your lord, respect your father, and interact harmoniously with your siblings, spouse, and friends, must lie in finding out the way and knowing how to apply it.

So when you aspire to the Way, you take the initiative to find someone who is adept at it to be your guide. If the person who is to mentor you acts in a contradictory manner, or if he speaks plausibly but is unclear in responding to actualities, leave at once and do not follow him. When you are steeped in the instructions of a false teacher for a long time, without realizing it you'll become further and further from the Way under that person's influence.

If you find no wise mentor anywhere in spite of seeking to learn from others in this way, you should turn your attention inward on your own. Turning your attention inward means that because the way of the wise is a teaching mastered only by sole reliance on the inherence of natural qualities, without any forced contrivance, as long as you have something to set your will on, the thing can be learned, as you can find out the basic idea by yourself. This is especially so in view of the fact that sages of old have provided maxims to guide people. If you work carefully on these, you should be able to find the great way of the sages in them.

Everyone acknowledges the order of the five norms and knows that there is a way of knighthood, but some affirm themselves and think that's enough, while some seem to strive to no avail trusting false teachers. These things happen because their aspiration for the way is weak.

Isn't this attitude what Confucius meant by "aspire to the Way"—

there must be a way, something that cannot be expounded arbitrarily. If not for effective aspiration, there is no means of attaining the Way. So it is called aspiring to the Way.

People who have become somewhat familiar with the world and pretend to be savants impose definition on the Way they think exclusive, insisting on their subjective opinions, thus becoming further from the way, ultimately failing to gain entry into the Great Way.

So even if you know the role of knighthood, without aspiration for the Way you may have knowledge but do not put it into practice and so do not consummate it. It is imperative to examine the principle most thoroughly.

3. Striving to Put Aspiration into Practice

Master Zeng said, "A knight ought to be broad-minded and strong-willed. 'When the burden is heavy, the road is long.' Isn't it also weighty to make humaneness one's responsibility? Isn't stopping only at death also a long way to go?" If a knight is not broad-minded and tolerant, he cannot bear heavy burdens and cannot get far. Even if you know your role and aspire to that path, unless you put that aspiration into practice it is just talk, not reality. And even if you put it into practice, unless you strive at it all your life and stop only at death, you'll give up along the way. Then there's no possibility of attainment.

Therefore diligent application is considered bravery in a knight. Confucius said, "A noble man wants to be slow to talk but quick to act." He also said that talk is easy, while action is hard. When it comes to recognizing your professional role, establishing your will, even though we speak of aspiring to the Way and learning the process of the Way, the focus is on making the effort to put it into practice.

Even so, diligent practice is hard to accomplish with an ordinary will. Even a minor habit of slight importance is hard to change without enormous effort when you've become accustomed to it. In particular, between gain and loss, wayward urgings of sexual desire, and opportunities for fame, if you linger over them for long, there will be no end, and those thoughts will arbitrarily take the lead. At this point, unless you have great strength within yourself, you'll be dragged down, and unable to be completely sincere.

To bring forth great strength in yourself depends on the depth of your will. If your aspiration is shallow, your striving cannot be deep. As far as will is concerned, this will does not emerge if you do not examine yourself and register profound shame at what is unworthy of humanity in you.

Therefore in *The Mean* Confucius says, "To like learning is akin to knowledge; to put it into practice diligently is akin to benevolence; to be conscientious is akin to courage." Mencius said, "One whom riches and rank cannot corrupt, whom poverty and lowliness cannot compromise, and whom threat and force cannot inhibit—this is called a strong man."

Riches and rank are things people like a lot, poverty and lowliness are things people dislike a lot, and threat and force are things people fear a lot. If your mind sticks to them at all, you cannot be called a strong man. A strong man is one who sets his will on the way of the knight and steadily strives to put this aspiration into practice. Unless you work this way on its attentive correctness, the basis of knighthood cannot be said to stand.

4. Mental Techniques: Cultivating Mood and Maintaining Will

There is a natural endowment in people's dispositions. That is to say, some are born with a positive disposition, while others have a dark disposition. This is called the natural state.

So a tiger is born with stripes, a phoenix naturally has five colors, a fine steed can run a thousand miles without training, a crane has six wings on a chick, white jade is lustrous without polish, gold is inherently brighter than tile or stone. These are each natural characteristics, with nothing artificial.

People are the same way. They are born with some good in them, but those who have not developed and sustained it may be in some respect like the clear moon or bright sun, but in another respect a dark indifference develops. So unless people set aside what they've attained in order to remedy their ignorance, transforming their disposition this very day, they are not fully human.

Mencius said, "I am able to foster an expansive mood." Even Mencius, however, added that he found it hard to say what "expansive" means, so I can't tell you just what it is like now. But since the mind may be disturbed or troubled by mood, consider it a matter of realizing this and employing principles of cultivation so that you are not in a mood of neediness. When you foster an expansive mood, it should be magnanimous and firm, able to expand beyond myriad things, undaunted by anything.

Because the mind depends on the mood, when your mood is calm your mind is calm. When your mood is agitated, then your mind is agitated. Since the mind and the mood are not in two separate states, there is no disparity between them. As the mood exteriorizes the agitation of the mind within, cultivating your disposition should be considered the basis of personal refinement and soundness of mind.

Cultivating means assessing the excesses and insufficiencies in your natural disposition, reducing the excessive and developing the insufficient, balancing action and repose in the midst of things. This is done in everyday activities.

The human body is made of five elements, but the most important are water and fire. Water is blood, which is heavy; fire is energy, which is light. With these two, blood and energy, the physical body is effectively complete. Water circulates because of fire, fire sometimes goes out and sometimes flares up because of water. But water normally takes to moisture, while fire normally takes to dryness; their substances differ in rising and descending. That is why people's moods are excitable and emotive.

Understanding this, if you cultivate your mood to make its cycle harmonious by balancing activity and calmness, not allowing it to be excited at random, with no vanity in your attitude, your mind should thereby be free from random arousal or absentmindedness.

Big Heartedness

If a knight does not have the heart to take on the greatest enterprise in the world and independently exercise that immense responsibility, he won't be big-hearted enough, but will become petty and narrow-minded.

So to have a big heart means to make your heart so free as to admit everything in the world, like an immense river that knows no end, or a towering mountain that shelters plants and trees and birds and beasts. The sky is open, letting birds fly; the ocean is wide, letting fish leap. When it is said that a real man must have this bigness of heart, it seems to refer to this attitude.

Guo Linzong[1] said of Huang Xian[2] of the Latter Han dynasty, "He is immense, like a tidal wave. He cannot be stilled, he cannot be disturbed. He is immeasurable." Zhou Yi[3] of Jin said, in response to Wang Dao, "In here is empty, nothing, able to contain hundreds of your ilk." Each of these refers to the person's big heart. If your capacity is not as broad as this, your power won't be robust.

Power means calmly putting everything in order, subduing the four seas while conversing and laughing. The earth supporting immense weight, the ocean immersing vast areas, the sky containing

---

[1] Guo Linzong was a very famous classical scholar of the Latter Han dynasty (25-219 CE). A private teacher, he is said to have had thousands of students. In spite of his literary accomplishments he did not enter government service, as would have been the expected norm for learned men of his caliber. According to some accounts, he was rumored to be a Taoist wizard.

[2] Huang Xian was awarded an honorary degree in his youth and summoned to service in the central government, but after a brief time in the capital he returned to his native place and never went into civil service again. He died at the age of 48. His popular epithet was Weixun, "The Little Prince."

[3] Zhou Yi: a model of integrity. He tried to save a certain official named Wang Dao from incrimination when Wang's cousin rebelled against the throne. Wang Dao was a trusted member of the cabinet of Emperor Yuan (r. 317-323), who founded the Eastern Jin dynasty (317-419), and later mentor to his son and successor Emperor Ming (r. 323-326) and Ming's son and successor Emperor Cheng (r. 326-343). Wang Dao's cousin Wang Dun was a successful military commander who had helped Emperor Yuan found the dynasty, but eventually determined to take over the throne himself and staged two uprisings. When Wang Dun rebelled, Wang Dao was thrown in prison because of their family relationship and presumed collusion. Unknown to him, Zhou Yi made great efforts to exonerate him and had him released. Later, when Wang Dun asked Wang Dao about Zhou Yi, the latter said nothing, so Wang Dun had Zhou Yi killed. When Wang Dao found out what Zhou Yi had done for him, he lamented, "I didn't kill Zhou Yi, but he died because of me." *Jin Shu* 69

everything, the sun and moon illumining everywhere—these are the powers of nature.

Thus, even if you stand in the center of the world and rule the people within the four seas, you do not take pride in this; even though you decide important matters by yourself, and impose important measures on the multitudes, you do not consider this great. If you cannot develop your psychological capacity this way, you'll be suffocated by things and won't be able to attain great expansiveness.

So it is said that one must act on bigness of heart. When our psychological cultivation is slight, and we have not established a sound will, our minds will be moved by gain and loss, likes and dislikes, our tempers will act up arbitrarily, and we'll lose reality.

When people feel pressed by things, that is because their mood is agitated and out of sorts. When you're agitated, knowledge is obscured by that, so everything you do is arbitrary. Then you have no breadth at all.

A man of mettle faces life-or-death situations, treading on naked blades, making swords and spears fly, evincing firm discipline, facing serious matters and making important decisions, all this without disturbance or upset in voice or appearance. The civil and military capacities to stabilize the world this way are to be found in greatness of heart.

Will

Will means the backbone and integrity of the aim of a man of mettle. If someone who would be a man of mettle sets his aim on something small, what he accomplishes and what he learns will be extremely slight; he is not a person of great capacity.

When Master Zeng and Mencius aspired to the Way, their will was such that they did not consider even the achievements of the likes of Guan Zhong[1] and Master Yan to be worth doing. Zhao Wen[2] of the Latter Han dynasty said, "A man of mettle should fly

---

[1] Guan Zhong (d. 645 BCE), was a founding philosopher of the Legalist school of political philosophy.
[2] Zhao Wen was minister of education during the reign of Emperor Xian (r. 189-220), the last emperor of the Han dynasty.

like a male; how could he lie like a female?" Chen Fan[1] said, "A man of mettle should make his way in life sweeping out all under heaven; how could he confine his concerns to one house?" Liang Song[2] said, "A man of mettle should be lordly in life, enshrined in death." Ban Chao[3] said, "A man of mettle should establish achievement abroad—how could he occupy himself with pen and ink?" Li Jing[4] of the Tang dynasty used to say, "The situation of a man of mettle essentially calls for him to gain wealth and status by achievement and repute—how could he wind up a mere man of letters?" Ma Sui[5] said, "When there's trouble in the world, a man of mettle should work for the welfare of all within the four seas—why become an old isolated scholar?" Gao Ang[6] of Northern Qi always said, "A man should go freely through the land, acquiring fortune and status on his own; how could he sit

[1] Chen Fan was a government official during the reign of Emperor Huan of China's Latter Han dynasty (r. 147-167). When Emperor Huan died and his widow Empress Dou took over the reigns of government, Chen Fan collaborated with her father to reform the government by recruiting able personnel and purging corrupt eunuchs, a major problem in Han politics. Chen's plan for getting rid of corrupt eunuchs was discovered by his enemies and he himself was murdered.

[2] Liang Song: a scholar and poet of the Latter Han dynasty, first century CE. Sent into exile when his brother, a high government official, was denounced and imprisoned, Liang Song was eventually exonerated, whereupon he returned to his native place and lived in seclusion. Ultimately he was again denounced, by an imperial in-law, an interest group that with the eunuchs played a major role in high Han politics, especially in opposition to the scholar-bureaucrats. Liang Song died in prison.

[3] Ban Chao served in several offices in the defense department of the Latter Han dynasty in China under emperors Ming (r. 58-76) and Zhang (76-89). He was assigned to campaigns in Central Asia, where he spent thirty-one years and is credited with establishing Han dominance over 50 states.

[4] Li Jing: a distinguished general who assisted in the founding of the Tang dynasty (619-906). He served in several capacities in central government, including Secretary of War, and also led Tang forces in the field against neighboring Turkic and Tibetan kingdoms. Author of numerous works on military science, Li Jing held numerous important posts under emperors Gaozu (r. 618-626) and Taizong (r. 627-649) of China's Tang dynasty. He was especially famous for engineering the defeat of powerful Turkic and Tartar nations of Central Asia, among the most redoubtable rivals of the Tang Chinese empire.

[5] Ma Sui distinguished himself in military service to the Tang dynasty under emperors Daizong (r. 762-780) and Dezong (r. 789-805). He was particularly known for subduing revolts against the central government staged by regional military inspectors from the imperial family. The regional military inspectors played an enormous role in the governance and dissolution of the vast and multi-national Tang empire.

[6] Gao Ang was a scholar who rose to high rank by military exploits under the Eastern Wei and Norther Qi dynasties in the middle of the sixth century C.E., before the reunification of China under the Sui and Tang empires in the late sixth and early seventh centuries.

up reading books and become an old professor?"

Each of these sayings has a defect in its design, so they cannot be considered maxims, but if a man's mettle is not raised to such high aspirations he will be stymied by petty matters and will not be able to accomplish what is most important.

In ancient times, people who would be ministers aimed to make their lords like Yao and Shun, considering it their own disgrace if even one person found no place. They considered it appropriate to treat their fathers as Master Zeng did, determined never to weary of it. This was because they all had high aspirations and were not concerned with small successes or minor affairs.

When Xu You[1] heard of the abdication of the throne, he washed his ears in the Ying River. Chao Fu declared that water unfit even for an ox to drink, and wouldn't draw from it downstream.

Fan Li[2] went sailing on the Five Lakes, not accepting overlordship of Yue for his achievement. Zhuang Zhou[3] used the simile of "a kite that's caught a rotten mouse getting angry on seeing a phoenix fly." Yan Ziling[4] didn't change his enjoyment of rivers and mountains for three lords.

Although each of these is not without defect from the perspective of the path of sages, in terms of having no ambition at all, for better or worse, not deviating from a place suitable to oneself even if one is a top talent in the land, their determination to stand firm can indeed be called the temperament of a man of mettle. The say-

---

1   Xu You was legendary sage of ancient times who refused the Chinese throne. When Xu You heard that the sage king Yao was going to abdicate the throne to him on account of his virtue, Xu You "washed his ears" to cleanse them of the very suggestion of worldly power. Another sage, named Chao Fu, learning of this, led his ox upstream to drink, away from the implied pollution.

2   Fan Li was a man of pre-imperial China's Spring and Autumn era, when the ancient Zhou dynasty was beginning to dissolve. He was appointed top general of the state of Yue for having encompassed the downfall of neighboring state of Wu, but he left the state without accepting the office.

3   Zhuang Zhou, commonly written as Chuang Chou, was Chuang-tzu, a philosopher of the Spring and Autumn era, the reputed author of the core chapters of the Taoist classic Zhuangzi or Chuang-tzu. This work lays great emphasis on keeping men of talent out of corrupt government.

4   Yan Ziling was a former schoolmate of the first emperor of the Latter Han dynasty. He was appointed imperial advisor, but declined the position. He took up farming and lived a long time, into his eighties.

ing that a manly man must have the mettle to flap his sleeves atop a thousand-fathom mountain and wash his feet in a three-thousand-mile river can be found in this kind of attitude as well.

However, if you only value high-mindedness without getting there by the Way of sages, you will value heretical nothingness and emptiness, regard the world as dust, consider the country chaff, and think it's alright just to suit yourself. That is why it is imperative to clarify their implications.

Mellowness

With a man of mettle being so big-hearted and high-minded, he will naturally have a certain mellowness about him. Mellowness implies depth and tolerance. It means keeping your virtues to yourself, covering your light, and not evincing anything extraordinary.

People of little intelligence and short on talent assert their knowledge, boast to others, and show off to society, because their capacity is so limited. When you're big hearted and good tempered, standing out above myriad things, there's no point in insisting on your merit and boasting of your fame any more. So there's no more atmosphere of vehemence.

When mellowness spontaneously manifests in your face, and the appearance of a humane man, a noble man, emerges in your interactions and associations with other people, you will be like sunny springtime, a blessing to all beings. This is the mellowness of a manly man.

With this mellowness, you can be caring, charitable, and helpful. When you see desperate refugees anywhere in the world, you take it as your personal pain, so you open your storehouses and turn your rice barrels upside down, expending your wealth and using up your money, happy only when the crisis is completely resolved.

This is the product of mellowness. This must be the sense of the saying, "Jasper hidden below, the stream is in itself beautiful; containing jade, the mountain conceals its luster. A man of mettle must have this mellowness." What an ancient referred to as dealing with things by being like an empty boat[1] is also impossible without profound mellowness.

Personality

By emphasizing only firmness, it may seem a man's manners must be rough. But this is not the intent of a man of mettle. So the saying that "a man ought to have the elegance of the moon over the phoenix trees and the wind in the willows" refers to an air that is not mundane manners but like a lustrous jewel spontaneously shining on people nearby.

Huang Shangu,[2] discussing the personality of Zhou Dunyi,[3] said his heart was as clear as unobstructed moonlight or a breeze after a shower. This means refinement with a healthy appearance.

Everything has a natural form. The lowly give an appearance of lowliness, the noble give an appearance of nobility. A wild crane has no common constitution; green pine contains the strength for pillars and beams.

After Mencius had an audience with King Xiang of Liang, he came out and said to people, "He doesn't seem like a ruler—when you are in his presence, you don't see anything to fear." This means that King Xiang didn't have the personality to be a lord of men.

When men's development isn't correct, some think that the rule for a man is just being hard and strong, while being cynical and slipshod about everything from attire, diet, and dwelling to speech and manners. This is a big mistake. For a man to age gracefully does not mean indulging in softness and calling that personality.

A transparent presence, like a crystal jar filled with pure water, or a white jade bowl of ice, without any crudeness or vulgarity—this should be called the personality of a manly man. Inwardly needing

---

[1] An empty boat is an image from the Taoist classic *Zhuangzi* (Chuang-tzu) referring to the practice of emptying the mind to be aloof and innocent of assertiveness and contentiousness.

[2] Huang Shangu was a famous scholar, poet, calligrapher, and civil administrator of Song dynasty China, ca. 1100. He was twice denounced by rivals and sent into exile.

[3] Zhou Dunyi was an 11th century scholar and bureaucrat in civil and military departments. He is best known as the founder of the Idealist school of neo-Confucianism and the teacher of the famous Cheng brothers.

to curry no favor, outwardly undaunted by anything, with an expansive mood, always on top of all things, like a bird flying in the sky, a fish frolicking in the deep, the moon over the phoenix trees, the wind alluring the willows.

Can you be unaffected by anything without having developed such a personality? Be very careful.

5. Distinguishing Righteousness from Profiteering

The means by which an upright man maintains his mind is simply a matter of distinguishing between the ethical and the advantageous. The distinction between the noble man and the petty man, the difference between the principles of kings and warlords, are all in the gap between righteousness and profiteering.

What is righteousness? Introspecting with a sense of shame and fear, self-criticism after dealing with matters; this could be called righteousness. What is profiteering? Indulging inner desires, pursuing outward comfort and leisure; this could be called profiteering.

Past and present, the process of learners entering the Way should consist of clarifying the distinction between what is right and what is profitable. That is because people find profit very attractive, and everyone gets obsessed with it. So in matters of life and death they like life and hate death; in matters of gain and loss they run to gain and flee loss; in matters of labor and leisure they dislike labor and take to leisure.

The needs of nourishment, housing, and clothing, the scope of looking, listening, speaking, and acting—anywhere that feelings occur, in each instance these feelings cannot but be. The teaching of sages and noble men is not to despise life and take to death, or run to loss and avoid gain, or labor without leisure. The likes and dislikes of sages and noble men cannot be other than those of ordinary people—the distinction is only in discernment or confusion.

What do I mean by confusion? Profiting yourself alone, without consideration of others—this I call confusion. If you want to gain something for yourself, so does everyone in the world; therefore, what sages and noble men do is distinguish relative importance.

Relative importance means that lords, fathers, elder brothers, and husbands are more important than subjects, sons, younger brothers, and wives. The world and the nation are more important than the individual. Looking, listening, speaking, and activity are less important than mind.

When you thoroughly investigate and reason out relative importance, confusion should stop. That is because in a life-and-death emergency, if there is imminent danger of harm to important others, such as the lord or the people, one should not hesitate to die without a second thought, while if those important to you are not in danger of harm the thing to do is take care to preserve your life. This goes as well for gain and loss, labor and leisure.

When you examine the principles of things this way in all events, then righteous and rational conduct will develop, while motivation by gain and loss will disappear. Even so, the distinction between what is beneficial and what is harmful is well-defined; the beneficial is truly beneficial, the harmful is truly harmful. When sages teach this to noble men, they do not force anything, but just let them recognize it themselves, and apply the reason for its inevitability to all things.

Realizing that this confusion is hard to analyze, people of ancient times devised various doctrines. As a man of stature, to abandon an obvious duty on account of personal interests is naturally shameful and appalling, extremely lamentable. It is because of this that people are proud when they gain small advantages, arrogant when they achieve success, pursue money and flee difficulty, seek to win by contention, want the bigger share, are discontent, wish to have all their ambitions fulfilled, and hope for any possible pleasure to the fullest.

When unlimited desires like this occur, there is no distinguishing relative importance, so one forgets the more serious and values the more frivolous, eventually neglecting the duties of lord and subject, father and son, elder and younger brother, teachers, colleagues, husband and wife, doing things as one likes, with unpleasant consequences in the aftermath. That's because neglect of duty involves violation of natural laws.

6. Making Peace with Destiny

What people suffer over are death, loss, disaster, difficulty, poverty, lowliness, isolation, and loneliness. What they enjoy are the opposite of these. When they suffer, their minds are uneasy on this account; when they're happy, their minds also change on that account. So their will changes in times of sorrow and joy; instability of mind is a normal state under these conditions.

A man of mettle keeps his wits about him at such times. This is what it means to be unaffected by riches and rank or poverty and lowliness. The *Book of Changes* says, "When there is no water in the wetlands, that is exhaustion; a noble man therefore lives out his destiny to achieve his aim." It also says, "When there is water on top of a mountain, it is halted; a noble man in this situation reexamines himself and cultivates character." This is the understanding with which a noble man makes peace with his destiny in times of distress and conditions of hardship.

Generally speaking, what we mean by destiny is impossible for people to create, but takes shape naturally and spontaneously, bringing those patterns and events into existence. This is called destiny, or fate. The saying that Nature produces people, and whatever exists has its rule, amounts to saying that every thing and every being has its individual destiny. Therefore Master Zhu[1] called it the Order of Nature in his notes, saying that destiny is like a command.

Master Cheng said, "In times of distress, when you've exhausted all preventative measures and still cannot escape, that is destiny." This is because in each such case it is an action of Nature of which humans are incapable. Confucius said he came to know the Order of Nature when he was fifty years old; he also said one could not be a noble man without knowing destiny. The saying of Mencius, "nothing is not destined, but accept it accurately" means that a person who is not at some peace with the Order of Nature will act arbitrarily and make mistakes, unable to be realistic.

---

[1] Zhu Xi (1130–1200), a Song dynasty scholar who collected and annotated works of the great masters of neo-Confucianism, including Zhou Dunyi, the Cheng brothers, and Huang Qu. The term Cheng-Zhu studies refers to the academic line following the work of Zhu Xi.

So when you've done all you can to take care of your health but your life span's shrinking, or duty is about to lead to death, this is destiny. When the time has come and there's nowhere else to go, your strength at last on the decline, even if there are savants there's no use trying to prop this up, so it comes to utter destruction, this is destiny. When King Wen[1] was imprisoned in Jiang Village, and Confucius was imperiled between Chen and Cai, this was destiny.

There are also those whose time never comes because of geographical isolation and lack of cooperation, yet cannot accept a simple life. Even though acknowledged and employed, Shi the Bandit[2] led nine thousand men on a rampage through the land, plundering all the lords.

There are those whose posterity flourishes, and there are those who are isolated and alone, who had few children and no extensive posterity. In any case, who arranged this?

In particular, people get confused by riches and rank and poverty and lowliness, sometimes currying favor by clever words and commanding appearances, or making a habit of obsequious and opportunistic flattery. In this the outstanding will of a man of mettle is entirely absent; it is no different from a lowly man preoccupied with monopolizing the market. It is the epitome of witlessness, most laughable.

Generally speaking, for someone to become established in the world is firstly a matter of timing; secondly a matter of being born in an outstanding family; and thirdly a matter of the individual having a temperament suitable to the times. Only when these three conditions are fulfilled can your time come. None of them can be cre-

---

[1] King Wen rallied the support of lords disaffected with the corrupt Shang dynasty in the late 12th century BCE, preparing alliances for the eventual establishment of the Zhou dynasty. King Wen was the elder brother of King Wu, who founded the Zhou dynasty, the source of classical Confucian cultural norms, in 1122 BCE. Wen had ruled the state of Zhou under the preceding Shang dynasty, entitled Lord of the West, but was imprisoned by the last ruler of the Shang in 1144 BCE because he was gaining support from other ancient states subordinate to the Shang dynasty. Wen was released in 1142 and put in charge of punitive military campaigns for the Shang administration to keep him at odds with other states.

[2] Shi the Bandit was a historical figure of China's Spring and Autumn era. This epithet is also used as the title of a chapter of the Taoist classic *Zhuangzi (Chuang-tzu)* criticizing predatory ambition.

ated by yourself; it can only happen naturally. Even if you're smart enough to acquire some property along the way, that's just being less poor, not sufficient to turn poverty into wealth.

Confucius said, "If wealth could be obtained by seeking I'd even be a driver! If not, I'll pursue my preference." What he meant was that if wealth could be obtained by seeking, one should not refuse to do a job even if it is incongruous with one's social status; but if it is something that effort cannot achieve, being in the order of nature, one should simply rest content with the principles one prefers.

So a pine is a pine, but the pine of Takasago and the pine of Sumi-no-E grow on very different ground, high and low, mountain and river. So one might be prized for its height, while another may be hidden and unknown because it is short. What determines that is the order of Nature, not human contrivance.

A man of mettle should always be at peace with this natural order, not being proud even of wealth and status, for these are the order of nature, as they are not one's own creation. Nor should one detest poverty and lowliness out of shame, where this is the order of nature and nothing that you can help.

Then neither poverty nor wealth, neither high nor low status, are objects of particular attention. When the year is cold, and the green pine survives alone in the valley, your psychological fortitude will become evident.

To insist on arbitrary action because you're not reconciled to your fate is something that men should be most wary of. If people let their minds go off according to their individual likes and dislikes, confusion will grow day by day. This, it seems, is the reason for working on soundness of mind by making peace with destiny in the present.

7. Integrity

If a man does not maintain integrity within, then gain and loss will occur to him in the course of public service and obedience to his father and elder brothers, and he'll lose his natural mind. Integrity means having no interest in bribes from outside, or in family wealth, standing upright and undaunted in what worldly people are incapable of doing. This is called integrity.

If you have no integrity within, your attention will be taken by the slightest gain or loss, so you lose your self-control and won't be in your right mind. So when Confucius refraining from drinking at Thieves' Spring, and Zeng Can turned his chariot around at the portal of Shengmu because the name means *overcoming mother*, were these not examples of integrity?

Even so, people whose conduct is so lofty as to refuse an enormous stipend but who are stingy with tiny things like a piece of paper or half a penny, are that way because their integrity is slight and so they become mean and stingy.

It is said that a man of integrity, with a view of clouds and moon, wouldn't even look into a pit of gold, wouldn't blink an eye at a mountain of cash. If you have no determination to keep your integrity, you'll naturally become covetous where no one sees or knows and it doesn't seem to matter if you take something. In ancient times a Mr. Ji of Yanling was traveling when he saw some gold someone had dropped on the road. He suggested to a man carrying firewood nearby that he take the money for himself. The man became very indignant and said, "Why is your rank so high but your talk so low? I may be a menial carrying firewood, but I have no interest in profiting from picking up gold that someone else has lost." Mr. Ji was surprised and asked the man's name, but he didn't answer.

Carrying firewood brings meager profit, while lost gold is very valuable, but a man who aspires to integrity has no business acquiring what he shouldn't have. There is an inherent sense of right here.

Depending on people's disposition, there are some who are naturally honest and have no greed at all. Although their temperament is in some sense superior to others, if they don't study and strive to bring this potential to perfect integrity, keeping their mind on this, they won't be able to extend it to all things. If you have the capacity for integrity, you should not neglect it on account of gain or loss, so here is where a man should strive most.

The integrity of Bo Yi[1] and Shu Qi in ancient times might almost be called the epitome of integrity. Mencius said, "Bo Yi didn't look at anything bad, didn't work for anyone but his lord, didn't employ anyone but his people. When there was order he stepped forward, and when there was disorder he withdrew; he could not bear to live where the government was corrupt and the people unruly. Among provincial people he seemed like someone in sitting in mud and cinders wearing court attire. In the time of Zhou[2] he stayed by the shore of the northern sea, waiting for the world to settle down. Therefore where people hear of the way of Bo Yi, even ignorant men become honest, and weak men acquire will." So to say Bo Yi was pure as a sage means he was uncorrupted.

8. Honesty

For a man to stand up in society, he has to be honest. Honesty means abiding by what is right, without wavering, correcting what needs correction regardless of relation or rank, without flattering people or conforming to convention.

As for those who say it's hard to establish yourself in society by standing on principle as such, without going the way of the world and following other people, as they refrain from correcting the lord's mistakes even while receiving salaries, not admonishing their fathers and elder brothers when they're wrong, going along with the times, getting big salaries and important offices, toadying to the age, saying they'll admonish the lord when the time is right, they wind up wasting time, never doing anything all their lives. This is very shameful, most ridiculous. How could they have a stalwart heart? Depending on their salaries, blinded by their offices, they'll lose their original mind and become objects of public derision.

---

[1] Bo Yi was among the nobles who went into self-imposed exile from the Shang dynasty during the reign of the last king; he is commonly cited as a purist. He and Shu Qi subsequently refused to recognize the Zhou dynasty supplanting the Shang, and starved to death in the mountains.

[2] Zhou here refers to the last king of the ancient Yin (Shang) dynasty, reigning from 1154 to 1122 BCE, commonly cited with King Jie of Xia (1818-1766 BCE) as an archetype of evil. Not to be confused with the Zhou dynasty or the Duke of Zhou, which connote good government in Confucian theory.

Mencius said that men of mettle will rise up even without a King Wen. When they depend on others' help and are eager for acceptance, people will admit criticism and correct errors even if they are not honest men. As for men of mettle, they will not expect or depend on any assistance.

A pine tree reaches the sky unbent, an orchid is still fragrant even if no one is there. This could be called the point where a manly man's honesty stands. As *honest, accurate,* and *significant* are expressions important in the *Book of Changes*, in working for your lord and your father, and becoming established in the world, at all times make true significance and honest accuracy fundamental. To be uninhibited by vulgar opinion, not setting forth anything to the lord that is not humane and just, coolly spanning the four seas in times of crisis, is due to keeping an honest mind.

9. Firmness and Constancy

A man in society will not be able to keep his right mind without a firm and constant will. Firmness means fortitude, not yielding to things. Constancy means keeping intact the aspiration one considers right, unchanging. If a man does not maintain this mentality, he will readily yield to his likes and dislikes, and his devotion to right will be uncertain.

Therefore I consider the practice of firm constancy to be establishing trustworthiness and rigorous devotion to right. Integrity and honesty cannot stand either without firm constancy. The path of knighthood in particular is normally based on fortitude, and practiced by unchanging adherence to its values.

What human being does not experience life and death, gain and loss, like and dislike? Inwardly examining principles with firm constancy to reach the point where you can meet death in peace, though death is most disagreeable; and you can accept loss in peace, though loss is extremely offensive; and you can easily abstain from luxuries, alcohol, and sex, desirable though they be, is something no one can do without maintaining fortitude and constancy at high levels.

Mencius said, "A man of will does not forget he may die in a ditch; a brave man does not forget he may lose his head." He also said, "A gentleman does not lose righteousness when in straits, and does not deviate from principle when successful." That is because of keeping the mind on this.

When this will is missing, even temporarily, you'll yield to the profit motive, drown in wine, and get infatuated with women, eventually forgetting duty and failing at the most important matter of life and death, changing your commitment in a crisis. How could this be called the aspiration of a man of mettle?

One who can distinguish the proper places of duty and profit, and act on this with contentment, is a noble man. A noble man is not easy to find in the world. This is something that scholars learn the hard way, by learning to get rid of their confusion. Scholars who would become men of mettle should always maintain firmness and constancy, accurately discern their presence or absence of mind in the midst of likes and dislikes, and understand how to be undaunted by myriad things.

Among the people of old there were those who were naturally firm and constant, yet while outstanding in one respect were ignorant in another. Scholars who have the outstanding disposition of the ancients ought to apply it to their present circumstances, then gradually develop it further to extend it to everything. As a knight, if you do not develop the spirit and physique of a man of mettle, that indicates the mentality of a lazy schoolboy—how could you have world class capacity and perception?

10. Refining Character and Perfecting Ability, Devotion to Loyalty and Filial Piety

The public life of a man involves service to the lord and participation at court; in private life he is attentive to his father and elder brothers, and manages his household. Thus he assists the affairs of the land and resolves the people's worries. When there are rebellious subjects, he personally accepts the responsibility of military command, devising strategy and rendering meritorious service of eternal distinction;

or he acts as an ambassador to settle a crisis without embarrassment to his lord's command; or he goes to his death, slighting his life, giving up a full lifetime at a single stroke of the sword. This is devotion to loyalty in the service of the lord.

Now then, doing all you can for your father and mother, looking after them to their satisfaction, continuing to be attached to them, sacrificing your life without regret—this is filial piety exercised to the utmost at home, is it not?

A man's responsibilities are very heavy. What I am talking about here is constantly cultivating your mood to be calm and quiet, keeping your presence of mind savoring principles, and transferring this to your lord and your father to clarify the realities of loyalty and filial piety. This is a knight's job—if you don't serve your lord virtuously and don't attend to your father and elder brothers sincerely, then there is no evidence of effort to cultivate the spirit and keep presence of mind.

To begin with, character means outward exercise of what is cultivated inside, with complete sincerity and thorough investigation of principles. That is called character. Even if you say you cultivate your spirit and maintain mindfulness, if your sincerity toward your lord and your father is inadequate, how could it reach anyone lower? In that case what you've cultivated, what you've kept, is only empty talk, without substance.

The Way of sages is actually the Way[1] only when it is exercised for the benefit of everyone in the world, so that the great and the small, the refined and the rude, are alike sufficed, and its influence reaches the four seas. If you only illuminate yourself and live a clean life as an individual, you are a complacent small person who always stands by his word and always finishes what he does.

---

[1]   The Way: in general, this term refers to expression of natural law, as in the Tao Te Ching, "The Way derives its laws from nature." Neo-Confucians of medieval China drew much of their metaphysics and meditative methods from Taoism. The subset termed the Way of humanity refers to the principles of an ideal social order. Humanity forming a triad with heaven and earth refers to human beings participating willfully in the natural order. This is a normal neo-Confucian theory of the natural origin of the social order. The expression way of sages refers to Confucianism, particularly in respect to social responsibility; this is contrasted to heretical nothingness and emptiness, which refer to typical nihilistic aberrations of Taoism and Buddhism.

So when you are unfailingly diligent in doing what you must in service of your lord and your father, and you accord with the appropriate principles, the world peaceful and the home trouble-free, always adapting without stagnating, this is like sky and earth covering and supporting all without exclusion. Is this not great virtue?

Therefore, to refine character, first work on loyalty and filial piety, being completely sincere in them, making faithfulness to nature basic in service of your lord and your father.

Thus in ancient times when Chief Yu brought the flood under control, and Gao Yao[1] became an officer, the principle in this was correct. Ever since Yi Yin and Fa Shuo[2] rendered distinguished service to Shang, and Dan Shao[3] the Duke of Zhou and Gong Shi[4] assisted the administration of the Zhou dynasty, successive generations of great ministers exercised utmost loyalty in governing society and helping the people, making their great accomplishments in times of peace. The Duke of Zhou's Taigongwang, Han's Zhang Liang,[5] and Shu's Zhuge Kongming maintained the principles of the Way in times of turmoil by means of achievements in war.

Guan Longfeng criticized King Jie[6] of the Xia dynasty, and got punished by being roasted to death. Bi Gan criticized King Zhou of the Yin dynasty, and got his heart ripped out. Shi Yu of Wei left his own corpse under a window to criticize Duke Ling.[7] Zhou She criticized the errors of Zhao Jianzi,[8] wishing to be a frank and straight-

---

[1] Gao Yao: a legendary minister of the ancient Xia dynasty of China, associated with The Strategies of Gao Yao, a treatise on political science included in the classic Important Documents.

[2] Fa Shuo was a legendary minister to the founder of China's Shang dynasty (1766-1122).

[3] Dan Shao, Duke of Zhou, one of the co-founders of the Zhou dynasty in the 12th century B.C.E, a major contributor to its cultural and legal system, was a model for Confucianism.

[4] Gong Shi is a traditional heroic figure, a minister of the early Zhou dynasty.

[5] Zhang Liang, a military hero, engineered an attempted assassination of the First Emperor of China, then later assisted in the founding of the succeeding Han dynasty.

[6] Jie: the last king of the ancient Xia dynasty, he acceded to the throne in 1818 BCE. Traditionally cited as a model of decadence and corruption., he was overthrown by Tang, founder of the Shang dynasty.

[7] Duke Ling of Wei lived in the time of Confucius, whom he met and consulted. Confucius walked out on Duke Ling after he asked about military matters.

[8] Zhao Jianzi was a prime minister of the state of Jin during the Spring and Autumn period. He fled the state when it was under siege, but later returned to fight back.

forward minister. Ji An of Han denounced Emperor Wu[1] to his face, Zhu Yun chastised Emperor Cheng.[2] Each of these individuals risked offending human rulers, without regard for their own lives.

When Wang Shu of Zhou City in Qi was overcome by the army of Yan, the King of Yan offered to make him lord of ten thousand households. He refused, however, saying that a loyal subject does not serve two lords, just as a chaste wife does not have two husbands. In the end he hanged himself.

Gan Guoqing[3] died after having his tongue cut off even as he was reviling An Lushan.[4]

These are examples of being absolutely loyal to the end. Did they not refine their character in service of their lords? If their character were not sound, how could they do as they did?

Now then, there was the filial piety of the great Shun, and Master Zeng,[5] the exertions of Dong Ying[6] and Wang Xiang,[7] the considerate care of Lao Laizi[8] and Huang Xiang,[9] the attachment of Zhong You[10] and Wang Pou,[11] the sincere feeling of Guo Qu[12] and

---

[1] Emperor Wu (The Martial Emperor) of the Han dynasty (r. 140-86 BCE) was one of the most powerful of all Chinese emperors, commonly classed with the First Emperor of Qin as a greedy and aggressive tyrant.

[2] Emperor Cheng of the Han dynasty (r. 32-6 BCE) enfeoffed the wily Wang Mang, who would eventually usurp the reins of government to terminate the Han and established the short-lived New Dynasty in 8 CE.

[3] Gan Guoqing is a Confucian model of loyalty. He was a political opponent of the rebel An Lushan, foreseeing An's treachery against the Tang dynasty, was taken prisoner by him and dismembered. He is said to have continued to berate An Lushan even as he was being hacked to pieces.

[4] An Lushan was a regional military inspector under the Tang dynasty in China. He staged a calamitous rebellion in 755.

[5] Master Zeng: a major disciple of Confucius. His three meditations are particularly well known: Master Zeng said, "I examine myself on three points daily. In planning for others, have I been disloyal? In relations with colleagues, have I been untrustworthy? Am I repeating to others what I don't practice myself?"

[6] Dong Ying married a "celestial maiden" who helped him take care of his parents.

[7] Wang Xiang was famous for breaking through ice in winter to catch fish to feed his stepmother.

[9] Lao Laizi would act like a child to amuse his parents even when he was seventy years old.

[9] Huang Xiang was a classicist and author, and was noted for devotion to his father.

[10] Zhong You was a distinguished disciple of Confucius.

[11] Wang Pou refused to go into civil service because the king had had his father killed.

[12] Guo Qu was famed for devotion to his mother, and is said to have found a buried pot of gold inscribed as a gift to him from heaven, representing celestial reward for his filial piety.

Meng Zong,[1] and the self-sacrifice of Yin Baoqi[2] and Shen Sheng,[3] all examples of perfecting sincerity in service of parents. How could those people get to be as they were without cultivating character?

So lords and fathers are the mainstays of social order, and if you don't serve them with complete sincerity the proper relationships between ruler and subject and father and son will not be clearly defined.

If you try to be completely sincere without cultivating character, your substance will be shallow and you may change in face of injury or death. In all things, if you cannot decide critical matters in major emergencies and upheavals, your character is undeveloped. Even in everyday mundane life, those who take care of their business on the basis of virtue are rooted differently. Even so, if it is not adequate in all things, its effectiveness is indistinct. Now if an extraordinary upheaval occurs under these circumstances, you will not be able to exercise complete sincerity as a subject or a son openly and obviously if your character is not upright.

11. Rely on Humanity and Justness

The virtues of the human heart do not go beyond humanity and justness. These are essentials of the order of Nature, and when you go along with those feelings without artificiality, you're just a heart-full of humanity and justness.

Therefore in a manly man's personal discipline he should make humanity and justness his bases of reliance.

Humanity is the life-giving heart of heaven and earth. When the feeling of sympathy emerges in proper proportion, this is the function of love.

Justness means being scrupulous in dealing with matters. This means external projection of inward scruples in proper proportion.

So without a humane heart, one cannot embody tolerance and

---

1   Meng Zong: a model of filial piety. He went into the woods in winter to hunt bamboo shoots for his mother and found them sprouting all over, as a divine reward.
2   Yin Baoqi was banished after being slandered by his stepmother, and yet was not embittered.
3   Shen Sheng was heir to a duke, but committed suicide after being slandered by his father's favorite concubine, who wanted to set her own son on the throne.

breadth of mind; and so one sinks in subjective likes and dislikes. This is why humanity is considered the source of sagehood.

Without a just heart, your dealings with matters will not be principled, so you will not be decisive.

When you work on humanity, you become courteous in the process. When you strive for justness, intelligence becomes clear in the process. This means that humanity and justness are the sources of courtesy and intelligence, just as water and fire are the bases of the five elements.[1]

What sages teach people is not beyond humaneness and justness. Humaneness is the basis of virtue, justness is its practical application. As for the path to which a man of mettle aspires, if he does not refine inner character on the basis of humaneness and justice, how can the reality be attained?

Now then, a man's daily activities do not go beyond serving his lord and his father outside while governing himself inside. When the principle of serving one's lord and one's father is established, here the conduct of subject and son is clear; then relations with colleagues, the status of brothers, and the distinction between husband and wife should naturally be orderly.

When you govern yourself inwardly on the basis of humanity and justness, myriad different functions and everyday activities are clear in this, so there should be no ignorance of the essence. Although many methods of personal cultivation of scholars since ancient times appear in books, the differing views of latter-day scholars should not be adopted. The sages set forth their teachings clearly; their doctrines are all in humanity and justness.

When you have your own experience of the function of humanity and justness, and actually sense the reason they are necessary to heaven and earth, then the source of the learning of sages will be clear in this. With no further need to speak of humanity and justness, everything you say will be humane and just.

---

1   Five elements: one of the most pervasive structures in Chinese thought. The five elements are water, fire, metal, earth, and wood. They are conceived of as producing and superseding each other in specific orders, resulting in corresponding changes in conditions.

Nonetheless, Confucians of past and present have drawn legs on snakes, producing wens and warts on the body, saying things with their mouths that are not in their hearts, filling myriad volumes with notes and commentaries on humanity and justness without being either humane or just. One might almost sigh in lament. Would men of mettle not be highminded enough to set their hearts to this?

12. Thoroughly Understanding Things

The functions of things each contain the universal absolute,[1] in the manifestations of which appear a variety of functions. Plants are plants, but there are outstanding orchids; chrysanthemums display an attitude of abandon; peonies show a sign of richness; lotuses have the qualities of princes. Wood is wood, but pine and cedar have the capacity to be ridgepoles and beams; the parasol tree has a clean constitution; apricot has a refined fragrance; cherry has a beautiful appearance. Willows are green, flowers are red. Their types, too many to tell, each have their laws. Noble men, it is said, gaze up at the heavens above, examine the earth below, and observe people and things in between. This is how they clarify the phenomena and events of sky and earth, among people and things, after which the aptitude of sages is freely exercised in order to respond to myriad things.

Since character is based on natural qualities, and humanity and justness are human principles, who would not rely on them? But even if you refine your character with humanity and justness, if you do not comprehend the qualities of things, from astronomy to geography, the thousands of differences and myriads of distinctions evolving from combinations of positive and negative energies, then your way of dealing with affairs is not free; you have not mastered heaven, earth, and society with your intelligence.

Everything is like this in service of your lord and your father, and in cultivation of yourself. For a man of mettle to save the people of

---

[1]   The universal absolute: This refers to a concept from the *Book of Changes* used by Taoists and neo-Confucians to refer to a primal stage in the evolution of matter prior to polarization of elemental energy into yin and yang or negative and positive charges.

an era, accomplishing an achievement of distinction for myriad ages, assisting the virtues of heaven and earth, exercising the sincerity of sages to the utmost, is all a matter of establishing this character and perfecting your intelligence and abilities. So even the august emperor, in his unsurpassed rank, must know about everything down to the work of lowly woodcutters, or there will inevitably be neglect in national government.

Even the sage emperors Yao and Shun directed Xi Ho, Xi Zhong, Xi Shu, Ho Zhong, and Ho Shu to make certain of the seasons, directed Yu to level water and earth, directed Ji to plant a hundred grains to fully utilize the earth, making Chief Yu[1] minister of public works, Qi minister of education, with Gao Yao becoming a judge. Shun directed Shui to be the master of the guilds, and made Yi the minister of mountains and wetlands, having him domesticate plants and trees and birds and beasts.

It would be impossible to detail all these things. How much the more, as a subject serving a lord and a son being filial to his father, you will invariably run into problems on every occasion if you are not thoroughgoing in everything. So you should savor books from the documents of Yu and Xia such as *The Plan of Gao Yao*, *The Plan of Great Yu*, *Yi and Ji*, and *The Contributions of Yu*.

Coming to the Zhou dynasty, Duke Dan of Zhou was the younger brother of King Wu, who was the son of King Wang; though he was the son of a king and the grandson of a king, he composed the *Songs of the Seventh Month* detailing the livelihood of the people; he admonished King Cheng with the composition *No Negligence*, informing him of the difficulties of agriculture; he defined the rules of the *Manners of Zhou* in exhaustive detail, clarifying etiquette and measure for human emotions. This was because he acquired thorough knowledge of things, and he was a genius.

To assist government in a time of peace, advising and aiding the ruler in establishing standards and laws for the empire, distinguish-

---

[1] Chief Yu is associated with the founding of the Xia dynasty, traditionally reckoned 2205-1766 BCE. As director of public works under his predecessor, he is credited with quelling a great flood in antiquity. He is traditionally said to have acceded to the throne in 2205 BCE as the last of the symbolic nonhereditary kings Yao, Shun, and Yu.

ing a meritorious design over myriad ages, is inevitably a matter of thoroughly understanding things. How much the more so when born in a state at war; if you are to handle major upheavals, raising troops for humanity and justice like Tang and Wu, subduing opponents' forces without fighting, preferring strategy and entering unpopulated areas, how can you master it without thorough understanding of the principles of things?

When Yin Yisheng of Jin negotiated with the Marquis of Qin at the Royal City, he secured the return of the lord of Jin to his homeland by answering the Marquis of Qin's questions well. When Que You of Wu was taken prisoner in Chu, he turned adversity into fortune. Lord Fu Bi went to the Khitan as an ambassador of Song and got the northern court to stop warring. In such cases, if they didn't individually exercise their ingenuity, they would have wound up disgracing their rulers' command.

So it is also with children serving their parents. Without thorough understanding of the principles of things, you cannot be completely filial. Nevertheless, if you try to encompass too many things, you'll be learned but lacking in moderation.

This point is most significant for scholars. If you do not thoroughly comprehend the principles but just go on ingenuity, your basis will be quite mistaken; you may even come to rely entirely on clever talk and eloquent flattery. To establish a stalwart will, exercise your abilities fully, serve your lord and your father, and master everything involved, can be called greatness of heart and breadth of capacity and perception.

13. Broad Study

The people and things of past and present are quite different; the languages and customs of other countries and this nation are very dissimilar. There are virtues comparable to heaven and earth, there is intelligence that extends to all things. What to use and what to leave aside is up to oneself. Records of these things are written in books, so one should read widely in books of past and present, discerning in detail how things work.

Scholars sometimes memorize historical facts and contemporary affairs to show off to the world; others amuse themselves with poetry and prose, considering scholarship to require verse and composition. Neither of these is the scholarship of a man of mettle.

To be an old professor occupied with a schoolboy's compositions, making a meager living by lecturing and writing for hire, crouching at people's feet, cannot be called the true aspiration of a man of mettle.

So what is scholarship? Rooted in the way of sages of old, assisted by tales of the acts of savants and noble men, understanding the changes of the present age and the principles of people and things is for broadening your perception and information, increasing your intelligence and ability, and improving your knowledge.

In later ages, books have been made into means of clever talk, a medium for memorization and literary amusement, incessantly deprecating contemporary people, elevating oneself and ridiculing others. Could this be called the scholarship of a stalwart?

When people are ignorant of past and present and do not comprehend changes, they are narrow-minded, their disposition is prone to prejudice, and their intellect is one-sided. That is because of taking education to mean learning the writings of ancient people. But if you study yet only work on yourself superficially, literary ability may become harmful because of this ignorance of how to use it. If you examine and understand your own present condition thoroughly, and then consider the times and ideals of past and present, all studies will increase your intelligence.

Books record things spanning thousands of years. How could we who are alive in the present day know about events hundreds of years ago, or consider the ways of remote foreign lands, if not for books? Therefore broad study of literature should be used to empower the intelligence.

The *Family Precepts of the Yan Clan* says, "The reason for reading and studying is to open the original mind, clear the eyes, and improve conduct. When worldly people need books, they can say this alright but cannot carry it out. This is why warriors and common officials ridicule them. There are also those who read thousands of books and then aggrandize themselves, looking down on elders and slighting contemporaries. People despise them like enemies, hate them like owls. In this way they seek to benefit from scholarship but instead they harm themselves. Not to study would be better." This is talking about errors in the attitude with which scholars read. If you give little consideration to inward refinement of character, personal development, and mental orientation, and only have external interest in scholarship, then all your vast learning becomes harmful and is not as good as not studying.

In such cases, people should consider self-examination and self-correction fundamental. Correcting the mind and governing the body does not depend on scholarship. Study is just a tool for clarifying intelligence and understanding past and present. When scholars have spare energy, in addition to practical application they should broaden their minds with books.

14. Self-Examination and Self-Discipline

A man of mettle should always examine himself and consider where his disposition is underdeveloped, calculate when personal likes and dislikes cause prejudice, and discipline himself to spur himself on where he is underdeveloped.

Master Zeng, an eminent disciple of Confucius, may have acknowledged a pervasive unity, but he still had a discipline of examining himself on three points every day. Zhong You, another disciple, was delighted to hear about his own errors. Each of these examples refers to self-discipline. Later Confucians wrote family precepts, noting what should be disciplined and corrected; this refers to self-examination.

Generally speaking, even though the affairs of the world may be well-established and their origins well-understood, they will invariably become corrupt if they are not examined and subjected to lucid review for a long time. Then mistakes will arise from reliance on them. That is, with the passage of time there is breakdown and there is collapse. So even if you thoroughly research principles when you start things, in order to bring them to completion it is necessary to consider the time and assess the situation, examine them from time to time and correct their corruptions, amending what is unsuitable to the time, or else you cannot achieve a complete conclusion.

Confucius said, "Isn't it delightful to learn and put it into practice over time?" To put it into practice over time means that there is no time when you are not practicing. Doesn't this mean making what you've learned habitual at all times, at every moment?

So while the actual exercise of the essence of the art of psychological development is to nourish spirit, maintain presence of mind, refine character, and perfect intelligence, when you examine yourself time and again in this process, correcting your own excesses, rectifying imbalance in your disposition, considering time and place to understand how things can work according to context, and also carefully examining and correcting yourself inwardly all the time so as not to drift off or lose control, then it will naturally become clear whether the things you do are right or wrong, crooked or correct. If you get stuck, you should strive with the help of a mentor to break through the impasse. This is the key to the art of psychological development.

The Confucians of the Song dynasty focused on the practice of maintaining attentiveness, warning against absent-mindedness. This is near to the understanding of self-discipline and self-examination. The *Good Words* of the *Elementary Learning*, the *Maxims* of Zhang Sishu of the Song dynasty, and the *Maxims* of Fan Yijian of the Song dynasty refer to self examination. Master Zhu of the Song dynasty composed maxims for the family, including verses on self-examination. These are all about self-discipline to correct one's own errors.

15. Detailing Dignified Manners; Unfailing Respectfulness

If you want to make the development of knowledge clear, comparable to the universal qualities of heaven and earth, ascertaining the original sources of the learning of sages, if you do not comport yourself respectfully, how can you acquire the key?

The art of comporting yourself respectfully must first be a matter

of correct standards for manners. Xu Wenzheng[1] said, "When dignified manners are outwardly correct, this is getting the general outline
of comporting yourself respectfully."

Now in terms of the standards for dignified manners, what takes
precedence? Not allowing looking, listening, speech, or action to be
affected by anything improper could be called the key to dignified
manners. And how can manners be correct? The *Detailed Courtesies*[2] says, "Don't be disrespectful." It's a matter of putting these three
words into practice.

Generally speaking, courtesy arises from the need of the individual's heart, with natural measures in regard to things, the dignity
of its expression inviolable. It ought to be elegantly articulated—this
is called courtesy. As all of your activity and repose is a function of
courtesy, each act, each restraint, each word, each silence, has its standard of courtesy. The fundamental standard of courtesy is all in the
three words "don't be disrespectful." If you wonder why, if you think
carefully as you speak or keep silent, as you act or desist, considering
how to meet those standards, even if you don't fully measure up you
won't be far off. If you just act on the moment, without any thought
or calculation, impelled by emotional inclination, discourtesies will
multiply and dignified manners will disappear altogether.

If you always think deeply in the midst of things, considering
them in detail, in each case you should be near a natural standard.
This is taught as not being disrespectful.

So it is said, "Don't be disrespectful; be solemn, as if thinking."
The expression "as if thinking" means not being negligent about
things, always being prudent and sober, not allowing carelessness;
one should consider carefully and think things through. This is the
idea behind referring to it as the basis of conformity to courtesy.

Respectfulness doesn't mean cowering silently, not saying or doing
anything. It means carefully examining and assessing the principles

---

[1]   Xu Wenzheng: A Confucian scholar in the time of Khubilai Khan (r. 1260-1295), the
warlord-emperor who completed the Mongol conquest over Song dynasty China and
launched two attempts to conquer Japan. Xu was drafted into government service as a
school master for the central university in the capital city.
[2]   *Detailed Courtesies* is a part of the Chinese *Classic of Manners*.

and reasons of things without being careless or inconsiderate. When you're careless and inconsiderate, you become negligent and thus lose control over your mind, letting emotions and desires take over.

According to a saying in the *Cinnabar Book* presented to King Wu[1] by his mentor Father Shang, "When respectfulness overcomes negligence, that is auspicious. When negligence overcomes respectfulness, that is destructive." Respectfulness and negligence are mutually antagonistic: when you're respectful, negligence disappears; and when you're negligent, respectfulness disappears. When negligence disappears, then the reasons of things are clear, so manners are correct; therefore it is auspicious. When respectfulness disappears, leaving only neglectfulness, everything you do is careless and slipshod, and so will soon come to naught.

The ways a man of mettle serves his lord and father and cultivates himself have to be particularly respectful. If there is any disrespect, years of effort are wasted all at once, disgracing your father and grandfather and bringing shame on your lord. This comes form slackening of respectfulness.

Cheng Yiquan[2] said, "Just be orderly and serious, and your mind will be unified. When unified, it will naturally be immune to untruth and insincerity." The expression "orderly and serious" explains the word "respectfulness."

So what does it mean to be orderly and serious? It is correctness of manners, with no impropriety in looking, listening, speaking, or acting. Therefore it is explained as proper dress, a noble gaze, and the like.

Mentality is all internal, while the interaction of physical activity with people and things, including looking and listening, is external. The internal and external are basically one, not separate. When manners are correct externally, moods are correct internally. When there is any external disarray, there is invariably an internal response to it.

---

[1] King Wu was the founder of the classic Zhou dynasty; his mentor Father Shang, also called Taigongwang, was Lu Shang, Wu's chief advisor. The Cinnabar Book that King Wu received from Father Shang is supposed to have contained writings on ancient practical philosophy and political science.

[2] Cheng Yiquan: 1033-1107 one of the famous Cheng brothers, Song dynasty patriarchs of neo-Confucianism.

If you clarify external manners thoroughly and keep them in accord with their natural laws, the keys to psychological technique should naturally become clear.

Manners are forms of courtesy. Courtesy is based on not being disrespectful. If those who aspire to dignified manners work on habitually avoiding disrespect, the way should not be much further.

Cheng Yiquan greatly admired the maxim, "A noble man grows stronger day by day when he is dignified and respectful. He becomes more irresponsible day by day when he is casual and indulgent." That is because the condition of ordinary people is that when they are at all unrestrained they become negligent and reckless day by day; but if they control themselves they become orderly day by day. This is the heart of dignified manners.

In the *Caution* chapter of the *Great Elegance* verses of the *Classic of Poetry* it says, "Respectfully careful about manners—this is the standard for the people." Also, in the verses of Wei it says, "Dignified manners are so rich you cannot choose among them." Beigong Wenzi of Wei explained, "To have dignity that is awesome is called being dignified. To have manners that are exemplary is called being mannerly. When a ruler has the dignified manners proper to a ruler, his ministers fear and admire him; they take him for a standard and a model. Therefore he is able to keep his country, and his command and his repute grow in the world. When ministers have dignified manners proper to ministers, their subordinates fear and admire them. Therefore they are able to keep their offices, preserve their clans, and comfort their families. The same holds true all the way down the social scale. In this way the higher and the lower are mutually reinforced." This appears in the *Zuo Tradition*.[1]

Dignity means not being frivolous, from your facial expression to your speech, with an appearance that is very solemn and awe-inspiring. Manners mean that everything from the way you appear interacting with others to the way you talk about things, based on

---

[1] Zuo Tradition is one main traditions of Spring and Autumn Annals, noting events in the ancient state of Lu from the eighth to fifth centuries BCE as the ancient Zhou dynasty disintegrated; a primary source of Confucian studies.

thorough examination of reasons, is suitable to be made a model that people can all take for a standard and an example.

This is attained by inwardly considering respectfulness and always examining the reasons for expression and speech. From the emperor above to the common people below, the key to personal cultivation is one and the same, a matter of fully understanding dignified manners. Dignified manners are no more than not being disrespectful. Scholars should certainly savor this.

16. Circumspection in Looking and Listening

Although the physical body is complex, it may be summed up in two terms, perception of the external and communication of the internal.

The ears, eyes, nose, and so on, all have the function of perception of the external, while internal functions, able to sense, can act externally.

When Confucius instructed Yan Yuan in the principles of mastering the self and returning to courtesy, he said, "Don't look at anything improper, don't listen to anything improper." What does improper mean? When you see and hear things, if you manifest a loss of dignity and you let your own selfishness take over, this is called improper.

Looking at the wrong sights and listening to the wrong sounds is not the only meaning of impropriety. Wrong sights and sounds come from outside; if we see or hear them unavoidably, without intending to do so, that should not be called improper looking and listening. Even though proper sights and sounds are not improper, moreover, if you lose your manners when you see and hear them, just letting emotions and desires take charge, this is improper looking and listening

Thus as lords and fathers look upon subjects and sons, as subjects and sons look upon lords and fathers, for each there are proper ways of looking, according to context. When lords and fathers listen to what subjects and sons say, and subjects and sons obey the directives of their lords and fathers, for each there are proprieties of listening to all voices that should be heard. If there is anything inappropriate to the occasion, it is not *proper*.

For a man of mettle to establish himself in society and make his behavior enough to be a model that myriad people can take as a guide, is initially a matter of circumspection in manners of looking and listening. In the *Detailed Courtesies* it says, "Don't eavesdrop, don't gaze promiscuously. When about to go in a door, always lower your gaze and don't look around. Generally, when the gaze is above the face it evinces arrogance; below the belt it evinces depression; glancing to the side evinces treachery." This is also referred to as the look being correct.

In the *Notes on Music* it says, "Ears, eyes, nose, mouth, heart, intellect, and all parts of the body are induced to act rightly by conforming to the correct." This is to see to it that there is no impropriety of ear or eye.

When you are inwardly negligent, to the point where you look without seeing and listen without hearing, your ears and eyes will follow their own inclinations, and improprieties will become quite conspicuous. When you keep aware of the caution not to be disrespectful, there is the caution to hear where there is no sound, to see where there is no form. When you look, your concern is to see clearly; when you listen, your concern is to hear clearly.

With an important person, first you look at his face, in the interim you look at his chest, at the end you look at his face. With your father, you let your eyes roam, but no higher than the face and no lower than the belt. There is courtesy in looking at his feet when he's standing saying nothing, and looking at his knees when he's sitting. So it's a matter of detailed determination of all courtesies of looking and listening in dealing with situations and people.

To sum this all up, there are three rules: looking, observing, examining. There are interactions of five normative social relations such as lord and subject, father and son. There are functions of seven emotions. Each of them has to have its proper manner, according to the specifics of various contexts.

Jia Yi's[1] *Norms of Appearance* says, "There are four guidelines for the gaze. At court, the gaze should be straight flowing and even. At ceremonies for spirits, the gaze should be as if they were actually there. In military formation, the gaze should be firmly planted and alert as a tiger. At funerals, the gaze should be lowered, eyes half closed." Cheng Yiquan of the Song dynasty composed guidelines for looking and guidelines for listening, to discipline himself in this respect; they are particularly suitable for comparative reflection.

After all, since looking and listening are functions of the eyes and ears, first rectify the manners of your eyes and ears, then correct your ways of looking and listening according to the people with whom you are interacting, and the changes in events, finding out their reasons, keeping looking and listening both in mind, using looking, observing, and examining to pursue their perfection. These would be the dignified manners of the man of mettle, never looking or listening improperly.

17. Circumspection in Speech

Speech is the act of communicating what is within. It is said that even be it a joke, it still comes from thought. Because speech emerges externally from internal activity, whenever you are restless you speak thoughtlessly. You're apt to be garrulous and flippant, speaking immoderately, talking too much, perhaps making up tall tales for the occasion, perhaps angering others by intemperate words.

This must be what is meant by the guidelines for speech that say it can create enemies and make friends, it can beckon fortune and calamity, glory and disgrace. If it is too easy it is pretentious, while if too complicated it is obstructive. Sages and savants since ancient times have all warned about easy talk without equivalent action. Generally speaking, though it is easy to open your mouth and talk, when you do not moderate your words you become excessively

---

[1] Jia Yi was a great scholar recruited by Emperor Wen of the Han dynasty (r. 179-156 BCE) to be a professor in the imperial academy. He rose rapidly in the ranks, and tried to change the calendar and revive rites and music. Running afoul of the resentment of the prime minister, he left the service of the central government to become a tutor for local kings. He died at the age of 33.

loquacious without added benefit, and because you can't put all you say into practice it often winds up empty talk and unfulfilled commitments. This is something to be very ashamed of.

Therefore, so that your words will always have measure, when you are going to speak on your own initiative, speak after having carefully calculated the opportunity and considered the occasion. This is the idea of the saying, "Prefer discretion in speech, as if you couldn't talk."

Words reflect on actions, and actions reflect on words. The determination to take care to do as they say in all things is what noble men of mettle esteem. You should see to it that you speak without being at all inappropriate, careful to be moderate even in agreeing with what others say, so as not to be inopportune or offensive in your words.

If you are careless and run off at the mouth, you'll talk too much and misspeak a lot, overworking yourself and being unmannerly in the process. It's no use for people to listen. The *Records of Manners* says, "A parrot may be able to talk, but it is still a bird; an orangutan may be able to speak, but it is still a beast." The point is that if you have no courtesy now as a human being, even though you can speak your heart is still that of a wild animal, is it not?

Next, there are courtesies for when you're going to speak. When you intend to speak, calm your mind, compose yourself, and don't be hasty; keep your voice low and even in tone, and speak quietly and calmly. An ancient said, "Calm your mind and soften your voice." In *Detailed Courtesies* it says, "Make your speech calm and steady." These are courtesies for when you're going to speak.

When you talk too fast, it is unmannerly, and hard for listeners to understand. When you speak too loudly, you startle people for nothing. Moreover, when there is a lot to say, if you start out in a loud voice you'll have a hard time getting to the end. This must be the sort of thing meant by the saying in the *Records of Manners,* "The mouth evinces repose, the voice evinces calm, the tone evinces gravity."

So when answering people's questions and inquiries, be sure to ascertain what is appropriate to the occasion, making your responses calm and assured. When some expertise is needed to make a statement or offer an answer, or when you hold critical discussions, or in cases involving private business, rumor, or hearsay, always be deferential to those around you; and when it is absolutely necessary to speak, be precise with your words. If you speak in haste and answer impulsively, pretending to be smart, the lack of courteous deference is undignified and unmannerly.

When people of ancient times spoke, they saluted those around them. Whenever you don't listen fully to what people say but respond as if you got it, because of carelessness your responses will inevitably be off; saying you know what you don't, saying you remember what you don't, you'll prove to be inconsistent. Here is an example of the ancient maxim, "Once a word is uttered a team of horses can't overtake it."

For this reason it is said that affirmation and agreement must be serious responses. Even if it seems to onlookers as if you have heard little, you must understand the inquiry fully and respond to it in detail. People of the world all value clever talk and an eloquent tongue, and often jump to hasty conclusions, responding in haste while others are still talking. Of course, this is not the way of a noble man.

In the battlefield, however, split-second decisions must often be made, and so everyday standards can't be followed. This is in cases of talk in the army.

Next, there are many courtesies according to the kind of speech, depending on the place, time, and people with whom you interact. There is speech for court, there is speech for home, there is speech for funerals and festivals, there is speech for debuts and marriages, there is speech for receiving guests, there is speech for the army. There is speech for lord and subject, father and son, older brother and younger brother, friend and colleague, and husband and wife. There is everyday speech, and there is speech for dealing with emergencies. If you do not thoroughly clarify these various categories, your speech will always be inappropriate, so courtesies will be confused and manners will be violated.

So in your speech at court, when you are on duty at the court of the lord, speaking in the capacity of a particular position, be careful that your speech is not beyond your position, with no personal talk, no communication of private business. With a calm mind and a gentle voice, listen carefully to what the elders say, and if there is any juncture at which you should speak, distinguish it clearly and don't let yourself be fawning.

When Confucius was at an ancestral shrine or in court he spoke eloquently but discreetly. When he spoke to the lesser grandees at court, he was firm and direct. When he spoke to the greater grandees, he argued mildly and cheerfully. This is how a sage was circumspect with his speech at court, with exemplary courtesy in speaking to senior and junior colleagues.

In *Detailed Courtesies* it says, "At court, when procedure is mentioned or procedure is questioned, reply concerning procedure. In the archives, talk about the archives; at the treasury, talk about the treasury; at the armory, talk about the armory; at court, talk about court. When you speak at court, you don't talk about hounds and horses; in an official venue, you don't talk about women." These are all traditional expressions of courtesy.

Now then, there are special words for court. Going to court is called appearing for service; leaving court is called retiring. There are lots of different words according to the era and the clan, but one should not discuss the present in terms of the past. Even though the courtesies of writing, defining standard forms, were established in the Koan era (1278-1288), the Shoguns have changed them from time to time over the ages. It should be a matter of focusing on the evocation of things, with clear understanding of what is appropriate to the time.

When you fully understand how you should be circumspect in speech at court, that speech must have certain qualities, and there must be certain manners of speaking, then you can figure out the branches from the root, a matter of inquiring from people who are knowledgeable, and also examining reasons.

To say there is speech for home means there must be speech for everyday life at home. If you employ court courtesies at home, that will seem pretentious. You can't speak the same way all the time. So at home, in referring to things, in coming and going, in the names of the attendant samurai and the process of organizing teams you don't use formal speech, and in your conversation you don't discuss official affairs and don't give personal opinions about official business. The *Detailed Courtesies* says, "Public affairs are not to be privately discussed."

The maxims of Fan Yiqian included these: "Don't talk about profit and loss, reports from the borders, dispatch of emissaries, or appointment of officials. Don't talk about the strengths and weaknesses or relative merits of provincial and prefectural officers. Don't talk about the errors and evils committed by the masses. Don't talk about opportunism or cronyism in office. Don't talk about how much money you have, or how you hate to be poor and want to be rich. Don't discuss female beauty in a licentious, demeaning, or disrespectful way. Don't talk about soliciting people to seek wine and women." These may be called admonitions for everyday life.

If you are as cautious about talking at home as you are at court, the appropriate harmony will be lacking, and this is out of order. Even Confucius was said to be "relaxed" and "genial." So then speech in everyday life is to be mild and harmonious.

Next are words for funerals and festivals. In *Detailed Courtesies* it says, "When viewing the casket, don't sing; when the casket is sealed, don't mill around. On the way to the grave, don't sing; hauling the hearse, don't smile. When attending a festival, don't be sluggish. At a funeral, don't talk about fun. At a festival, don't talk about trouble." These are manners of speaking for funerals and festivals.

When you are in a situation where there is sorrow, there should be no joy in your speech, so as not to forget sorrow in the heart; how much the more so when you are the one in mourning.

As for festivals, when you are not serious they're just formalities, becoming either farcical or something for show. Is this the original intention of honoring spirits? That is why the words used must be most serious.

In all funerals and festivals there are courtesies of reference associated with ritual objects, rhetoric, and writing. Thoroughly study their reasons, and don't discuss them subjectively.

Next are words for debuts and weddings. Debuts are ceremonies marking adulthood. Weddings conjoin two families, so this is a very important ceremony. Therefore the words used on these occasions should not be random or arbitrary; research fully, question thoroughly, and follow what is appropriate. When you have a detailed understanding of the rites of passage and matrimony, and carry those ceremonies out correctly, then your words are clear.

Next are words for guests. These are courtesies of deference and respect exchanged between guest and host when visitors come and go. For example, it is said that one who enters as a guest defers to guests in every house.

When guests are invited, there are courteous expressions for prior response to the invitation, and there are courteous expressions of thanks for visiting. When guests arrive, the host greets them with expressions of courtesy, and they politely defer to each other. When guests leave, the host sees them off and thanks them. There are also courtesies for guests' expression of gratitude for the invitation, before and after; and there are courtesies for the sendoff and the welcome.

Giving thanks for the hospitality, appreciating the excellence of the food and drink, commenting on the house and grounds, the scenery, and the flora, apologizing for being unworthy of such considerate treatment, appreciate the intention. In this, assess the relative status of host and guest, and consider the occasion in deciding whether to thank someone in person, or use a messenger or intermediary, or send a letter, as there are different degrees of importance in courtesy and deference.

Next is speech in the army. Jia Yi's *Norms of Appearance* says, "Bated breath and hushed voice—this is speech in the army." Since the army is mustered for military action, one does not speak of defeat in everyday terms, and one does not utter words of weakness. Everything has its manners.

Next is speech between lord and subject, father and son. When a lord or a father gives directions to a minister or a son, speech should be mild and understandable, with detailed instruction and clear direction. When little is said but the implications are deep, ministers and sons have a hard time understanding at once.

Anyone who would have authority over others ought to employ subordinates only after observing them, noting their ignorance, and instructing them thoroughly. Therefore speech should be mild and harmonious, so that the feelings of subordinates can be communicated comfortably.

When subjects and sons get directives from their lords or fathers, they should circumspectly acknowledge each detail, not prefer their own opinions but listen carefully to the words of their lord and father, comprehend their aim, and then do the task. If you disregard the directives of your lord or father, putting your own opinion first, this is acting clever, not the consideration of loyalty and filial piety.

The *Detailed Courtesies* says, "When your father calls you, don't say 'Yeah.' When your teacher calls you, don't say 'Yeah.' Say 'Yes!' and get up." It also says, "When one who is going on a mission for his lord has received his orders, the word of the lord doesn't stay overnight—once the word of the lord arrives, the man of the house goes out and bows to the favor of the lord of the land."

The *Courtesies of Social Interaction* says, "Reference to a lord refers to employing ministers; reference to a grandee refers to service of a lord." The *Detailed Courtesies* says, "When comparing people, compare them to their peers. When asked about the age of the emperor, reply that you've heard he was so many feet tall when he made his debut. When asked the age of the ruler of a state, reply that he is well versed in politics. If he is a boy, say he is as yet unable to participate in politics. When asked about the son of an official, if he's grown up say he can manage; if he's a child say he can't manage yet. When asked about a scholar's son, if he's grown say he can handle inquiries; if he's a child say he can't handle inquiries yet. When asked about a commoner's son, if he's grown say he can carry kindling; if he's a child, say he can't carry kindling yet. If a lord wants a knight to shoot but he can't, he refuses on the grounds of infirmity, saying he aches from carrying kindling. Asked about the wealth of the ruler of a state, reply with the size of the territory and the produce of mountains and wetlands. Asked about the wealth of officers, say they have stewards, live on tax revenues, and don't need to borrow ceremonial implements or attire. When asked about the wealth of knights, answer with the number of their chariots. When asked about the wealth of common people, reply with the count of their livestock. If a ruler of a state is going to leave his state, to stop him say, 'How can you leave the earth and grain shrines?' In the case of an officer, say, 'How can you leave the ancestral shrine?' In the case of a knight, say, 'How can you leave your tombs?'"

In *Discourses and Sayings* it says, "The lord of a country calls his wife Madame and himself Boy. The citizens call her Lady. To those of other countries she is referred to as the Little Lady, while the citizens of other countries still call her Lady."

Generally speaking, such expressions are not all of the same class. It is simply essential to study them and understand them thoroughly. When the words of lord and father and subject and son are correct in this respect, then the words of brothers, spouses, and colleagues should all be in accord. When you speak to your father or older brothers, you honor and respect them like lords, but when you mention them to others you humbly call them your *stupid father* and *stupid brother*. You refer to the children of your father and elder brothers the same way.

Just consider the situation and take into account the occasion, and adjust your level of gravity according to the people you're dealing with and the proprieties of the matter concerned, based on the fundamental intention of not being disrespectful.

In particular, when the speech of men and women is not appropriately mannerly, with men imitating the speech of women and women using masculine speech, they are both out of place. It is therefore imperative to observe the precept that men should not speak of domestic affairs and women should not speak of public affairs. Since all words come from thought, one should be most circumspect.

Next, there is speech for ordinary life and there is speech for emergencies. That is to say, in times of tranquility fast talk and hurried speech invariably startle people. When we talk fast or speak hurriedly, it is because of being inwardly careless and inconsiderate. When there is an emergency, whether a natural disaster or man-made trouble, that's the time to startle people with fast talk, speaking quickly to get them thinking as soon as possible. This is not a situation or an event to be dealt with in a quiet and relaxed manner.

On this account, abnormal events have to be dealt with in unusual ways. This is when you accurately address the reasons for normalcy as well as abnormality. If you always think in the same way and keep to one line of reasoning, without mastering situational adaptation to change, in any case you'll just get stuck.

Considered in this light, since words and speech are manifestations of the internal, if you are at all careless in this respect your manners must thereby be disordered. A noble man's care to avoid discourteous speech is much to be appreciated.

Discourtesy does not refer only to vulgar or improper talk. Whenever you open your mouth immoderately, that is discourteous. You must realize the magnitude of the admonition not to say anything discourteous.

Next, there are precepts for talk. This refers to what to be consistently conscientious about in conversation between lords and fathers and subjects and sons, between brothers, spouses, and colleagues. This amounts to the need to assess the timing. This means figuring the proper occasion to speak, the right time to say something.

For example, when you cannot reason something out, if you speak of it without considering the proper place, the matter concerned cannot be reasonable. Assessing the time means figuring when it would be good to speak out in the proper place, which of the four seasons, and whether in the morning, noon or night; and considering your own age and that of the person you're talking to. Considering and determining each issue is assessing timing.

The saying that you should not talk while eating or speak in bed presents precepts for timing. To speak on a sudden impulse is failure of timing.

The *Detailed Courtesies* includes a precept that a son should not use the word *old* in everyday speech to avoid allusion to his parents' aging, saying that speech should accord with the situation. What this means is that even if something could or should be said, there are situations in which it shouldn't be said. When said in the wrong situation, everything causes harm. This is why forms of speech at court and at home are different.

Accordingly, there are things to be said and affairs not to be mentioned, according to the person. As you speak of humanity and justice in front of your lord, likewise consider all your social relations and conduct your conversation accordingly.

Confucius said, "There are three errors in attendance on a lord. To speak of something before it is time to talk about it is called haste. Not to speak when it is time to talk about something is called concealment. To speak without noting facial expressions is called blindness."

Conversation generally to be cautioned against is talk about sex, matters of gain and loss, luxuries, and longings for amusement and leisure—these are not to be topics of conversation. In principle, one should not engage in abstract philosophy of nature, mind, and nothingness, or self-laudatory, conceited talk. As for vocabulary, neither vulgar words nor effete and ornate expressions should be employed. All this is language to beware of.

Next are the uses of language. Confucius said, "In speaking, one thinks of loyalty." He also said, "One should be loyal and trustworthy in what one says." The classic *Manners* says, "In converse with the crowd, speak of loyalty, faithfulness, kindness, and good prospects. When talking to children, speak of respect for their fathers and elder brothers. When talking to officials, speak of loyalty and faithfulness." Whenever you talk to people, you should do so in a way that will benefit them. That is a way to help others. To speak so as to profit oneself alone is not the way of a noble man. To benefit oneself without considering the welfare of others is always the act of a petty person. This is what is meant by Master Zeng's saying, "Am I unfaithful in my considerations for others?"

Talking all day, wasting words, to make a point of your own cleverness, repeatedly showing off verbally, is something noble men detest; it should be called useless eloquence. Petty people are used to turning anything that's said to their own advantage. There is no impropriety of speech worse than this. One must guard against it most carefully.

In Zhang Sishu's maxims it says, "All speech must be loyal." This is indeed something always to be cautious and careful about. As for loyalty and trustworthiness, loyalty means being completely sincere in consideration for others. Trustworthiness means not fabricating falsehood, being correct and clear. Since these are problematic points in speech, everyone should beware.

18. Be Careful of Appearances

Appearances are the substance of the vessel into which nature and mind are placed by the natural order. When inner thoughts are improper, appearance is influenced by them, the manifestation being outwardly evident. If you want to rectify your appearance, you have to correct and clarify what you think inside.

With thoughts inside, facial expressions appear outwardly; since the inside and outside, the external and the internal, the root and the branches, are a natural continuum, you can no longer consider them separately.

The way that noble men of old were careful about appearances and particular about rules of etiquette is worth considering. In *Manners* it says, "A noble man appears relaxed." Relaxed means an unhurried, quietly deliberate manner. The *Minor Manners* section says, "To guests, respect is principal; at ceremonies, reverence is principal. At funerals, sadness is principal. At parties, liveliness is principal. In the army, you hide your feelings and prepare." Since the manifestations of outward appearance are each induced by inward thoughts, when you examine and clarify your inner thoughts to correct them according to what's involved, your appearance will conform to this. Duke Xiang of Dan said, "A noble man rules his body by his eyes; his feet follow along. This is how you know his mind when you see his appearance." That is because there is no place for the mind apart from the appearance.

Now then, appearances change in consideration of the time, depending on the situation, in the particular context. In Jia Yi's *Norms of Appearance* it says, "There are four appearances. At court, the appearance is studied, composed, neat and respectful. At ceremonies, the appearance is meek, humble, orderly and gentle. In the army, the appearance is cautious, solemn, firm and fierce. At funerals, the appearance is grief-stricken, fearful, as if one would never return." This is a traditional description of appearances.

To elucidate, there is an appearance proper to court. When serving at court, the appearance is always to be respectful, never forgetting one is in the lord's place. Comings and goings should be anxious, deferentially respectful, so as not to be unmannerly. Descriptions of Confucius' appearance in the presence of a lord as *nervous* and *polite* exemplify appearance for court.

There is an appearance for home. This means that when you stay home, you let your appearance relax. At leisure, when there is nothing to do, you should cultivate that mood. Even so, to be lazy and slovenly is certainly not the way of a noble man. It's just a matter of making your facial appearance relaxed and gentle. This must be the meaning of the description of Confucius at leisure as being *relaxed* and *at ease.* Annotations say that being relaxed means that the face is relaxed, while being at ease means that the expression is cheerful.

So there are appearances for funerals, appearances for debuts and weddings, appearances for guests. In each situation you should respond in kind, having clarified the case. It's all a matter of rectifying your appearance by being respectful. In the *Jade Spread*[1] it says, "Whenever there is a ceremony, your appearance and facial expression should be as if you were seeing the entity being honored. The proper appearance at a funeral is emaciation, while the facial expression is downcast and dejected. The look is furtive and glancing, the voice is muffled."

In *Minor Manners* it says, "On auspicious occasions, honor is important; at funerals, familiarity is important; with guests, respect is

---

[1] Jade Spread is a section of the Chinese Classic of Manners. The image Spread in the title refers to a cloth spread on which precious stones are laid out for display.

essential." There are courteous appearances appropriate to rites of passage and wedding ceremonies, moreover, indicating comprehensive manners and courtesies. You should cultivate your appearance with this in mind, fully understanding what is appropriate to each occasion.

Next, there are appearances for war. The *Jade Spread* says, "The appearance proper to combat is resolute strength. The manner of speech is stern. The facial expression is severe and solemn. The gaze is clear." *Kong's Collection*[1] says, "The custom when the general is present is that when you're in the ranks with your helmet and armor on and your weapons in hand you don't bow even to your lord or your father. If the army is unfortunately defeated, then ride by relay to deliver the news, without carrying scabbard or bow case. The emperor, wearing plain clothes, mourns outside the armory gate."

In *Minor Manners* it says, "When you ride war chariots, have your blades before you when you go out, keep your blades behind you when you come back." In the *Charioteers' Art of War*[2] it says, "Of old civil manners were not brought into battle, while military manners were not brought into the civil domain. If military manners were brought into the civil sphere, the people's morals would be lost; if civil manners were brought to war, the people's character would be weak. So in the civil domain words are civilized and speech is warm. At court, be respectful and deferential, disciplining yourself to attend to others, not showing up when you are not called, not speaking when not asked, stepping forward reluctantly and withdrawing readily. In military formation you set up resistance, on the move you chase opponents down. Men in armor do not bow, in war chariots they do not salute. They don't run on ramparts, they don't weaken in danger. Courtesy and law are outside and inside; the civil and the martial are left and right." This concerns military manners.

---

[1] Kong's Collection: By Kong Fu, a 9th generation descendant of Confucius. He lived during the Qin dynasty (255-209 BCE). When the First Emperor ordered books burned and scholars buried alive, he concealed his copies of the classics inside a wall and went into hiding in the mountains.

[2] The Charioteers' Art of War is a famous Chinese military manual, attributed to Tian Rangju, composed between 356-320 BCE.

So all domains of social relations have their courtesies and manners. Even so, nothing compares to keeping the appearance correct and respectful. Master Zeng said, "Control your manners to avoid roughness and carelessness." *Records of Manners* says, "Do not let an arrogant, distorted mood become established in your body," also referring to correctness of appearances.

Next, concerning the function of facial expression and tone of voice, since facial expressions appear and tone of voice changes along with attitude, the thing to learn is to keep your attitude right. Although all appearances depend on thoughts within, among them the facial expression reveals the humors and the tone of voice depends on the agitation or calm of the temper, so one should keep their correction in mind.

Norms of Appearance says, "Attitude has four occasions. At court the attitude is quiet, serene, and solemn. At ceremonies the attitude is calm, thoughtful, and harmonious. At war the attitude is angry, wrathful, intense and severe. At funerals the attitude is dejected, mournful, grief-stricken and sorrowful. When the four attitudes take shape within, the four expressions show outwardly. It is as if the attitude manages the expression."

Minor Manners says, "One who is buoyant and cheerful has the expression proper to bells and drums. One who is sad and quiet has the expression proper to funeral wear. One who is full of bustle has the expression proper to weapons and armor. At funerals one must have a look of sadness; in armor one has an appearance of inviolability. Therefore the noble man is cautious not to lose face to others."

The *Jade Spread* also says there is a look of luster, generally talking about the expression on people's faces being mild and agreeable.

When a lord had him receive an ambassador, Confucius had a tense look on his face; when he left, on descending a step he relaxed his face and looked pleased. These were Confucius' expressions of respect for a ruler's order. The saying "flying high and flocking" refers to noble men going into action on seeing an opportunity.

Being severe of mien but soft inside is what petty people are like, according to Confucius, like thieves who make holes in fences and tunnel through walls to rob houses. This refers to a contradiction between inside and outside. Master Zeng said, "When the facial expression is correct, this is close to faithfulness."

Each of these examples illustrates reasons for being circumspect about facial expression. There are, however, petty people who employ clever talk and imperious expressions without changing their attitude inwardly. There are villains of mild countenance, and there are those who manipulate expressions to put on the appearance of a noble man. These are acts of extremely dishonest people with perverse ambitions; though adequate to deceive others for a while, eventually the error of their ways will surely be discovered. How much the more since noble men see right through petty people, so there's no way to hide. Even if they want to cover up evil, there's nowhere to conceal it.

Now then, tone of voice is where the breath of speech appears. The *Jade Spread* says, "The breath is to be quiet." *Norms of Appearance* says, "Talking fast, spraying spittle, and a whining, disagreeable tone, are all taboo." The expression "with bated breath" refers to Confucius' tone of voice when in the presence of people of the highest nobility. "Humbly, with a cheerful voice" describes the courtesy with which a filial son attends his father.

Records of Music says, "Music is produced by sound. The root of this is in the human mind's sensitivity to things. For this reason, when people feel sorrow their voices are choked and stifled; when they feel happiness, their voices are cheerful and relaxed. When they feel delight, their voices are excited and expansive; when they feel anger, their voices are rough and harsh. When they feel respect, their voices are plain and clear; when they feel love, their voices are gentle and soft. These six are not spontaneous; they come into play after feeling something."

Even in the sounds of music their expressive tone emerges from impressions of feeling. From this perspective we should be very careful about the manifestations of tone of voice. Duke Lu of Ying[1]

---

[1] Duke Lu of Ying: A distinguished minister of the Northern Song dynasty (960-1126).

said, "Disposition can be seen in speech, manners, and bearing, in relative gravity and pace." These are reasons for taking tone of voice seriously.

Here we have noted a general outline of types of appearance. Appearance includes action, and every action has its manners. This must be the sense of the saying, "Don't act improperly."

Now then, the principles of action include measures for one's everyday abode. There are rules for sitting. *Norms of Appearance* says, "Sit in the standard sitting manner. Not crossing your legs and not showing the soles of your feet, the gaze level, is called normal sitting. Sitting slightly bowed, the gaze on the knees of an honored individual, is called sitting in company. Sitting with your head up and your gaze within ordinary range is called dignified sitting. These are appearances pertinent to sitting." *Detailed Courtesies* says, "Don't sit cross-legged; sit like a lord." This is the rule for sitting.

It is written of Confucius that he was informal at home. Speaking from this perspective, there must be rules for every situation—sitting at court, at home, in fortune and adversity, in the army as well as at parties. In all social relations, of course, you need to have an understanding of how to sit with honor and respect, how to sit with equals, how to sit when at ease. Wherever a man of mettle is, he must always keep a respectful attitude without forgetting the possibility of emergencies occurring. Even if you're home at leisure in peace, you should never become slipshod, lazy, or slovenly.

So the task of a noble man is to remember standing up when he's sitting down, to remember the advantages of action when he's at leisure.

In *Detailed Courtesies* it says, "When sitting parallel, don't let your elbows protrude to the sides." This is the rule for sitting next to people. The statement that "in the company of others, you shouldn't choose your own convenience" means that you shouldn't prefer seating suitable to yourself alone, such as seeking the coolest spot in summer and the warmest spot in winter.

Guan Ning of the Han dynasty, it is said, sat on a single wooden chair for over fifty years without ever crossing his legs, and the seat was worn through where his knees were. Cheng Mingdao of the Song dynasty, it is said, used to sit up straight all day like a clay manikin. Each of these examples refers to not letting one's appearance be slovenly even when sitting alone, cultivating one's ordinary presence. When there is nothing to do, you sit quietly and cultivate your disposition; standing, you do not display an attitude of arrogance and lassitude; dealing with people, sit respectfully, with a mild air. These are rules for the way a man sits.

If you sit cross-legged spread out like a winnowing basket, your arms and legs uncontained, you appear lazy and indifferent. If you get up the minute you sit down, and sit down as soon as you stand up, restlessly and randomly, your mind will not be composed. Is this the way of a man of mettle?

In the *Jade Spread* it says, "At home on vacation, one is warm." Being at home means one's abode is peaceful. It also says, "At home, a noble man always faces the door," meaning that one faces the light.

Next, there is the appearance when standing. Here appearances are already in motion. In the *Jade Spread* it says, "The way to stand is not to stoop in a servile manner. The head and neck must be centered; stand steady as a mountain, act when it is timely." *Norms of Appearance* says, "Jaw firm, gaze straight, shoulders square, back straight, arms as if embracing a drum, feet two inches apart, face straight, hat laces tied, legs straight, feet aligned, the body not moving the elbows—this is called the normative way of standing. With a slight bow it is called standing in company. With a bow at the waist it is called solemn standing. With the belt-ornaments hanging down it is called lowly standing.

In *Detailed Manners* it says, "Stand as if at a ceremony." It also says, "The manner of standing indicates character," describing conformity with the proprieties of standing.

So when you're going to stand up from sitting, relax your limbs, pay attention in front of you and behind you, to your left and to your right, consider the proprieties of the situation where you're standing, and then stand up. To consider how to stand before you stand up is good manners in standing. If you stand up whenever it occurs to you or whenever you feel like it, as you try to stand up you may find your limbs have gone to sleep, and you may stumble and offend those around you; even if you manage to stand up your posture won't be right. When you stand without correct posture, it's hard to stay standing for a long time. If you're holding something, you're bound to lean and bend.

If you can stand, you can walk. If you don't stand straight, you won't be able to walk properly. This is the meaning of making your manner of standing correct. In public and private behavior, first check your manner of standing: settle your center, keep your spirit taut, your navel firm, your shoulders square, and your back straight. These are all manners proper to standing.

Next, there are manners proper to walking. There are ways of walking at a sitting and in an audience hall; there are proprieties for court and for home. There is a way of walking down the street.

In the *Jade Spread* it says, "Walking corresponds to the music *The Model of the Warrior*,[1] running corresponds to the music *The Succession*[2] and *The Downpour*.[3] The ordinary stride should be straight and swift; in the ancestral shrine, orderly and solemn; at court, dignified and respectful. In an auditorium, take short steps; in a hallway, stride more freely; inside a room, don't walk around."

In *Norms of Appearance* it says, "Walk in a slightly bowed manner, without swinging your arms, without your shoulders going up and down, without your body leaning to one side, moving serenely. This is the way to walk."

So when you get up to walk from a seat, be sure to look carefully in front of you so as not to step on or soil anyone or anything. That is

---

[1] The Model of the Warrior is a classical musical composition celebrating the overthrow of the corrupt last king of the Shang dynasty by King Wu of the Zhou. A note in the original says, "The sound of the jade ornaments hanging from the belt is slow, after The Model of the Warrior."

[2] The Succession is a classical musical composition that celebrates the succession of King Shun to King Yao; these were sage kings of old (3rd millennium BCE), and the succession is famed in Confucian philosophy for having been nonhereditary, based on ability rather than birth.

[3] The Downpour is supposed to be the music of Tang, respected founder of the ancient Chinese Shang dynasty (1766 B.C.E.). A note in the original says, "It matches [the pace of running] because it is fast."

why you shouldn't leave your seat while your legs are still numb.

Even when you go someplace where nobody's around, call out to let your presence be known in case there's someone inside. Don't go unannounced. In *Detailed Courtesies* it says, "When you're going to go into a building, always call out. If there are shoes outside the door and you hear talking, then go in. If you don't hear talking, don't go in. When about to go in through a door, always lower your gaze. When you go in the door, salute politely; don't look around. If the door was open, leave it open; if it was closed, then re-close it. Don't step on any shoes, don't step on any seats. Go along the edges of the room, careful to acknowledge others."

One does not rush off because one wants something. One should not leave in haste on account of dissatisfaction. This comes from the *Minor Manners*, meaning one should not come and go hastily. Then one will always be careful of one's walk, not allowing one's appearance to be sloppy, so as to maintain respectfulness. Even if there is an urgent matter, to act in a flurry is not the mentality of a mature man. One should never forget the sense of the saying in *Minor Manners*, "Even when you enter an empty place, act as if someone were there."

When there is some business with one's lord or one's father, however, one should be as intent as if one were inexperienced.

When walking on the street, always be on the alert for anything out of the ordinary. Keep your attendants and servants in a straight line, be fully prepared; leave room for others coming and going, and don't act violently toward wayfarers. Concede the right of way, don't walk spread out across the road.

Don't look for byways or shortcuts. Caution attendants and servants in front and behind not to get in the way of people coming and going. Don't let them push anyone down or drive them off the road. Don't let them mess with merchants' goods.

Scouting should be furthest in rain and snow, at dawn and dusk, to clear the way ahead of time. If the road is muddy and makes for a difficult passage, you should have them go by a better route on this account; go yourself, having them wait a while before setting out.

If there is an incident on the way where your underlings have been uncivil to people on the road, as the master you should come immediately and politely apologize. Don't pass by as if unaware.

When you arrive at someone's place, dismount on the side of the gate, compose your appearance, and request admittance. Caution your entourage beforehand not to stroll around, sit in front of the gate, or talk or laugh loudly. When you go into people's houses uninvited on account of hunger and thirst and drink hot water, or go into eateries for wine and food, you must be very careful to establish appropriate rules.

When coming and going in the dark of night, use lamps in front and behind to let people get out of the way and prevent trouble. When it's dark, use sound to enable people to avoid you.

Even when you return home, send someone ahead to announce your arrival. Unexpected comings and goings always involve the ill consequences of lack of coordination between inside and outside.

These are manners for coming and going on the road. Just keeping respectfulness in mind, clarify the appropriate usages to establish comprehensive rules. Otherwise, in the event of an emergency dignified manners will be lost and you'll lose the reality of a man of mettle.

It is said that when you go out the door you should be as if meeting an important guest. It is also said that when you go out the door you should be as if seeing an enemy. Each of these is an admonition to maintain respectfulness and not be disorderly.

When Ziyou became governor of Wucheng, Confucius asked, "Have you found personnel?" Ziyou said, "There is a certain Dantai Mieming who never takes shortcuts and never comes to my office except on official business."

Ever since meeting Confucius, Gao Chai never stepped on [his parents'] shadows, didn't kill hatching insects, didn't break plants or trees. During a rebellion when he was governor of Wei, he went out and shut the gate. When he was told there was a shortcut out, he said, "I've heard that a noble man does not take shortcuts." When told there was a hole in the wall, he said, "I've heard that a noble man doesn't go through a hole." After a time a messenger came, and he opened the door and emerged.

These were both students of the school of the sage, illustrating their manner of action. But not going by shortcuts and not going through holes are not precepts of the sage, they are only accurate understandings on the part of Mieming and Gao Chai. A sage may take a shortcut, and may also get out through a hole. This can be inferred from the fact that Shun secretly tunneled an escape hole as he was digging a well, and Confucius passed by the state of Song in humble clothing.

Therefore Master Zhu noted, "Not taking shortcuts or going through holes is fine for times when there are no problems, but if beleaguered by brigands, why sacrifice your life by keeping these precepts? This can be seen by observing how the Sage passed through Song in humble clothing."

There is also a way of running. This means the proper manners of running to go fast. In the *Jade Spread* it says, "Running fast requires drive, so don't let your hands and feet get out of alignment. If you go in a straight line, jaw down, you'll be swift as an arrow."

In *Minor Manners* it says, "Don't run outside a curtain or a screen. Don't run in an auditorium. Don't run on top of a rampart. Don't run holding valuables." In *Norms of Appearance* it says, "Running is done slightly bent. Floating lightly, shoulders as if streaming, feet like shooting arrows—this is the way to run. When turning, do so slightly bent. Go into motion with an elegant alacrity, turn firmly and cleanly. This is the way to turn around."

Abroad it is considered courteous to pass quickly by persons of high estate, not stopping in front of them; that is why there is a courteous manner of running. Running is proper in all emergencies, but one does not run when it may startle people or cause an accident. This is the sense of the statement in *Minor Manners* that "Once back home, one doesn't run."

Next, there are manners of holding things. In *Detailed Courtesies* it says, "When presenting something to someone standing, one does not kneel; when presenting something to someone sitting, one does not stand. Whatever you present is held at chest level; whatever you carry is held at waist level."

In *Minor Manners* it says, "Pick up what is empty in the same way as you pick up what is full." Whatever you hold in hand, even something like a scepter or fan, you shouldn't bend over. In particular, books and utensils you present to your father or lord should not be carried any lower than the waist. When your hands are tilted, what you are carrying is not straight; or your body may lean to one side on this account, or your legs might bump into what you're carrying, which is extremely discourteous.

When a man is facing a battlefield with sword and spear in hand, along with bow and arrows, are these not all forms of carrying? It is imperative to be most circumspect.

Next are manners of rising and reclining. That means that in people's everyday usage it is normal to rise in the morning and go to bed at night. In *Domestic Rules* it says, "A son serving his father and mother gets up when the roosters begin to crow." This is the courtesy of early rising. It seems that the norm of early rising only refers to dawn, when you can see people's faces clearly and go about your business with the lamps off. This is when you can get up and function efficiently, in both public and private life. If you want to be prepared for work, you have to get ready from when the roosters begin to crow, otherwise you won't be on time. Therefore since antiquity the norm for early rising has always been when the roosters begin to crow.

The rule for retiring at night is generally that when the sky has become too dark to work, you should stop your outside job and go inside. Let your employees rest. Then stretch your limbs, bending and stretching in a relaxed mood. These are rules for rising in the morning and retiring at night.

The *Jade Spread* says, "Always sleep with your head to the east." The east is the direction of life-giving energy, so this is the direction for the head. In *Detailed Courtesies* it says, "Don't sleep lying face down." The *Discourses and Sayings* of Confucius says, "Don't lie like a corpse." These refer to avoiding an appearance of laziness in your reclining posture.

Rising and reclining are the flexing and stretching of the four limbs and whole body. Their norms should be kept in accord with the timing of sky and earth, the affairs and interactions of the day, and your degree of fatigue. Otherwise, leaving it to feelings and desires, you'll inevitably fall into self-indulgent laziness; giving up the courtesy of early rising, abandoning the rule of retiring at night, you turn night into day and day into night. Administrative business will then be neglected, and care of the physical body will be lacking. One must be very careful about this.

Next is the matter of hobbies and arts. All cultural and martial arts, ritual, music, archery, riding, writing, and mathematics, either train deportment and manners, or limber up the hands and feet, or refine the perceptions, or regulate the production of the voice. This is completely consistent with the principles of correcting inward thoughts, making external behavior orderly, serving one's lord and father as a stalwart, devoting oneself entirely.

So if you are born in a military family, and of a status where you would aspire to be a man of mettle, regulate your conduct with courtesies, make your movements harmonious by means of music, and practice archery and horsemanship as the job of a knight. Making these all everyday activities, always practice their proper usages carefully to refine appearances.

Writing does not necessarily mean no more than writing something. Writing also refers to reading, memorizing written characters, and gaining knowledge of things past and present.

Mathematics refers to enumerations of natural phenomena and reckoning of quantities of things. If you are not familiar with mathematics, you don't know measures.

These are all bases of dignified manners as one appears in action.

So when we speak of courtesy, there are specific courteous measures for good times and bad, for war, diplomacy, and celebration. There are courtesies of food and drink, there are courtesies of clothing, there are courtesies of housing. There are courtesies for all kinds of questioning and answering, handling of implements, carriage and speech. Considering the *Detailed Courtesies* thoroughly, comprehending the past and present systems in this country, choosing according to what is right for the time, we should conform to what is suitable.

Dogs, horses, swords, wine, foods—rules for each of these are set forth in the *Detailed Courtesies*, but I haven't written them here because they can't be applied in the present day.

In music, this country is also said to have eight instruments,[1] but I am not familiar with that system. Recently, enjoyment of pantomime music is considered the music of the warrior caste. It has a very fast tempo, and its songs are full of superstitious nonsense, while its dances are odd and extravagant, so it cannot be considered substantial. Its performance only employs flute and drum, so it is limited to bamboo and leather. It cannot be discussed in the same year as ancient music, but this is not the current custom. It is so low it cannot be reformed. The pantomime music with songs containing real events is unmatched by the bawdy sounds of popular music, so it can still qualify as musical art.

As for the rules of archery and horsemanship, manners and rites detail the methods of shooting and riding. The rules for riding have disappeared. In this country, the systems of archery and horsemanship are very detailed. You should learn and practice them fully, studying their manners, to arrive on the path of the noble man.

In *Principles of Archery* it says, "In archery all your movements must be mannerly; only when your mind is focused correctly and your physical posture is straight can you hold bow and arrow steady. Only after you can hold bow and arrow steady can you talk of hitting a target. Thus can efficacy in action be observed."

Archery and horsemanship are the work of a man of mettle. If you have any time off at all, you should never neglect everyday practical physical training. There are many various kinds of manners involved in archery and horsemanship, furthermore, to be studied in detail.

---

[1] Eight instruments: A classical Chinese categorization, referring to instruments of metal, stone, string, bamboo, gourd, clay, leather, and wood. Japanese music tends to employ mostly string, bamboo (woodwind), and leather (percussion) instruments.

Calligraphy, writing, and reading are instruments for focusing the mind when at leisure. Cheng Mingdao was very punctilious about calligraphy. He once said to someone, "It's not that I want fine calligraphy, it's that this is study."

All uses of hand and foot involve manners; so to perform them carelessly is the root of negligence. Even an idle diversion, if unbalanced, is indicative of someone's state of inner development. Therefore absent-mindedness is also to be avoided in calligraphy. A maxim of Zhang Sishu was to always use formal characters for calligraphy.

Be even more careful to avoid slovenliness in your manner of reading. If you read in a sloppy way, whether propping yourself up on a pillow or reading lying down, nothing will record inwardly because your attention in this condition isn't right. Especially since the deeds and fame of sages and savants and emperors and nobles of past and present are recorded in books, how could it be the intent of a man of mettle to gloss over them?

In the *House Maxims of the Yan Clan*[1] it says, "When you borrow someone else's books, take good care of them; this is one of the hundred practices of a man of mettle. If volumes are spread in disarray over a cluttered desk, they'll often be stained by children or maids, or be damaged by wind and rain, or insects and rodents, a real blot on your character." This is why you should be careful.

Mathematics is for calculation and measurement. Sky and earth, people and things, are not beyond these numbers. Consider carefully to keep accurate accounts of the day's business. If the figures are not clear, there will be either excess or insufficiency, which will be off in either case.

Next, regarding the practicing of hanging jades from the belt, the *Records of Manners* says, "Noble men of ancient times always wore jades. On the right side they word jades sounding the notes *cheng* (sol) and *jiao* (mi), on the left *gong* (do) and *yu* (la). They ran with the rhythm of the music *Gathering Herbs* and walked with the rhythm

---

[1] House Maxims of the Yan Clan: By a scholar recruited to tutor the crown prince during the founding era of the Sui dynasty, which reunited long-divided China in 589.

of *Relaxing in Summer*.[1] They turned like a compass, cornered like a square. When they stepped forward it brought them together, when they withdrew it made them move; then the jades rang like music. So when a noble man is in a vehicle, the sound of gold bells is heard; when he walks, it causes his belt jades to jingle. In this way perverse thoughts don't enter the mind." This is a system whereby the sounds made by the jades worn on the left and right are harmonized in standing, sitting, and walking, without the slightest lapse of attention, to prevent unrestrained activity. If movements are at variance with courtesies, the sounds of the belt jades do not harmonize. Having belt jades hanging from the waist is used for correcting appearances and manners, as these may be likened to virtues. Putting bells on vehicles and harmonizing their sounds corrects the manners of the drivers, alerting against inward negligence, calming their minds.

In sum, the intention is that one's manners become correct through the use of the jades hung from the belt to the left and the right. This is standard for noble men.

After you have made your appearance orderly in these ways, then the principles of dignified manners should be clear. Only when a man of mettle attends to ordering his person this conscientiously can he enter the path of the noble man. If he acts out of place, thus becoming disorderly in manner, his inner mental focus will naturally slacken, and his character will not be correct. Dignified manners of appearance all connect to inner character. Their importance should be recognized.

19. Moderating Consumption of Food and Drink

Living things cannot survive physically without food and drink. This is the explanation of the doctrine of mutual production of the five elements. Wood grows nourished by water, metal is produced by the nutrition of earth. Humans, being the most intelligent of creatures, receive the nourishment of all five elements together, which when complete make a full life possible. Even a single day without food

---

[1] Gathering Herbs and Relaxing in Summer are names of ancient Chinese musical compositions.

and drink, and this life is reduced. This is why people require food and drink.

When Zigeng asked Confucius about government, Confucius said, "See that food is ample, that arms are sufficient, and that the people trust you." Of the eight ministries of the *Universal Guidelines*[1], food is first. That is because each one has a basic object.

Now then, drink refers to liquids, food depends on the five grains. If you go for water and prepare food when you're already thirsty and hungry, you eat and drink immoderately. If you eat and drink so that you're always satisfied, you can also be excessive. Therefore sages came to get people to space their meals so they could live out their natural life span. That is the reason all living things must have food and drink.

How is the proper measure to be calculated? Just enough that you do not become extremely hungry or thirsty. Now to extend this discussion further, when people's food and drink is neither too much nor too little, they eat at an interval of six hours, and drink once in between. That is to say, after getting up in the morning they eat and drink between 7 and 9 a.m. Then six hours later they eat and drink again between 1 and 3 p.m. This is the proper spacing of morning and afternoon meals.

Natural changes are all triplex. The human digestive system too processes food and drink in six (2x3) hours.[2] One should drink in half that interval. People of ancient times defined this system, initiating the practice of eating at certain times in the morning and afternoon to take care of hunger and thirst.

These are inevitable natural measures. When you exceed them, your spleen and stomach are impaired and you put on excess weight, weakening your energy and circulation. When you don't have enough, your spleen and stomach are undernourished, you lose weight, and

---

[1] Universal Gidelines (Hong Fan) is a work in the Chinese classic Ancient Documents, consisting of an ancient proto-constitution, a design of government. The eight ministries outlined therein are: 1) foodstuffs; 2) commodities and money; 3) public rites and religious affairs; 4) infrastructure; 5) education; 6) the penal system; 7) diplomacy and foreign affairs; 8) military affairs.

[2] In the original it says "three hours" because 'hour' in the old 12-hour system was equivalent to two hours in the modern 24-hour system.

your energy and circulation are unsound. In either case it is because of deviation from natural measure. People who deviate from this measure will naturally have a change of disposition.

This alone should be considered proper measure. When two meals are not enough, the rule is to eat at noon when the days are long and eat at night when the nights are long. If you take to this when there is no insufficiency, you will eventually lose proper measure.

The sky revolves in relation to the earth. For the human being, food for spleen and stomach is earth. Without food, energy doesn't circulate, just as the sky is not defined but by the earth.

Next are regulations for food and drink. People should regulate food and drink in accord with their salary and position. People of high rank with large salaries live on the best quality of food. Those of middle and lower ranks should act accordingly. Within that range it's a matter of being more frugal than your status requires, because excess and extravagance are endless and involve a lot of expense.

In *Regulations for Kings* it says, "Feudal lords do not slaughter an ox without a reason. Grandees do not slaughter a sheep without a reason. Gentry do not slaughter a dog or a pig without a reason. Commoners do not eat delicacies without a reason." This means people have regulations for their food and drink according to their rank, within which they opt for frugality.

According to the *Manners of Zhou*, one hundred and twenty dishes were served at the emperor's meal. The formal practices of the nobles and grandees can be surmised from this. Commonplace scholars repeatedly emphasize frugality without acknowledging these distinctions, ultimately to become obsessed with gain and loss, to the point where they accumulate massive wealth. Even so, they invoke King Yao's spinach soup and King Yu's bland diet as justification. This is quite ridiculous.

Yao came after Shaokang and Shun (26th century BCE), and reigned in a primitive era, so regulations for food and drink could not have been spelled out. As Yu quelled the Flood, as long as the work had not been completed throughout the land he lived modestly to spare expenses in the interest of the public project for the whole land. In each case, the premise of relative importance was quite reasonable. Coming to the Zhou dynasty (12th century BCE), both embellishment and substance were organized, standards for clothing, diet, and housing were best adapted, and systems of dining and cuisine were completed.

Are these not adjustments over the ages? Ignorant of the appropriate discretion, filling storerooms with possessions having no purpose for the world or the nation, abstaining from food and drink appropriate to rank and salary, is to enrich your storerooms at the expense of your body. This is not the practice of a noble man.

If a knight does not have the position and his salary is small, and yet he craves delicious food, he is not a real man of mettle. If you have no endurance even in respect to food and drink, what can you endure? Confucius said that one who aims for the way of the knight yet is ashamed of poor clothes and poor food is not worth talking to. He also praised Yan Yuan for living on one container of food and one gourd of water without that altering his happiness. In each case, it was because they were satisfied with their lot.

Wang Xinmin[1] of the Song dynasty once said, "If people ordinarily eat vegetable roots, they can accomplish a hundred tasks." Hearing this, Hu Wending[2] applauded. That is because one should not have ambitions out of proportion to one's position. When society deteriorates and customary norms are abandoned, people all crave food and drink in excess of their position, and repeatedly prepare delicacies. At this point they become obsessed with flavor and physically flaccid, losing the will of a man of mettle day by day.

These are due to errors consequent upon loss of measure in food and drink, whereby those with high ranks and rich salaries eat poorly, while those in petty offices who are impecunious enjoy rich food. This seems to be the meaning of Mencius' saying, "People devoted to food and drink are despised by others, because they nourish the small while missing the great."

---

[1] Wang Xinmin lived in the 11th century. He obtained a master's degree in the civil service examination and was recruited for employment in a central ministry, but declined. He was noted for strength of character

[2] Hu Wending was a distinguished educator.

There are also measures appropriate to age. In terms of age, there are the young, the adult, and the elderly. If children aren't raised on good food, then physical development will be compromised. In old age, supplement their failing energy with fish and meat. This is the meaning of the saying that at the age of seventy one is not satisfied without meat.

Just as there are differences in the three stages of life, there are differences in people's constitutions. It is imperative to be circumspect about their nourishment.

There is also the weather. Considering the degree of cold and heat, dryness and moisture, eat warm food in cold weather and mainly cold food in warm weather. Dryness and moisture both follow this. If you deviate from these measures, you'll inevitably develop an internal ailment, and then you won't have any taste for food and drink anyway.

There are also regional differences in cuisine, and differences in richness and quality of ingredients. One must consider these in regulating eating and drinking. This is not to mention ceremonies, entertainment of guests, and drinking parties—the ancients have already defined regulations for them. It's a matter of taking these into account and following what is suitable for the time.

Ceremonies, entertainment, and parties each have distinctions of upper, middle, and lower. There are courtesies from above to below, and there are courtesies from below to above; normal social interactions use these exclusively. The system differs in the various contexts of fortune, calamity, warfare, diplomacy, and celebration. This requires thorough study.

Then there are usages of diet. Rice may be polished as white as can be, but should be prepared with consideration for the quality of the rice and the soil where it was produced. Rice grown in wet soil has a high moisture content, while rice grown in dry soil has a low moisture content. Rice grown in normal soil is firm and flavorful. Rice grown in uncultivated soil is weak and flavorless. Sandy soils and rocky soils are each different. Places like this have to be assessed.

As for salt, newly evaporated salt is biting and spoils, whereas salt from ancient seashores is mild and doesn't spoil. This is added to soybeans to make what is popularly called *miso*. The method of preparing the soybeans, the method of boiling them, the method of adding salt, or the method of adding malted rice, the amount of grinding needed and the proper vessel for storage—there are all these things to consider. In this country everyone uses salt *miso* to make soup. Rice *miso* is very important for care of the spleen and stomach. The application of the method of manufacture must be carefully considered to make it full-flavored.

Now then, vinegar, soy sauce, and *sake* are used to season vegetables, fish, and meat, so it is imperative to make sense of the flavors of these three items. Vinegar produces blood, *sake* increases energy, soy sauce has the function of retaining fluid in the intestines. Vegetables have mild flavors and pacify the stomach. As for fishes and meats, some diminish physical energy while some increase it. There are five types of spices, whose quality may be good or bad. There are pleasant and unpleasant aromas, which improve or worsen the mood. It is imperative to regulate their uses carefully, adding warm things to cold things and putting cold things in warm things, to mitigate their harm.

These are all used for food and drink. Rarities and exotic foods should not be consumed recklessly. Rarities refer to items that appear in the world ahead of time; exotic foods refer to items that are not of this country. If you eat a lot when you first try a rarity, you'll get sick to your stomach. Therefore you should eat a little at first, then gradually increase the amount. Exotic foods should not be consumed at all. All interest in rare and exotic foods is due to obsession with taste. Some take to them claiming that they are medicines for the spleen and stomach, or that they have the function of increasing water in the kidneys.[1] This is not the motivation of a man of mettle.

---

[1] Kidney: In Taoist terminology adopted in traditional Chinese medicine, also used in Japan, *kidney* is used to refer to both urinary and sexual systems, so in this context kidney water can be used to mean urine output or seminal fluid.

Sustaining the body with ordinary food, one should not be greedy for life. Moderating wine and sex, one should not want to increase kidney water. Even so, to take the usual food as it comes, whether or not it is well prepared, is not the way of the noble man either. The regulation of food and drink is a basis of manners. Proper preparation and seasoning should not be neglected. In the *Discourses and Sayings* of Confucius it is written, "Rice cannot be too white, mincemeat cannot be too fine. Rice that has soured and fish that has spoiled he does not eat. What is discolored he does not eat. What is foul-smelling he does not eat. What is overcooked he does not eat. What is out of season he does not eat. What is improperly cut he does not eat. What has no proper sauce he does not eat. Even if there's a lot of meat, it is not allowed to overwhelm the flavor of the rice. Wine alone has no particular measure except that he does not drink so much as to become disorderly. Commercial wine and jerky from the market he does not consume." These are the usages of Confucius in respect to food and drink.

In the *Records of Manners* there are details on types of rice, types of dish, types of soup, filtering of wine, all sorts of food and drink and the ways to prepare them. In general, the norm for rice is compared to the season of spring, in that it should be warm; the norm for soup is compared to summer, in that it should be hot; the norm for sauce is compared to autumn, in that it should be cool, and the norm for beverages is compared to winter, in that they should be cold.

In terms of blending, in springtime the sour is increased, in summer the bitter is increased, in autumn the pungent is increased, in winter the salty is increased. These are adjusted with sweetness.

Commentary says, "According to standard method, sour flavors are not used in food in springtime, bitter flavors are not used in food in summer. In each of the four seasons, the flavor of the season is reduced. The discrepancy here is that what is being referred to is the standard method. When the seasonal energy is at its strongest, the flavor of the season is reduced to mitigate the energy in its full force. What this classic is talking about is using food to nourish people, wary of lack or compromise of energy; therefore the flavor of season is increased to nourish energy."

"For wild meat, use plums. Quail soup and chicken soup are prepared with minced water-pepper." These are methods of flavoring. Statements such as "this is extracted from meat" and "this is made with fish" are methods of preparing meat and fish. The statement that "At a grandee's meal, if there is mincemeat there's no jerky, and if there's jerky there's no mincemeat; a knight does not have both meat soup and sliced meat together" refers to the manners of different social classes.

Insofar as the system of a different country is inconsistent with the rules of our country, here I have given some indications for the sake of demonstration. If the system of dietary usages is incomplete, you will not be properly nourished, and will be unable to attend to your lord and your father properly. The logic of this should be thoroughly examined.

Next, there are rules for the acts of eating and drinking. In *Detailed Courtesies* it says, "When eating in company, don't eat to satiety. When dining together, don't wipe your hands. Don't roll rice into a ball. Don't overeat. Don't slurp. Don't smack your lips. Don't gnaw on bones. Don't put back fish or meat you've touched. Don't throw bones to the dogs. Don't grab. Moist meat is torn with the teeth; dried meat is not torn with the teeth. Don't gulp down roasted meat." These are the table manners of people of ancient times.

Generally speaking, dignity will be missing without proper table manners. So when sitting down to eat and drink, first be correct in your appearance, be considerate of those around you, and don't begin until the senior present has picked up his chopsticks. Each one should do this after being acknowledged by the senior.

Don't take big mouthfuls, don't look around when you're eating; keep your facial expression composed. Pay attention to the way you hold your chopsticks, and to the posture of your shoulders and back. Don't favor one dish, even if it is excellent. If you gather a whole mess of garnishes, or drip juice as you chew fish or meat, or scatter bones or dirty serving dishes, that is extremely unmannerly. Loud lip-smacking and slurping that can be heard at a distance are behaviors of small people. Since ancient times, those who touch foods with as much as two inches of their chopsticks are considered vulgar people. While eating and drinking, it is not mannerly to discuss mundane affairs or to laugh and talk with your mouth open.

These are generalities. It is necessary to devote further attention to understanding the rules.

If you have the occasion to eat in the presence of your lord or your father, first get their permission; don't go ahead and start eating and drinking on your own. Only if it's something that has to be taste-tested should you eat or drink first. Be solicitous of your lord or father, greet those around you, and present a respectfully courteous appearance. Compose your face, keep your mouth straight, don't make sounds in your mouth. Receive each dish respectfully, either bowing or saluting, not touching the serving plate, barely touching your bowl, putting any bones and pits in your inside pocket. Wine you taste first yourself.

Although the courtesies are numerous in their entirety, you can keep them by the three words *"Don't be disrespectful."*

In the *Jade Spread* it says, "No one presumes to eat until the lord has finished. Once the lord is done, rice and sauce are taken out and given to the attendants." In *Manners of Meeting of Knights* it says, "When the lord has a feast, taste all the dishes and drinks before the meal, then wait; when the lord orders you to eat, only then do you eat."

In *Detailed Courtesies* it says, "If you partake of fruit in the presence of your lord, if it has pits put the pits in your pocket. If you're dining with the lord and the lord gives you his leftovers, transfer everything but what is in utensils to be washed."

In the discourses of Confucius it says, "If a lord made him a present of food, he always straightened his seat and tasted it first. If a lord made him a present of raw meat, he'd always have it cooked and served. If the lord made him a present of a live animal, he'd always keep it."

These are courtesies for attendance at meals with your lord or your father.

In *Detailed Courtesies* it says, "When attending meals with elders, if the host personally urges food on you, then bow and eat it. If the host does not urge it on you personally, then eat without bowing."

In the *Jade Spread* it says, "Fruit is eaten after the lord, cooked food tasted before the lord."

In *Detailed Courtesies* it says, "When attending elders drinking, if wine is presented, rise and bow, and receive it from the senior. The younger one then goes back to his seat and drinks when the elder gives the word. The younger does not presume to drink until the elder has emptied his cup."

These are courtesies of attendance on elders at meals.

In *Detailed Courtesies* it says, "When presenting food, meat on the bone goes on the left, cut meat on the right. The rice is placed to the person's left, the soup to the right. Minced or roasted flesh is placed on the outside, savory sauce is placed on the inside. Steamed onions are placed at the edge, with wine and beverages to the right. When the meal is over, the food and condiments are removed by kneeling before the guest and handing them to the server. The host rises, thanks the guests, then afterward sits in a guest seat."

In the *Jade Spread* it says, "If the guest calls it a feast, the host refuses the compliment, saying it is not worthy of being considered a feast. If the guest says it is delicious, the host refused the compliment, saying it is plain."

These are courtesies between guest and host.

In addition to these, there are many usages related to eating and drinking, such as rules of service and presentation, and wine-drinking manners, but they are different from the fashions of our country. The appropriate deportment and demeanor should be learned from those who have thoroughly investigated the principles, following what is suitable to the time.

Next, there is the matter of the noble man keeping away from the chopping block and the kitchen, as it is said. The chopping block is where birds and animals are slaughtered and prepared; the kitchen is where they are cooked. If a noble man gets near them, thoughts of gain will occur, or greedy or miserly thoughts may occur, or even pity for the fish and fowl being slaughtered, and a slack attitude develops. These are all disagreeable. There may also be an unpleasant smell of roasting, or the sight of food being prepared may cause a loss of appetite. Therefore these are places a noble man should not be near, so one should avoid them. In *Records of Manners* it says, "A noble man avoids the chopping block and the kitchen; living creatures do not slaughter themselves." A noble man ordinarily makes it his way to care for nature; that is the reason for such consideration.

20. Dignified Housing Design

Housing is something people have no choice but to arrange. Even if you have food and clothing, if you are exposed to rain, dew, frost, and snow, vulnerable to wind, cold, heat, and humidity, then food is not enough to support life, and clothing will be ruined by the elements. So housing is constructed to avoid these problems.

Now then, in remote antiquity people were always outside, going about their activities, digging holes in the ground for dwellings, concealing themselves inside to avoid the wind and cold. Sages thought about this, gathered bamboo and wood, cut hay and reeds, and made the first houses. The *Book of Changes* says, "In high antiquity people lived in burrows and slept in the fields. Sages replaced this with houses, putting a ridgepole on top and eaves below, against the wind and rain." This is why housing evolved in human life.

Once houses are being built, everyone knows how they're constructed, craftsmanship is highly developed and tools are adequate, then the rules for construction of housing have to be comprehensive.

The saying that "the abode affects the mood" is a warning from Mencius. When a person's residence is not right, his mood changes because of this, and his manners cannot be correct. If you enter a room full of orchids, you sense the fragrance without seeking it; if you go into a room with rotten fish in it, you naturally take in the smell. When you go into a winemaker's house you want to drink wine; if you go to a merchant's house you become aware of the profit of commerce. This is because the mood is developed differently according to the abode.

Phoenixes roost in parasol trees, nightingales perch on hilltops, fish frolic in ponds, unicorns appear in rural groves. The fact that they each have a reason for their preferred place is the principle on which dwellings are constructed. For the residence of a lord or grandee, only when a suitable location is selected and the manner of construction adheres to the guidelines of sages, following the rules and providing for convenience, with all forms and functions organized, can it then be a comfortable abode. People who don't care about their houses, wherever located and however constructed, are primitive cave-dwellers; this is not a motivation for the present usage of balance between decoration and substance.

Considering that the housing system is said to distinguish social classes, it is a matter of considering the person's official rank and salary, figuring how many people he has to support, and assessing the accommodation of guests, official functions, and gatherings, to conform to that social class.

Then there are adjustments according to the person's age and physical condition. Of course, the fashions of the age and the climate also figure into the structure. Where the house is located, how far it is from a city, whether it is urban or rustic, its position relative to mountains, and the courses of rivers—the construction should be based on each of these considerations.

Therefore the classes of knights, farmers, artisans, and merchants must be defined, and their personal estate, so that even if one is rich one does not design a house beyond one's class, and even if one is poor one locates in an appropriate place. Only then can the rules for housing be clear. Based on these rules, the distinctions in size and layout should be made meticulously.

Although lightness is valued in a house, it may be made large or small according to one's social class. There must also be differences in structural dimensions within an individual house as well. Rooms are divided into inside and outside to separate the sexes; from the inside they do not talk about the outside, from the outside they are not allowed to look into the inside. With separate entrances and different walls, empty space is maintained inside and outside to keep males and females from gathering together in one place. This is a regulation that has come down from ancient times.

When the logic is examined thoroughly in this way, so that the high and the low and the great and the small all keep to their stations without any looseness, everyone will naturally keep to their class, master their work, and have no wish for anything else.

This is the housing system. Next, to discourse on the types of rooms, the first concern is where to put people. Of all people, a room for your parents should be your first consideration. If they are no longer alive, first make a shrine, then lay out rooms for family members. This is the modern-day house with a residential extension.

Next is the place where you yourself stay. Make the structure where you normally stay large, constructing a small room inside for a place to meet intimates. Construct a bedroom in between. This means that your personal abode is divided into a living room, bedroom, and drawing room.

Next, lay out guest chambers. Whether large, medium, or small should depend on the person. Here too build three sections, to entertain guests who come, whether relatives or strangers, of high or low estate. Arrange an antechamber here, either storing weapons or posting guards, to prevent disturbances inside and out, and to make it easy to relay communications and provide service.

Next is a kitchen compound. This is laid out in three sections. There is a place for butchering and dressing fish and poultry; there is a place for cooking; and there is a place to draw water and store firewood, and to keep fish and poultry, vegetables and fruits, wine and soy sauce. If the proper usage of each is not defined, the organization is inappropriate.

Next is a room to store goods. For rare and precious utensils, works of art, weapons and armor, build a storehouse with thick brick walls to keep out thieves and prevent fire. For items to which you need daily access, such as utensils, clothing, and money, build closets and set up lights. Bung up mouse holes, guard against burglars, and establish a place where all your refuse can be discarded.

This is the layout of a residence. The inner apartments for the womenfolk can be inferred from this pattern.

Next, lay out roofed corridors to join the large and small structures, with walkways everywhere, sheltered from wind and rain, setting up guard posts at appropriate locations to keep watch over that area, with space left open above and below the yard.

When it is like this, the design of a residence is complete. So, considering this in terms of the individual, there is personal space, which is one's everyday living space. There should be facilities for guests, a place to prepare food and drink, a place to store personal accessories, and a place for servants. Even in a one-room cottage no more than ten feet square these principles are inescapable.

If you extend this to the construction of huge mansions, even palaces and multi-storied buildings, you can calculate from a ten-foot-square cottage all the way to guest apartments up in the clouds and towers blocking the sky from view.

This is internal design. When you build walls of earth and stone surrounding this, either with high ramparts or deep moats, it can be a design for a castle. Systematizing the elements of a residence on this basis is done in order to define the rules of sages, establish standards, and promote thorough study of their logic.

Next, there are practical rules for residences. Carefully consider the season, be cognizant of the people's labor; don't interfere with the farming season. In all matters, such as the appropriate times to cut wood and bamboo, or when it is convenient to transport earth and stone, if you don't do them at the right time you'll toil to no avail. Calculate the appropriate pacing, relaxed or hurried, solely in terms of the season.

A preface to the *Classic of Poetry* says, "'*Beta Pegasi* right in the center' is praise for Duke Wen of Wei. Duke Wen moved his residence to Chu Hill, where he founded a city and built a palace, constructed in the proper season. The peasants were delighted at this, and the country prospered." *Beta Pegasi* is a star in the north, the Housebuilding Star. This star is right in the center at dusk in the tenth lunar month by the current calendar. This is the time for building houses, when the people have free time, in accord with the season. In cases of unavoidable necessity, just go with what is most urgent. So it says that the construction of gates and doors, the repair of roads and bridges, and the walls and moats of a castle are necessary no matter what the time. You should not wait for a particular time to attend to these.

Next, if construction is done without assessing the location, the construction won't be good. There are places where the atmosphere is extremely cold, and some places where it gets very hot, because of the environment. There are places where snow reaches the roof. Although it's normal for a northern exposure to be cold and a southern exposure to be warm, there are differences depending on the region. Considering east, west, north, and south, taking account of mountains and rivers, sea and land, assessing the quality of the soil and considering water use, be guided by the natural environment.

Next is the work of construction, figuring how much labor is needed, setting up supervisors and appointing foremen; earth and stone construction, bamboo and woodwork, providing everything necessary for the carpenters and journeymen, paying particular attention to the distribution of labor and formation of teams, always attentive to oversight of the construction. Dignified manners are to be maintained here, so appoint a manager and visit daily to check on everyone's industry or idleness, to find out who deserves reward and who deserves punishment. Then the construction will naturally be done correctly and completed quickly.

Qiu Wenzhuang[1] said, "When men of old undertook projects, they always did so in accord with the season, having examined the lay of the land and made sure of the suitability of the ground, not only doing everything humanly possible but also consulting ghosts and spirits on this. After all, building a house unavoidably puts a burden on people and costs money. You should always avoid it if it can be avoided. If you absolutely have to do it, do not fail to climb to high ground to survey, making sure the exposure and configuration are appropriate. Go down to low ground to look, examining the

---

[1] Qiu Wenzhuang: Imperial librarian of the Ming dynasty, ca. 1500.

suitability of the soil. Considering the sunlight, check to see if the exposure is in the right direction. If everything is all good, then and only then mobilize the workers and start construction."

Generally speaking, the key to construction is in the importance of lightness. Abroad they have couches and chairs. The rooms all being floored with planks, they put couches and chairs for people to sit, while the spaces where people walk are earth, stone, or tile. In our country everyone uses plank flooring for convenience; this is because people consider their own advantage without minding the expense to the land.

The places that require special attention to be made thick and heavy are as follows: care must be taken with the pillars, the earth must be made firm, the ridge and crossbeams must be well made, and the roofing must be made waterproof. To expend labor and money on unnecessary items is all frivolity, just to show off to people, leading to extreme extravagance. That's why it is said that lightness is valued.

Now then, it is said that distinctions in social class are defined by relative height. What this means is that an upper level, middle level, and lower level are constructed in a house, surrounded by inner walkways and outer walkways; people of high rank sit in a high seat, while people of low rank sit apart, keeping to their places, either on the middle or lower level, or sitting politely on the inner or outer walkways, so there can naturally be no disturbance among the lowly, and it is hard for them to act unmannerly. Because there is a distinction of high and low in the house, that is inherently adequate to maintain status and correct manners. Even more so when sitting in a high place, because any unmannerly behavior is readily evident below. Therefore those of high and low rank naturally have to correct their manners.

Next, it is said that with no place to hide, separating inside and outside naturally corrects misbehavior. What this means is that if the place where one stays is hidden, improper behavior will inevitably occur on this account. If where one stays is not hidden from view, the inner and outer apartments are strictly segregated so males and females do not come and go, the orderlies stay in their posts, the elderly, adult, and young are all segregated, and there is no space or seat hidden from view, then who can misbehave?

This means that manners should spontaneously be correct because of the structure of the residence. Otherwise, if you sprawl out idly, getting in the way of the orderlies, occasioning alienation and antagonism, administrators don't consult privately anymore, and you always keeps yourself hidden behind screens, these are all indications of a household where the people misbehave.

A noble man, a man of mettle, has nothing to be ashamed of. Examining his domestic situation, he has no sense of guilt. He has nothing to hide, inside or out. When he needs to rest, he should go to his bedroom. There is a time to retire to your bedroom; at the wrong time, it should be considered an impropriety.

So it is said that a noble man does not seek ease in his abode. Seeking ease in one's abode means acting like a retiree with an inclination to rest, neglecting work out of self-interest—this is what the admonition is directed at.

Next is the maxim to be on the alert for disturbances. That means if you only think of convenience and don't recognize the need for security, in being cultured you forget the martial, ignoring the negative on account of the positive. So lock your gates and doors, post soldiers on guard, stock the equipment necessary for preparedness against disturbances, prepare torches and lamps to keep nighttime security tight, post sentries in the hallways where people have to pass, and stockpile short and long weapons to facilitate prevention of any disturbances that may arise inside or outside. All exits, routes of passage, and gathering places should be posted with sentries to guard against disturbances.

These are precautions against disturbances caused by people. For this reason the design of a residence focuses on internal and external defense, with an understanding of these disturbances. So you set up a street sentry post outside your gate to guard outside; establish sentry posts left and right of doors, make simple guard houses wherever there are comings and goings, posting small numbers at each point to check exit and entry. Inside the house, install sliding screens so that they make a lot of noise opening and closing; position sentry stations so they can take in all four directions and easily look outside.

With this the arrangement is complete, so as long as people are at their posts there will be no disturbances from outside; thieves and robbers will naturally not come.

Next is the matter of fires. If the organization of the residence is fully functional in accord with the foregoing design, fires inside and out should be mostly avoidable. The reason for that is as follows. In terms of the four seasons, people concentrate on fire in winter and spring, the two seasons when the wind is strongest. In terms of day and night, they are concerned with fire when they cook their two meals and when they get up at dawn. The places where fire is kindled are where food is cooked and water is boiled, where charcoal and kindling are gathered, where candles and lamps are placed, and open hearths. Fires are kindled when guests come, when someone is sick, on occasions of fortune and disaster, and at times when a lot of people gather.

Studying the pattern of these categories, make thick clay linings for the fireplaces where fires are going to burn; see that they are near water, ram the earth below and cover it with stone, and don't put anything overhead that shouldn't come in contact with flames. Set up a separate building at a distance where most of the cooking and boiling are to be done, leaving empty space and keeping a supply of well water. When the fire is hot, have a steward check the color of the flames and the smell of the smoke. When a lot of fires are lit, send stewards around to check each place, and when a lot of guests have come, to watch for sparks from the torches of their attendants, making the rounds inside and outside to check. This constitutes a system of watch and signal.

If a fire occurs outside, have a rational system of duty delega-tion—a team to go up on the roof to prevent the fire from catching, a team to carry out valuables, a team to escort your wife and family, a team to go along with you. Have plenty of fire-fighting equipment, with a system of signals for their use.

When you follow these procedures, you should logically be able to fight fires. Even if you cannot help getting burned out, however, it should be said that your bearing should still not be disordered. Therefore even if you face an emergency, as long as the organization of your residence is right, there should be no change in your manners. If your home is haphazard, disorderly, and things are done in an arbitrary way, when a disturbance arises you will get confused and upset and lose your composure.

Occasionally there are those who stolidly discount worldly matters, who even in times of disturbance or fire say it's fate. Though they don't lose their composure, this is only an unexamined and unorthodox nihilistic view of the order of nature. Even though they don't lose their composure, their doctrine is forced. It isn't practical.

Noble men of mettle go by the guidelines of heaven and earth from beginning to end, so when they build houses they consider the environment, calculate the space, and coordinate the season with human affairs. As they make the design complete in this way, they are familiar with their residence and fully prepared to protect it, without mention of fate. When everything has been done to safeguard it and yet there is an unavoidable incident, then this is attributed to fate.

Therefore the reasons for strictness in organization of a residence and correctness in everyday manners become clear when dealing with disturbances. That is because there is a culture of dignified manners in the home.

Scholars who lack this understanding espouse the frugality of the eras of the sages of antiquity. In *Historical Records* it says, "When Yao had the land, his palace was elevated only three feet, the timbers were not planed, and the thatch was not trimmed." According to Confucius, "I find no flaw in Yu. His residence was humble and he devoted his energy to water drainage." They say this means we should strive for virtue without concern for housing, leaving housing however it may be. This is due to extreme literalism without reasoning.

If it's a question of how to master oneself and how to develop character, the evidence thereof is obvious in the uses of clothing, food, and shelter. That doesn't mean we should concentrate on our houses at the expense of self-cultivation and character development.

Virtuous conduct is in personal behavior in professional, social, and familial interactions. In professional, social, and familial interactions, personal conduct is not unconnected to adequacy of clothing, food, and housing. So, with careful consideration of proper proportion for our position, we should follow the ideas of the sages in organizing these arrangements, eliminating both excess and insufficiency. Here is where manners should stand.

In Yao's time, the world was still not far from a primitive condition, so systematic formulation was not yet applied to housing. It's not that they rejected housing, but because there were still many more important things to make. The same applies to Yu. Because flood control left the people no leisure, it was no time to build a splendid palace. Now that the land is at peace, all crafts are available, and there is no need to use the strength of the country for water drainage, for the emperor and lords to try to emulate the example of Yao is anachronistic. How could it be practical?

Were Yao and Yu to emerge today, they would build their palaces high to show the dignity of emperors and lords. Even so, excessive expenditure of money and belaboring of the people on extravagant residences is bound to result in destruction, like the Grand Palace of the First Emperor of China and the Separate Palace of the Sui. This is why the sages warned against such extravagance. To argue arbitrarily without understanding their words is something corrupt Confucian pedants do; it is not respected by noble men.

The design of a residence requires great care. Selecting the building codes of this country, compare them with the examples of Tang dynasty China, study construction all over the world. Even though styles of construction have been defined from generation to generation since, they tend to be extravagant or too cheap, not conforming to the proper principles of construction. Noble men of mettle should only focus on the fundamentals determined by sages, not being influenced by the fashions of the times, avoiding the wrong attitudes. All implements used along with a residence are made differently; they cannot be treated carelessly. To please others' eyes, or devote yourself to partying, are not what sages care for.

21. Clarifying the Uses of Implements

As things that support the body—clothing, food and drink, and housing—cannot be dispensed with for even a day. Now then, since there is clothing there are tools for tailoring it, wardrobes for hanging it, and chests for storing it. Food and drink cannot be handled by hand, so various utensils evolved. In antiquity they made holes in the ground to serve as bowls, and drank from them with cupped hands. They used clay drumsticks to beat earth drums. These are ways of high antiquity.

If you have a house, you should have all the utensils that go along with a house. In addition, there are all sorts of personal conveniences, beginning with armrest and cane, brush and ink-stone. There are implements associated with good and bad fortune, warfare, hospitality and diplomacy, celebration, ritual, music, archery, horsemanship, writing, and calculation. Military equipment, from armor and helmet to swords, spears, bows, guns, and their accessories, as well as articles of riding gear, are countless, but basically they are no more than the cultural and military implements to facilitate practical convenience and guarantee security.

Here the designs of implements all have their rules. There are many such designs, past and present, crude and fine. However, one should set out items that match, crude or fine according to social status, indicative of character and importance. One should not waste money on fancy implements just to impress people and show off.

So vessels for food and drink, for example, should be elevated, removing anything unclean underneath, preventing servants from touching with their hands where your mouths touch the vessels. In particular, vessels for presentation to nobles are put on a high stand to elevate the dish. This discourages menials from bending over and reaching out to pick them up. This arrangement is a measure of unavoidable necessity, to prevent people from assuming discourteous postures.

Everything should be understood in this way. Even if a utensil is only a decoration, it is inscribed with a maxim or inlaid with a saying, and people not allowed to get it dirty, so that the words are understood when seen, and as they are remembered over time they come to convey a lesson.

Therefore no implements ought to be carelessly misplaced or mishandled. In particular, documents or papers bearing the names of sages, even a single sheet, should not be soiled. Needless to say, books and writings should not be handled carelessly at all.

A man of mettle normally devotes his greatest attention to weaponry. You should inquire of men who have them to consider and calculate their advantages and disadvantages. A person's physique has more or less flesh depending on the season, and body weight changes from year to year, so the suitable size of weapons cannot be known without constant consideration and calculation. Since ancient times knights have all kept them by their seats and studied their uses from experienced predecessors. This is because men of mettle do not forget danger when at ease.

To keep any of your equipment from touching your feet, be it your weapons or your riding gear, they should be placed to one side when coming and going.

Horses are the legs of men of mettle. Without a horse, how can you travel long distances and cross steep ground? How could you treat your horse inconsiderately? You should take good care of it. There are systematic rules for this, which you should study thoroughly.

Next, there are the individual uses of the advantages of implements. That means they should be organized according to the occasion. If they are not used according to the occasion, their use will be out of place and inexpert. Every implement has its occasion. The place ought to be considered as well; figure out suitable locations to organize them in their places. If they are not put in proper places, things will soon be damaged.

There are people put in charge of this. If no one is in charge, thorough inventory is not done, and things are mishandled. Even if there is a magistrate in charge, still appoint a supervisor to check, making rounds of inspection.

When kept under wraps for a long time, implements inevitably get damaged by exposure to moisture and dryness. Military equipment in particular has to be checked carefully, as it may be rendered useless by infestation of insects or by rot.

Articles for everyday life facilitate convenience, whereas military gear is equipment for protection in times of disturbance; so if it is misplaced, that is the basis of major defeat in an emergency. The supervisor should check diligently, correcting the errors of administrators, dealing out rewards and punishments.

These are principles for organizing implements. All use of implements among people should be detached and mannerly. To give too much attention to them is not the attitude of a noble man. Hu Wending said, "People should be simple in their tastes—there is no need to appear rich and highly placed." Mencius said, "Even if I had a house forty feet high, a dining table ten feet square, and hundreds of maids in attendance, I wouldn't have fulfilled any ambition of mine."

Tastes refer to things like diet, attire, and residence. This also applies to the use of implements. If they are not handled with courtesy, though, dignified manners will be lacking in this, so even if they are handled with detachment it is essential to maintain courteous formalities and not confuse social order.

Next, there is the use of precious implements. Generally speaking, implements conventionally called precious are compared in qualities to heaven and earth, including atmosphere, beauty, and elegance. Only when implements induce people to examine themselves are they to be called precious implements. When people accomplish this completely, they are called sages. When birds and beasts have this adornment, they are called phoenixes and unicorns. When implements have this they are called auspicious treasures and precious articles. These have been respected since time immemorial, because people can take them as standards.

Even so, though precious implements and such as unicorns and phoenixes are famous in the world, this only refers to their atmosphere and elegance. As for sages, they lack nothing of the virtues of heaven and earth, so their character is thus sound, their knowledge thus universal, their courage thus outstanding. That is why sages have rarely appeared in the world over thousands of years, while gems are not rare.

Now then, next to this, if things that benefit the world and are useful to people are considered precious, then the energies of wood, fire, earth, metal, and water produce grain, clothing, plants and trees, fish and fowl, salt and greens, and enable the making of implements and swords—all of these are treasures of the world, indispensable even for a day. There is profit in gold, silver, and copper cash, moreover, when used for exchange, as what people have is profitably traded for what they lack. This is how money began to be treasured.

Considered in this context, speaking in terms of the benefit of convenient utility, even a single vessel or a single object, small as it may be, is a treasure when its time comes. For example, a sharp sword capable of killing is a treasure for the one who kills but an instrument of ill omen for the one who is killed.

Something that is good for only one function or one task, nonetheless, without universal application, is not called a treasure. Money is called valuable because it can be exchanged profitably. No asset is more convenient than this for getting through the world—that is why it has been valued from age to age. Jewels are the treasures of nobles, of no particular practical use, and no value as currency. Therefore common people don't treasure them.

When a society does not consider jewels precious treasures, that is because people value profit, not quality. Those who do happen to value jewels do so because they want to exchange them for gold and silver.

In ancient times, emperors, lords, grandees, gentry, and even commoners always wore jades. Emperors came to wear jades hanging from their belts. In the *Documents* it says, "Gather jades designed for dukes, marquises, earls, esquires, and barons; interview the regional governors at court every day during the first month of the year and distribute the jades to the governors." This means the emperor distributes assorted gems to the lords, indicating that everyone should emulate richness of character like the qualities of these jades, and should perfect sound intelligence like the luster of jade. When the lords come to court, they present the jades bestowed on them, never forgetful, never careless. This represents the fulfillment of character and intelligence.

Even so, as society degenerated, the purpose of the jades given to the lords as gems of evidence to check their character and intelligence was lost because they didn't know what treasure is.

According to the *Manners of Zhou*, six kinds of tablet were made of jade and distributed among the feudal states. Kings took the tablet of peace, dukes took the tablet of war, marquises took the tablet of trust, earls took the tablet of status, esquires took the grain gem, and barons took the reed gem. Six vessels were made of jade for rites to the sky, earth, and four directions.

Also it says that the imperial treasurer manages the treasury and security of the ancestral shrines. The treasures of the nation are stored here. *The Mean* speaks of setting out implements of the ancestors, and the *Documents* say what those ancestral implements are. All of them are treasures of the nation, valuables passed down from previous generations and carefully kept as hereditary treasures, likened to the virtues that stabilize the state.

Qiu Wenzhuang said, "Past Confucians have said that jade has the refined energy of pure positivity, so it is most treasured by sages. When they were going to propitiate heaven and earth and the four directions, they had no means of tendering their sincerity, so they made six implements of jade."

Jade has existed everywhere in China since ancient times. This can be seen by perusing the *Classic of Mountains and Seas*. In the time of Yao and Shun, they were already using it to make tablets and scepters. In the time of *The Contributions of Yu*,[1] there were already gemstones in the tribute from the three provinces of Yang, Liang, and Ying. The jade presented by Bian He[2] during the era of the

---

[1] Contributions of Yu is a work in the classic Ancient Documents concerning the ancient sage king Yu, who according to tradition founded the Xia dynasty in 2205 BCE.

[2] Bian He figures in an ancient story supposed to represent faithfulness. He found a rock that he recognized to be a jade matrix, and presented it to his king. The king thought it was just a rock and had one of Bian's feet amputated to punish him. When Bian presented it to the next king, again it was not recognized for what it was and Bian had the other foot cut off for his trouble. In the end the value of the jade was finally recognized by a third king.

Warring States came from Mt. Jing. In Han times, Indigo Fields in central China and Jade Fields in Yu province both had jades. In those days, Central Asia was not yet in contact with China. Currently we don't hear of any places in China that produce jade; all the jade in use comes from Khotan. Khotanese jade is of three kinds; white, dusky, and green. All of them come from the rivers. This is different from what ancients referred to as the mountains shining with gemstones. This is because Chinese jades come from stone and must be chiseled out, whereas foreign jades come from water and must be sifted out.

How could jade have differences of time, place, and organic matter? Jade is the purest of gemstones; is there a limit to where it is produced, can it ever be mined to exhaustion? People of ancient times associated jade with virtues, so they were never without them for no reason, making implements of them to use. The kinds used for belt chimes have to be multiple. Those for which ideographs have been devised number more than two hundred kinds, so it is obvious that they had a lot of jade in ancient times, and many ways of using it.

In the present age, there are peasants who don't know of jade. Why was it so plentiful in ancient times but so rare today? The reason people of the world don't know that jade is a treasure is because they focus on utility and indulge in subjective desires, so they tend to regard money as treasure. From this they value objects that delight the eye, please the ear, or stimulate the palate; or they treasure art and calligraphy, or rare antiques, because they are scarce and uncommon; they prize things by looking, listening, handling, or wearing them. When they ask their price, they think expensive things are great treasures. This is very much the behavior of small people, not the philosophy of noble men.

For a stalwart's weaponry, sword and spear have the greatest function, so they could be valued as treasures, but something that is sufficient only to kill a single person and protect one individual is not a treasure. The function of the three-foot sword of the Exalted

Ancestor of the Han Dynasty of China,[1] in pacifying the land, was far reaching. The long sword of this country has a chilling shine that makes foreigners fold their arms. These are worthy of being considered treasures.

Even so, when something used by your father and grandfather is needed for your house, then it is a family treasure. An ancient said, "As for the valuable articles rulers keep from preceding generations, those that bear the marks of their handling, those in which their spirit is lodged, are set out when there are events at the ancestral shrine, to show that they are being preserved. When the emperor is dying, these are set out to show their complete return." This is not a trivial matter. *The Mean* uses this to illustrate the capacity of inheritance and bequest; the *Documents of Zhou* uses this to represent the preservation of heritage. They say that if you are someone's descendant, heir to the status of your ancestral clan, keeper of your ancestral profession, how can you be filial if you don't keep the heirlooms left by your ancestors?

Speaking in these terms, while it may be reasonable to keep heirlooms of your ancestors carefully as family treasures, if you store a lot of useless articles on the pretext that they are treasures of your ancestors, on the contrary this will bring disgrace on your ancestors, and even amount to teaching your children and grandchildren to be greedy.

There are a lot of fellows known as men of mettle who nevertheless treasure utensils, even those who usually don't care about gain and loss, because they have no aspiration to the Way, don't know the intent of the sages, and have not reasoned these matters out thoroughly. Beware of this.

Generally speaking, treasure as applied to the multitudes of people everywhere on earth logically refers to whatever brings fulfillment. Cash is extremely useful to poor people, whereas rich people don't need it. Even a hobby is a treasure to someone who has none,

---

[1] Exalted Ancestor of the Han refers to the founder of the Han dynasty (r. 206-194 BCE) who had been one of the leaders of revolts against the government of the first Chinese empire. A traditional theme of righteous rebellion in China is of a sword from heaven inspiring a new leader to rise up.

whereas one with more than enough isn't interested. Thus they should not be classed as universal treasures. Scholars should pay attention to this.

22. Dignified Manners in Ceremonial Functions

Generally speaking, the function of ceremony is what manners hinge upon. Courtesies concern conduct in every single matter, in regard to every single thing. Therefore, from the physical body all the way to utensils and implements, what noble men of mettle value is understanding the guiding principles of each case. Among ceremonies, the major ones in the social structure are rites of majority, marriage, funeral, and ceremonies honoring spirits and ancestors; and rituals for hospitality, military organization, interviewing, and celebrating.

Majority means the rite carried out on someone's attainment of adulthood. In terms of ceremony, there is the ritual of the capping of the knight, which is also respected in Japan. Military leaders have observed this generation after generation. In recent times the institution of cap and gown have gone out of fashion, so the knight and commoners don't learn about it, the capping ceremony is neglected, and the rites of attaining adulthood are unclear.

In the *Manners* it says, "Males from the ages of fifteen to twenty may all be capped. This should only be carried out if there is no mourning in progress for their father or mother, or requiring a year or more." That system is very detailed, but it's not used today, so I omit it.

Sima Guang[1] wrote, "In ancient times capping was done at the age of twenty. The reason everyone valued the rite of attainment of adulthood is to charge the individual with the responsibility for his actions as someone's son, someone's younger brother, someone's subject, someone's junior. Therefore it is necessary to emphasize the importance of this with a ceremony. In recent times people have become more superficial; few keep minority status past the age of ten. Even if you charge them with the responsibility for their actions in their various roles, how could they comprehend? In case after case

---

[1] Sima Guang: A famous scholar and information officer of the central government of Song dynasty China during the latter half of the 11th century.

they remain equally ignorant from youth to maturity. That is because they don't know the ways of adulthood. Even if it is impossible to reform all at once now, if you wait from the age of fifteen until they master the *Classic of Filial Piety* and the *Discourses and Sayings* of Confucius and they have a rough knowledge of rites and manners, and then you cap them, this will still do."

Although current custom does not practice capping, the front of the scalp is shaved between the ages of fifteen and twenty as a rite of passage to majority, and the childhood name is replaced with an adult name. So this amounts to a capping ceremony. Could it be proper to neglect it?

Thus before the actual ceremony signifying attainment of majority, boys should be taught all about adulthood, so when the day comes they can perform the ritual in the presence of their parents and adopt an adult name. This is what is referred to by the expression *a guest gives a name to the one being capped.* This guest is one chosen for this function from among friends, one who is wise and mannerly. The name here refers to the adult name. So the capping involves meeting one's parents in the ancestral shrine, having an audience with honored elders, and going through a celebratory ceremony, seeing to it that manners are correct.

Courtesy to guests is shown by the ritual of offering three cups of wine. As for giving thanks to guests, that is done with bolts of cloth and mounts. The details are in classics and traditions and commentaries on manners and rituals.

Master Cheng wrote, "With the capping ceremony obsolete, there are no adults in the land. Or some wish to cap at the age of twelve. This will not do. Capping is to convey the responsibilities of adulthood, and twelve years of age is not the appropriate time to hold people responsible as adults."

Girls also debut at the age of fifteen. This is their rite of adulthood. Once people have formally become adults, there are proper ways for a person to be a person, from clothing, diet, and housing to physical carriage and attitude. Can these legitimately be neglected? This is why the capping rite is considered important.

Marriage joins two families in friendship and produces progeny, whereby the process of succession to parents in carrying out responsibilities is consummated. Since it is a major rite for men and women, it should not be made a matter of convenience.

Funerals and services for the dead are rites for remembrance of successive generations of parents. The procedures should be studied carefully, and consideration should be given to the proper timing. The courtesies of receiving guests, the process of hospitality, and the courtesies of drinking wine require greatest circumspection in regard to dignified manners.

As for military operations, this is a function of knights, with a most serious bearing on questions of life and death, survival and destruction. It cannot be explained all at once; research thoroughly, think everything through, find out what everything is for, acquiring an understanding of war strategy and military science. Your only aim should be to become a king's warrior.

Audience refers to a minister's first meeting with the lord, or a visit to a teacher or elder. These are called audiences, and the proper manner is to show the courtesies of a knight in audience. You should examine all of the types and thoroughly understand their applications.

Rites of celebration are systems of propitious times and ceremonial days for all observances of auspicious events.

The foregoing rites are all important observances. As a man of mettle, if you don't know courteous manners but are just hard and strong, you will be so mean as to merit the epithet of a northern brave.

Even though bravery and strength are basic for a man of mettle, if you neglect manners and obey subjective desires, you cannot have cultural and martial capacity and intelligence. If you don't have cultural and martial capacity, as you only make techniques your basis, how can you attain real courage?

Courtesy is basic for people, including social relations and the designs of utensils and objects. When courtesy is violated here, then proper measure is lost. Without proper measure, all action and speech will fall into either excess or inadequacy, and cannot accord with the requirements of natural principle.

Sages of ancient times valued courtesy, and established various kinds of regulations to prevent people from falling into evil. So if a man of mettle puts it in his heart to avoid disrespect in all things, making his lifestyle conform to courteous usages, thoroughly studying their principles, only then can he live up to the standards of dignified manners.

23. Circumspection in Daily Activities: General Discussion of Everyday Affairs

In the *Book of Changes* it says, "The people use it everyday without knowing." In *The Mean* it says, "The Way is not to be left for a moment. If it can be left, it is not the Way." People's every action in the world is not beyond this. I call this the Way. While I don't know, heaven and earth gave me a physical form, equipped with reason enabling it to function. In ancient times sages systematized ethics, defining inevitable rules. Even though there are no sages here, in age after age thenceforth people observed these of their own accord, so the Way exists in their everyday usages. The fact that the Way has degenerated gradually over the ages, and people and things have changed, is because of departing from this Way.

Even so, no incident can take place independent of the Way. Speaking from this perspective, from peace and war, flourishing and decline on a large scale, down to changes and movements in one event or one thing, there is no departing from the laws of heaven and earth. Noble men of mettle can only talk about the Way when they have actually experienced what this means.

Considering this body, then, it has ears, eyes, nose, mouth, four limbs, and hundreds of parts. Inside, there are distinctions of nature, mind, emotion, will, and temper. On employing this body there are functions of walking, standing, sitting, reclining, looking, listening, speech and action. To support this body there are clothing, housing, utensils, and necessary objects. There is a distinction between appetite and sexual desire. There are interactions of lord and subject, father and son, husband and wife, old and young, colleague and friend. In that context there come to be rituals for good times and bad, for war, hospitality, and celebration.

When we consider this body of ours, all of these things are inseparable. Although there are individual differences of status and wealth, none of the aforementioned items is dispensable. With this body and this mind, to depart from these things is only possible in death. In the meanwhile, thoroughly studying their principles, harmonizing with the Way that cannot be departed from, keeping the rules of heaven and earth in everything you do, in everything you arrange, with everyone you meet, even when sitting alone, organizing everything with heaven and earth as the embodiment of humaneness may be called the everyday practice of a noble man.

The principles I explain are not remote, but inescapable. In their everyday activities, everyone refers to what makes them happy as the Way, and what is offensive they call human greed. With only these two alternatives, can everyday activities be taken lightly?

24. Correcting a Day's Activities

A hundred years is considered an advanced age in terms of the human life span. A man of mettle should only consider the activities of one day, today, to be the limit. Individual days accumulate into a month, individual months accumulate into a year, individual years accumulate into a decade, decades pile up into a century.

One day is still a long way—it's in a single hour. An hour is still long—it's in fifteen minutes. Fifteen minutes is still too much—it's in a minute. In these terms, the accumulation of even thousands of years comes from one minute and concludes in one day. If you're negligent for a minute, eventually that will become a day, and may ultimately turn into a lifetime's laziness.

The continual creation of life by heaven and earth does not stop for a minute; blood and energy do not stop circulating for a minute. In this way heaven attains eternity and earth perpetuity; in this way life flourishes forever.

When virtue and intelligence circulate like this, one is a sage. Great Yu valued even a minute of time, Confucius contemplated flowing water. This must be the sense of the saying that the circulation of virtues is faster than the conveyance of commands by relay.

Considering a day's activities here, first get up early, wash and groom yourself, dress properly, including accessories, and sit quietly with your hands folded, making your appearance and manner correct. Nurture the mood of dawn,[1] and contemplate the principle of heaven and earth ceaselessly producing life.

Then acknowledge your debt and duty to your lord and your father, and think about today's work, a matter of considerate contemplation. "The physical body, hair, and skin, are received from father and mother; not daring to injure them is the beginning of filial piety. Establishing oneself, carrying out the Way, leaving a reputation to posterity that will distinguish your father and mother is the end of filial piety. Serving your lord with total devotion, planning for the benefit of others, is loyalty." The meaning in this is deep and far-reaching. Above all, you should observe subtle impulses.

Once daylight dawns, open the door and clean, sprinkle, and sweep the walk. Here the energy of heaven enters in, here the veins of earth grow. If there are household chores, give instructions with all the necessary information. In the meantime, if visitors come or messengers are waiting, see them promptly and respond to them promptly, not causing them any delay.

If you are in the service of a lord, go to work early. If you are taking care of your parents, see if they are all right. If you go out to work, be thoroughly circumspect about where you situate yourself and what you say, and don't plan beyond your position. If you are attending an elder, be polite and respectful, treating him like your father or elder brother, being deferential and not arguing.

Generally speaking, the course of service in public office is to go to work early in the morning before others, and leave work in the evening after others. When you get home, look in on your parents. With a mild manner and gentle voice, settle in your seat and inquire

---

[1] The mood of dawn is an image from Mencius. The mood of dawn means mental calm, freshness, coolness, and clarity.

about affairs in your absence, assess their relative urgency, and do what needs to be done.

If there is free time, change out of your court clothing, sit quietly and contemplate, reviewing the day's activities. If you have time to spare, then read, reflecting on the words and deeds of people of old, getting to know the designs of sages and savants.

When the sun has gone down, then give instructions for night security, making sure of mutual arrangements. Then go to bed, relax your body and rest your mind. Have attendant samurai go on and off duty at regular times.

These are the habits of rising early and retiring late, working at the office and looking after the family.

These are precepts for knights when at home. They ought to be observed with care. A tradition says that in an official career forty is considered the age of strong service. This is the time when one's planning in public service is apt. Nevertheless, taking the number of progeny into consideration, on the command of his lord or father one should be allowed to get experience in office even if only around twenty years old.

Even if knights serve in office, their work load is little and they always have a lot of free time. Sometimes they are given leave and live at home, or have unfortunately never served a lord, or their parents have passed away early, or they are too far away to go on duty from morning to night. When leisure days living at home go on for a long time, your will slackens, becoming unrestrained and indulgent; calling yourself the one man of leisure in the world, you don't look after your professional work and eventually degenerate into an animal. This is what Master Zeng meant when he said, "Small people living at leisure will do anything immoral."

So discipline is required when living at leisure. Generally speaking, a man of mettle does not relax his discipline because of distinction, and does not become lazy in his conduct because of obscurity. Thus he first gets up early in the morning, cleans himself, grooms and reflects, acknowledges and contemplates, then goes out and greets the knights, attends guests, and may watch archery or go horseback riding, then has a quick meal. If there are guests who showed up without an invitation, then don't change your simple fare. Share a cup of lees.

When you've finished, rinse your mouth and straighten your appearance, dignified in your manner. If you have no business to attend to, practice the arts of swordsmanship, archery, shooting, or spear fighting, strengthening your physique and perfecting your maneuvering. Invite experts, or go to their places, never being lazy. If you slack off for a long time, you'll become clumsy, uncoordinated, out of condition, sluggish, inadequate for the job.

A man of old carried bricks to develop his strength. Both his determination and his effort ought to be observed.

If you still have free time, read books and study military science and martial principles, researching the reasons for the things involved, clarifying the designs of the relevant equipment and operations, based only on what the sages say.

Once the sun sets, then have your evening meal, repeating the morning ritual. Morning and evening meals are best simple and quick.

As the day grows dark, light candles early to distinguish objects and dispel doubt. If something comes up, go ahead and see to it. Otherwise, if there's nothing going on, then quietly rest your mind.

While a man of mettle is staying at home, if he is this circumspect even in solitude, then he will have a clear conscience. He does not neglect manners whether in view or out of sight. Here his mind is broad, here his body is robust, here his attention is focused; his will has a definite direction, and no ideas of license or indulgence occur to him.

These are precepts for living at leisure.

25. Use of Money; Ethics of Receiving and Giving

If you have money but can't use it, then money isn't valuable. If you have a use for it but don't calculate the amount of money needed, then the use isn't practical. Money is valuable because of need, needs are practical because of money. There is no distinction between money and its use.

Money is quantifiable, needs can be met. Money functions properly to provide for the poor, to help the indigent, to look after the needy, to invite the wise, and to recruit knights. It is a medium of exchange, whereby what people have can be exchanged for what they have not, and trade is made profitable. If it is used effectively it is valuable; otherwise, miserly feelings occur day by day, and the calamity of extravagance happens from time to time. Neither of these is the way of the noble man.

A man of mettle thinks only of duty. If you treasure money and amuse yourself with possessions, you'll be remiss in military duty, unable to forget home in an emergency. If you think so much of home that you abandon duty and flee death, you become an object of derision and you disgrace your father and grandfather. What is enjoyable about having a human face but an animal heart?

History abounds with people who had an abundance of gold, silver, money, and goods, but lost their countries and wrecked their families, or traded themselves for money making. But outstanding men disdain empire and state. There is the example of one who washed his ears in a river, and those who gathered ferns in the mountains. You should reflect on their high-mindedness.

Even so, this does not mean that if you have money you should discard it in the mountains or toss it in the sea, treating it the same as dirt or rocks. It's just a matter of making sure of its measured use.

The riches of the world are the riches of the world, not the riches of one man. Money makes trade and profit possible, applying to all things; that is why it is called wealth. People who have money say they don't want to waste it, and don't know how to spend it. If gold and jade fill your rooms, and money and goods lie in storage, and yet you don't know how to put it to use, then the riches of the world stagnate inside individual treasuries and are not useful to the world. What is more wasteful than this?

When people like money, they're generally miserly with it. That is why sages didn't consider money as treasure and did not value hard-to-get goods. Indeed, to store pottery, paintings, calligraphy, and vessels of copper and iron, and call this treasure, spending thousands in gold on these things, is extreme confusion.

The principles of giving and receiving, the duties of ruler and subject, superior and subordinate, and the courtesies of interactions with peers, should be carefully observed by knights.

All things great and small involve duties, whether giving or receiving. So if disbursal is not done in a principled and just manner, people will not be pleased and knights will not enlist.

A tradition says, "Men of justice cannot be hired for money. Even a beggar won't accept food used for enticement." How can we not be careful? If it is right to receive something, then it should be accepted, no matter how valuable it is. If it is in any way unjust or unprincipled, even an immense salary, or leadership of the world, should not be accepted.

So when you give, consider the relative value of the thing, determine the way to do it and act accordingly, including a note. No matter how small or meager, it represents an intention and maintains an ethical principle. How could the recipient not be appreciative?

As for the proper way to receive something, usages of sendoff and welcome, restraint and deference, how can these be overlooked? If you don't do it right, giving is without feeling and receiving is without pleasure. You should focus on circumspection in the context of giving and receiving. Someone said, "Rather than be miserly and accumulate money, let a knight be generous with it, and he'll have even more."

26. Prudence at Parties

Knights are not lazy either in public or private; sharpening their will, they are diligent in their activities. This is their job. Treating savants as savants and familiars as familiars, they organize parties and drink wine, and frequently gather to listen to music. These are occasions when guests are entertained.

Bathing in the wind wearing the clothing of spring, hiking in the mountains, enjoying the moonlight in the valleys and the clear breeze on the rivers, they follow the flowers and willows. These are the parties of men of mettle. Why just occupy yourself with reading and writing, becoming a stuffy little man? Here your heart expands, here your taste is purified.

Nevertheless, drinking wine must have discipline, and diversions must have measure. Each excursion, each diversion, as a model for lords, does not involve streaming music or an idle waste of time. In the sacred park of King Wen, the doe and deer were fat, the swans were white, fish danced in the ponds. This is a lesson of the ancients, to share their enjoyment with the people. Whether in falconry, hunting, or fishing, should a man of mettle lose measure and become obsessive? One must be very careful.

BOOK TWO

The Warrior's Rule

By Tsugaru Kodo-shi

I. The Basis of Order

1. Martial Virtues

Warriorhood is a word for unflagging bravery and ferocity for justice. It has wide application, and there are many kinds.

When someone is fierce and powerful by nature and developed in skill, able to lift heavy weights and leap long distances, cross rivers and travel far, going all day without tiring, wielding sword and spear without blinking or quivering, winning every battle at will, such a man is called a warrior. This is someone who has attained one type of warriorhood.

There are those who issue strict orders, grant generous rewards, and impose severe penalties, who employ soldiers like herding sheep, coordinate armies by rules and regulations, plunge in where there is nowhere to go, gain total victory in every battle, expand the territory and revive the nation. One like this is called the warrior leader of a country in combat. Sun Wu[1] of China and Shingen of Japan were examples of this.

There are those who think deeply and silently descry patterns of change; who know what has gone by and perceive what is to come, free of confusion; who find out the hidden and fish out the obscure, without error; who prefer strategy to contests of strength, who spend a lot of time contriving and act indirectly so as to overcome enemies. Kongming[2] of China and Kusunoki[3] of Japan were examples of this.

[1] Sun Wu, often cited as Sun-tzu or Master Sun, was a successful military strategist whose treatise *The Art of War* is a perennial classic in its field, still widely studied.

[2] Kongming refers to Zhuge Liang, (ca. 180-233), a distinguished civil and military leader of the Shu Han, or so-called Minor Han, one of the Three Kingdoms into which China was divided following the dissolution of the Han dynasty in 221 CE. Shu refers to the region of Siquan, where a remnant of the Han dynasty was set up and held out for forty-four years.

[3] Kusunoki Masashige (? - 1336) was a distinguished warrior of the Japanese era of the Northern and Southern Courts, a time of civil war when rival branches of the imperial family were backed by competing warrior clans. Kusunoki became governor of two provinces, and was also a member of several organs of imperial government under Emperor Go-Daigo. A great hero of Japanese history, Kusunoki died fighting the warlord Ashikaga Takauji, founder of the second samurai dynasty, centered in Muromachi, Kyoto.

Those who are capable of balance without wavering, who are centered and unbiased, who cannot be compromised by wealth and honor, who cannot be moved by poverty or disgrace, who are not affected by the senses, are stalwarts of the teachings of sages and savants.

Thus while their types are not the same, they are all consistent with the great basis of warriorhood, merely differing in scale and relative refinement. When you seek precedents of people of old, or require literal explanation, it's hard to penetrate the profundities in an explanation of warriorhood.

Virtue means attainment. When we attain this we thereby feel at ease; where others attain this, they rest easy in their places. This is called virtue.

To improve oneself by warriorhood is the beginning of martial virtue. To govern knights by warriorhood is the end of martial virtue. To rule the world by warriorhood is the ultimate achievement of martial virtue. To master the whole process beginning to end, root and branch, omitting nothing, is true martial virtue.

As a martial state, Japan has been governed militarily ever since Lord Yoritomo,[1] so if the basis of order and peace is not established by martial virtue, the root and stem will be weak, and easily collapse. The substantiality of martial virtue is most profoundly important.

Overall, the function of martial virtue is spontaneous strictness without disobedience even if the military leader doesn't enforce rules severely, having knights flocking to one's court to serve even though one is not always giving out rewards, and everyone trembling as before battle axe and halberd even though one is not angry. These are signs of the external efficacy of martial virtue.

If you wonder what path or what principle to go by to get to where people submit in fear like this, the basis is the warrior leader's personal realization of warriorhood.

To be devoted to warriorhood as much as to sensuality, to use it as constantly as food and drink, to respect and believe in it as

---

[1] Minamoto Yoritomo (1147-1199), founder of the first Bakufu, or central military government of Japan.

in ghosts and spirits, to regard it with the gravity of the greatest mountain—these are preliminary tasks of self-improvement by way of warriorhood, the root source from which to extend martial virtue to the four seas.

Whatever reaches outside is invariably rooted inside—this is the condition of all beings. Therefore, when a foundation rooted within is small and slight, what emerges outwardly is accordingly not far-reaching or grand. For this reason, if a warrior leader wants the full effect of martial virtue, it's a matter of first attending seriously to the path of self-improvement by warriorhood.

Now the evidences of martial virtue outwardly evinced are two— awe and obedience. This is called martial dignity. When martial dignity is outstanding, people submit and fear; being awed, they also obey.

Awe and obedience are two things, but in effect they are one. Without awe and fear, others may outwardly obey but be inwardly opposed. If they are not submissive, they may be afraid at first but will eventually rebel. In military science this is called the rule of controlling yet inspiring, by means of awe and admiration.

To the degree you are awesome, people will find this intimidating; to the extent you are admired, people will become attached to you. Therefore fear and admiration are the sources of all actions. The expression of martial virtue being awe and admiration, the practical effects of awe and admiration are fear and submission.

Therefore to work unceasingly on warriorhood by yourself is to have virtue within you. Where people can rest in peace is where virtue is consummate. When inside and outside, other and self, find their proper places, this is the totality of martial virtue.

What effectuates this is knowledge; what implements this is duty; what completes this is courage.

When the generals are rich in martial dignity, even if there are external troubles with rival states there is no anxiety for the homeland—any who may come to try to invade will themselves be toppled and fall. Thus the state will endure. Does ease not ensue upon attaining this?

When the multitude of knights comes under the influence of this virtue, they discern duty on their own, volunteer with courage, despise discourtesy, and keep the law. Thus there is joy within and delight without. Does ease not ensue upon attaining this?

Those who take leisure and amusement for ease are as if slicing off flesh from their own bellies to eat in order to satisfy their own hungry guts. One occasion's pleasure turns out to become many incidents of injury. Therefore taking it easy without a basis in martial virtue is the conduct of a weak leader.

As a general category, martial virtue has two main aspects, cultural and military. Internal order is cultural, external deterrence is military.

Even in other countries, rulers who started their careers with armaments seem to have founded their states by martial virtue, but that is not what the warriors of our country mean by martial virtue. It corresponds to the military classification, but that militarism is still not the same as our country's militarism. Iron and lead may both be metal, but the difference in their durability is as that between sky and earth. You can't even talk about them on the same day.

Abroad, what is called the virtue that governs all within the four seas functions on the basis of humaneness, so it is cultural virtue. What warriors call the virtue that governs all under heaven functions on the basis of duty, so it is martial virtue.

This country and other countries are all within the same world; the reason their ideologies are so contradictory seems to be due to the influence of ancient ways continued through the ages by habit, turning into conditions of human nature in the world. So whereas they originally received the form and energy of earth and water, they unavoidably came to have different preferences and aversions. Therefore when virtuous government is established taking all conditions into account, even if not exactly perfect it is not far off.

Things have three active ingredients: to have all three is called virtue. One is called potency, second is called ability, the third is called purpose.

For example, when a sword has an unfathomable efficacy, such that its energy shoots the North Star or sprites shrink from it, this is the potency of the sword. Cutting through iron helmets and piercing rhinoceros hide armor is the ability of the sword. As for the purpose of the sword, it is to accompany a man in action and repose and do what it is supposed to do.

To have exemplary dignity in conduct and activity, to have awesome sternness in correctness and uprightness of speech and behavior, is the potency of a commander. To be unafraid in face of peril and unerring in strategy, to lead a small force to attack a large one, achieving victory a hundred percent of the time, is the ability of a commander. To motivate oneself unceasingly, not become conceited about talent and ability, accept criticism without refusal, and persevere in education out of compassion for the ignorant, are examples of the purpose of the commander.

When these three things are combined, this is called martial virtue. Until you have attained these three, you cannot reach the ultimate goal of being able to rest in peace.

2. Warrior Wisdom

Clearly understanding warrior ways and martial matters is called warrior wisdom. Even if you read through books of ancient and modern history and exhaust the literature of Japan and China, as long as you are ignorant of the ways of warriors you cannot yet claim the wisdom of the warrior leader.

Wisdom is a function of intuition and intellect, while talent is a function of wisdom. Knowing a lot by learning from precedent is wisdom; to build it up inwardly and apply it to oneself, able to employ it in the ways of warriors today, adapting to their changes, is talent.

What is crucial in cultivating warrior wisdom is in knowing the conditions of victory and defeat. Victory means controlling events and people; defeat means being controlled by events and people. Of all the things we face—heaven and earth, people and things—it is only considered important to control people.

People have inner and outer states. It is easy to control the outside, hard to control the inside. To effectively control both inside and outside and not allow opponents to rise against you is the reality of victory. This alone is the reason why the military class is constituted as a warrior caste—simply because there is this matter of victory and defeat.

When that wisdom builds up over a long time, it produces a sensitive and perceptive mastery within. When it is abundantly stored and long accumulated, that mastery becomes more and more complete, so that it intuits and discerns everything about warrior ways and martial matters, great and small, specific and general. Its uses are inexhaustible; it can be drawn on endlessly. When it reaches perfection, it is coextensive with sky and earth, metamorphosing like ghosts and spirits. This is the total attainment of warrior wisdom.

When ordinances are issued and rules are established without the clear discernment of warrior wisdom, few principled knights will keep them. When principled knights are satisfied, in the end the common crowd will ultimately submit. When the knights submit, the three common classes go along too. This is how the military class spreads its influence by means of warrior wisdom.

Martial virtue is the substance of warrior wisdom, while wisdom is the function of virtue. Substance and function are rooted in each other, and are never separate. Virtue is expressed by wisdom; wisdom is stabilized by virtue.

3. Warrior Justice

Justice is a term for dealing with affairs and people appropriately. Appropriateness means that all parties find their place, so that they are happy. This is what is appropriate. If you yourself are the only one to enjoy a benefit, you may be happy about it, but others are not. Though something may seem all right from one point of view, from another it may, on reflection, prove to be objectionable in some way. In such cases, that cannot lead to happiness in the end. So justice means judging and settling matters between people to the satisfaction of all parties.

Making judgments and decisions appropriately is something even the three civilian classes do, according to their roles. The justice of the warrior's way is determined by martial virtue and warrior wisdom; that is why it is called warrior justice.

Judgment by cultural virtue has less authority. When there is little authority, there is more amusement than fear. When judgment is made by martial virtue, it is authoritative and inviolable, welcomed yet feared. This is martial justice.

People who are fixated on cultural virtues are influenced by erudition to be indecisive in judgment. This is the trouble with education that cultivates intelligence exclusively in literary terms. As long as there is indecisiveness and hesitancy in judgment, legal codes won't help people much in the end. This is far from warrior justice.

The form of warrior justice is righteousness. To be right means to conform to rules and guidelines. This is represented by the square. When you draw a square, the lines must be straight and the angles right. Using this as a standard of correctness, in being correct one is honest.

Upright honesty seems cutting, but it is not so. What is cutting is sharp, and sharpness injures whatever it touches, unable to bear the weight of anything. A square, being straight and upright, can bear great and small, good and bad. So when you are about to stand out in a way that seems like it should not be deemed honest, all angles being crooked, then you don't rest content here; this is the form of honesty.

The ultimate principle of square and round cannot be fully expressed in writing. Therefore righteousness accepts people but is not influenced by them. Those who are cutting sometimes suffer from inflexible egoism on this account. When warrior leaders treat their followers inflexibly and egotistically, then the hearts of the multitude rebel. It is a matter that calls for extreme prudence and caution.

Justice requires credibility. If you make a decision but change your promise afterward, or you eat your words, the feelings of the multitude turn against you. When they are against you, then the troops will not obey orders in emergencies. When they are insubordinate, their battle lines will inevitably crumble. This is how you get your state taken away and lose your territory. Should we not be careful?

If you want justice to be true, that is in knowing the guidelines of the four foundations of courtesy, righteousness, honesty, and shame. In military science this is called the cross square. The uprightness of the vertical is straightened by means of the horizontal, while the straightness of the horizontal is set by the vertical. At this point the vertical and horizontal determine their paths. This is uprightness and rectitude, and hence is warrior justice.

Those who are not prompt in making decisions, or who are errant in the logic of their judgment, are that way because of weakness of wisdom. Weakness of wisdom is due to paucity of virtue.

In the duties of the warrior leader, there are things for which consultation with administrators is appropriate, and matters on which consultation is inappropriate. In general, matters that may affect martial authority are not for consultation. What requires inquiry and consultation with influential officials is the civil order.

4. Warriors' Work

Warriors' work refers to the affairs of the warrior's ways, the occupations of warriors. There are many differences of grade and type among them.

The interactions of warriors are all part of warriors' work. When you come to know the work of warriors, its wisdom is realized and its duty fulfilled. In cultivating the wisdom of martial science, where to begin is of utmost importance.

Although there are very many kinds of warriors' work, yet the general principles cannot vary. Some things call for inquiry from a master of the way, some things should not depend on the words of predecessors. It's all a matter of attaining the necessary principles by the necessary means.

What is essential in martial science is to read the classics to become acquainted with the customs of a martial state, understand the underlying ideas of the warriors' rule, and still question predecessors to comprehend the inner essence. Studying military books to discern the conditions of victory and defeat, or debating the gains and losses of ancient wars to know the present day, thereby you should plumb the wellsprings of victory.

When you get to this point, facts and principles are generally clear. When it comes to martial arts, horsemanship is most important. Swordsmanship is next, and then archery, shooting, and so on. This should be the order in which military leaders should learn martial arts.

There are so many kinds of weapons that it would not be easy to thoroughly examine past and present manufacture and the history of changes. It is imperative, however, to test the actual advantages and disadvantages of weapons, and to clarify the principles of complete preparedness and omission.

There are many weapons and military arts abroad, but few are worth taking up and employing. Among them, the works of Taigong,[1] Sun and Wu,[2] the *Three Strategies*,[3] and Li Jing contain excellent principles and are most useful for the art of war. Also, the principles of Zhuge Liang's *Eight Battle Formations* are absolutely outstanding.

The ancient military arts of Japan also contain little that can serve to guide, especially in situations such as standing shield to shield on the field, or requiring the art of archery to shoot from horseback. However, many of the military methods of the last two hundred years are very useful. In the case of Shingen in particular, though he naturally excelled in the use of weaponry and so there is nothing in his ordinary conduct to serve as a guide, nevertheless he had considerable attainment in the art of war and should be studied.

---

[1]   Taigong is an abbreviation of Taigongwang, "Father's Hope," an epithet of Lu Shang, mentor of King Wen, one of the co-founders of China's Zhou Dynasty, regarded by Confucians as the Golden Age. Lu Shang assisted King Wen's older brother King Wu in overthrowing the decadent Shang dynasty in the 12th century BCE. A famous text known as *Liu Tao or Six Strategies* is attributed to Taigong.

[2]   Sun and Wu refer to Sun Wu and Wu Qi, outstanding military strategists and authors of famous treatises. Sun Wu is noted above; Wu Qi was a successful tactician of the Warring States era, and his work is a classic of military strategy.

[3]   *Three Strategies*: a famous military text, said to have been transmitted to Zhang Liang, a strategist for the founder of the Han dynasty of China in the 3rd century BCE, by a certain Huang Shi, who was allegedly a wizard. A distinguished historical figure, Zhang Liang is also noted in Taoist annals, and Huang Shi is supposed to have been a shenren or "spirit man," either mythical or an unknown. The famous unknown is a stock figure in Taoism, which advises people of extraordinary abilities to keep an unusually low profile.

While this is so of all cultural and martial studies, when it comes to military science and the arts of warfare it is particularly imperative to consider every element carefully and clearly understand. This is because evidence of their accuracy or otherwise is not manifest on the same day, but in a life and death situation it's not easy to call back a strategy once it's been set in motion.

5. Warriors' Preparedness

Strict military preparation when you have no opponents is called the preparedness of warriors. The preparedness of warriors is critical to the rule of warriors. Without the warriors' preparedness, as a knight you have nothing to grip and nowhere to stand; it's like being in a boat on the ocean without an oar—what will you do if a storm comes up?

Only when military preparedness is complete can the world pillow on stable peace. But this completeness is not easy; it is to be attained by strictness in what the art of war refers to as the five stages of security. Only after having attained this has the state attained the martial spirit.

6. The Courage of the Warrior

Courage means being unafraid and unyielding, making progress through experience, strengthening yourself unceasingly.

Being fearful means you are controlled by external things, so that you become psychologically passive. The spirit of knighthood is normally forward in action, but if you see no advantage to going forward and so you withdraw strategically, it's because in actual effect this is really advancing. As long as you don't know the actuality of that advance, you won't be able to advance and withdraw to the appropriate degree.

Loss of virtue in warrior leaders is ordinarily due to indulgence in desires. The source of the sickness of indulgence in desires is superficiality of courage.

Inside there are desires associated with the emotions, outside there is desire for fame and desire for gain. When it comes to insatiable consumption of delicacies, using silk like burlap, forgetting the pains of the people while oblivious of one's own extravagance, in extreme cases like the First Emperor of China[1] and the Martial Emperor of the Han Dynasty[2] degenerating into absolute ignorance, this is all because of being captivated by external things and losing inner control.

Now then, when you are not seduced by external things, avoid sensuousness and restrain indulgence, regulating your desires so your constancy is not taken from you by external things, this is called not yielding to things.

A common shortcoming in the world is to start out striving diligently but eventually become lazy—hardly anyone makes virtue last. The transmission of martial virtues to eternity, and the extension of the warriors' rule to the four seas, is a question of the depth or superficiality of martial valor. This is the key to a military leader's exercise of power.

The courage of the warrior is the sum of all practices of the way of the knight; will is the source of all practices. When courage is superficial it's hard to establish will, and without will courage cannot be. When will is established, that is courage; when courage is developed, will is also established. Courage and will are interdependent.

The way to make martial valor great-hearted and perpetuate its discipline is first of all in magnanimity. Magnanimity means breadth of mind. If you get angry at small things, delight in small gains, and fear small injuries, eventually you'll be taken over by external things—how can you acquire the strength to bear the great responsibilities of the world over the long run? To endure trouble and toler-

---

[1] First Emperor of China: Qin Shi Huangdi (r. 221-209). Uniting the ancient states, the first emperor founded the Chinese empire on Legalistic principles, which emphasized primary production and aggressive warfare. In Confucianism the First Emperor is a prototype of a tyrant; in Taoism, he is a prototype of a man undone by greed and ambition.

[2] Han Wu Di (r. 140-88 BCE) was one of the most powerful rulers of the Han dynasty in China (206 BCE -219 CE). He abolished semi-autonomous principalities to establish absolute central rule, and established a state school system based on a uniform curriculum to indoctrinate civil servants. Like the First Emperor of China, he took an interest in esoteric arts and tried to become immortal; this is traditionally interpreted as an indication of their absolute greed and aggression.

ate hardship, never yielding to them, in order to accomplish a monumental work, is the magnanimity of a great man.

Second is a matter of conscience. When rulers are unguarded outside of audience, they will inevitably become careless in the bedroom, unmindful that there are ways of surreptitious access at every door, forgetting that ridicule may reach the young. This is because of having no shame before heaven, earth, and humanity.

The essence of conscience is in clear understanding of duty and principle. If you know these two things effectively and practice them sincerely, eventually you will attain the reality of martial valor, the courage of the warrior.

Wielding a sword with short clothes and unkempt hair, killing people like cutting grass, undisturbed in mind and appearance even with boiling cauldrons in front and swords and bone-saws behind, is also a kind of martial valor. Referred to as being able to stomp down naked swords but unable to be balanced, this is not adequate to regard as the courage of a military leader. It is the boldness of an assassin.

When people get old they hope for gain, but as they become feeble they practice temporary benevolence, in extremes believing in Buddha in hopes of the happiness of heaven. In the days when Emperor Wu of Liang[1] was whipping his horse in ancient times, who could have foreseen that he'd eventually starve to death? These are examples of small courage without a broad basis, losing constancy in the end and winding up in extreme ignorance.

This is how insecure the human mind is. The lessons of the warrior's courage are most serious.

II The Way of Rule

1. Establishing Will

The direction of feeling and thought is called will. To be established

---

[1] Emperor Wu of Liang (r. 502–549) established his domain of Liang in southern China during the period of division in Chinese history known as the era of the Northern and Southern courts. Alleging repenting of the bloodshed he caused in his rise to power, he became an ostentatious patron of Buddhism, draining state finances. In the end he was overthrown by an erstwhile ally and vassal who rebelled against his rule.

means standing tall and not collapsing. Even minor tasks cannot be accomplished unless the will is established; how much less success in the warriors' rule! When the will is established, anything can be achieved. When the will is not established, all works are unsuccessful.

Confucius' sage virtue at sixty was all there in his aspiration at the age of fifteen. "Who was Shun? Who am I?"—this was Yi Yin's[1] aspiration. When your will is established, you can become even a sage or a savant; when it is not, you become ignorant and ignominious. Establishing the will is the means by which to begin and finish everything. This is a matter of establishing it by striving.

In ancient and modern times there are examples of founders of states who seemed to have will in the beginning but eventually became lazy when they had attained riches and rank. If you are going to establish a robust will that ends only on death, it is a matter of making the will the leader of energy.

Everybody's feelings are each based on benefit. Therefore wherever the energy body contacts there is a tendency to want to linger over this minor gain. When you follow it desirous, energy employs will. On this account, will wears out along the way.

So if there is an impulse to linger over minor gains along the way, restrain it strictly with the awareness that it is a robber that will deprive you of the character of the warrior. If you are careful to keep the will in charge, it never wavers.

Everybody who discourses on the duties of the Way knows it, but what is hard to put into practice is this: one may indulge oneself in a respite, or one may indulge oneself in something small, but once one indulges oneself, one becomes more and more indecisive, until one ultimately loses one's will forever.

The discipline of being careful even when alone is not to be taken lightly at all. Wanting some time off, or some trivial thing, is an

---

[1] Yi Yin: a legendary minister of the Shang dynasty (1766-1122) of ancient China, often cited in Taoist literature. Yi Yin (d. 1713 BCE) was a minister for Tang, the founder of the Shang dynasty, and for his grandson and successor. Shun was an archetypal sage leader of antiquity. Yi Yin's rhetorical question "Who was Shun? Who am I" stands for the idea, emphasized by the Confucian apostle Mencius, that all people have the capacity to be a sage.

impulse of an internal thief. To refuse to be captivated in such situations and remain aloof as you do your work is the will of a great man.

The roots of human feelings are the two poles of like and dislike, that's all. The will inclines to what we like and turns away from what we dislike. Human feeling likes benefit and dislikes harm. What average people like is of small benefit, what they dislike is of small harm. Accomplished people are the opposite; they like great benefit and dislike great harm.

Great benefit means peace on earth and perpetuation of the nation. Small benefit means personal ease and temporary pleasure. When the will is established it inclines to great benefit; when it is not established it admires small benefit.

Whenever you seek small benefits, invariably small benefits do not last, and calamity comes along. Even a lord who settles for those small benefits and seeks ease cannot but hope for peace and perpetuation of the state. He has the feeling of hope, but his will runs only to objects that ruin what he seeks all the time. There is no worse confusion of the human mind. How sad!

The richest and highest ranked man in the land, as the lord of the land, has all officials kowtow; to go by him is like passing a tiger's cave, to say a word is like grabbing a tiger's whiskers. So he becomes accustomed to having others agree with whatever he says and does. His palate is sated with rich and delicious food, he always wears light and warm clothes. For this reason, as everything to which he is accustomed easily gets him involved in acquisitiveness, so he also has his will easily taken away.

Wealth and poverty are as different as ice and coal, but both involve a lot of problems associated with the mood manipulating the will.

The basis of establishing the will is in the aim. A warrior leader of the four seas makes complete peace his bullseye. Never giving up, even in death, as long as you haven't hit the bullseye, is the will of a hero.

2. Personal Cultivation

For a warrior leader to extend martial rule throughout the land, the first task is personal cultivation. Cultivation means governance. Being reasonable and consistent, with clear principles, refraining from improper words and acts, is called personal cultivation.

The existence of a warrior leader in the world is like the sun in the sky—even bedroom secrets and dalliance in cloistered chambers eventually leak out and are bruited abroad. If anything incorrect or weak is said or done, the knights of the kingdom will be contemptuous of him in their hearts. When they are contemptuous, his martial authority collapses. So the existence of a warrior leader in the land is like walking over springtime ice bearing a heavy load. The need for personal cultivation is very serious indeed.

The functions of the human body are at most of three kinds—speech, conduct, and mind. What a warrior leader watches out for in the course of personal cultivation, is in not becoming lazy and weak. This is done in terms of these three things, among which mind and conduct are fundamental and conduct is crucial.

Speech is a way of outwardly expressing inner qualities, so its use is important. The speech and action of a warrior leader should, as a rule, be only what is necessary and natural. To cultivate cleverness of rhetoric for artfulness and euphemism is the work of orators; to strive for an attitude of courteous deference is the business of courtiers. The words and speech of a warrior leader are to be simple and straightforward, with clear and consistent logic. Whether to be deferential or dignified depends only on the rule of necessity. Those who strive for literary embellishment do so because of being inwardly afflicted with weakness.

As for social relations and responding to events and people, these are important elements of conduct; those instructions are under the heading of ordering the home.

The mental method has two principles, rectifying the mind and nurturing energy. Rectifying the mind is the substance, nurturing energy is the function. The condition of all things is that the substance is established through the exertion of the function, while the function is accomplished through the establishment of the substance. Therefore the way to rectify the mind is all in nurturing energy.

Ordinarily the essences of energy and blood are called the energy of the immaterial soul and the blood of the material soul. When the immaterial soul and the material soul combine to produce inconceivable effects, that is called nature. As an overall representation it is temporarily called mind. What is always active within is called ideation, and what emerges outwardly and has aftereffects is called emotion. What ascertains inwardly is called thought, what aims is called will, and what fills the body is called energy. So when mind is mentioned, it refers both to its nature and its conditions.

Rectification of mind means the education to examine the responsive function of the mind and make it conform to certain standards. When inward thoughts and outwardly expressed ideas and feelings of like and dislike are all normal and undistorted, this is rectification of mind.

Once that which is master of the whole person acts in accord with regular standards, how could there be any difficulty in personal cultivation?

What fills the body, enabling the eyes to see, the tongue to taste, and so on, is energy. Nurturing means cultivation, fostering and guiding in the duties of the warrior.

Inward changes in arousal and repose make unlimited adaptive actions, depending on external advantage and injury. So whenever the ears, eyes, nose, palate, and limbs have contact with anything, energy accordingly transmits the good or bad or advantage or injury thereof to the natural mind. Natural mind functions responsively as it senses the attraction and repulsion of this energy. How can we but be careful about external habituation altering inner qualities?

Therefore when you are always reading military texts or always practicing martial arts, your energy expands over everything, unyielding. From here you come to attain rectitude of mind. So in the path of personal cultivation it is important to rectify mind and nurture energy.

3. Ordering the Home

Ordering the home means social relations, lessons about matters in quarters. Here the principles become complex and cannot be learned completely from books. Ordering the home means that all social relations and matters in quarters are regular, with nothing out of order.

The way for a warrior leader to order the home is not entirely the same in other countries as it is in our sacred court. This is a matter of considering the teachings of sages by the standards of the teachings of warriors.

Generally speaking, the social relations of warrior leaders are based, as in the art of war, on awe and admiration only. Awe may be principal and admiration auxiliary, or admiration may be principle with awe auxiliary; or awe and admiration may be half and half; or awe may be instilled alone, or admiration may be instilled alone.

When there is awe there is courtesy. When there is admiration there is harmony. When awe and admiration are thus in proper proportion, then social relations are accordingly correct. If you want to achieve that proportion, it is a matter of observing everyone's state of mind and doing one's best in everything. As for matters in quarters, it is essential to make rules strict and prevent indolence.

Housing, attire, diet, and articles of daily use are all functions of ordering the home. In all affairs of warriorhood it is essential to be simple and plain. To make efforts at ornamentation on the grounds that this is ritually correct is the beginning of loss of the substance of warriorhood.

The decline in the authority of the Divine Warrior of the Precious Lance[1] and the abandonment of the virtues of the royal courts seems to have started with the importation of customs from foreign countries. In the warrior profession we must be wary of this, especially of keeping many concubines and indulging in orgies. For warriors this kind of leisure enjoyment is more harmful than locusts

---

[1] Divine Warrior of the Precious Lance: the Shinto god Izanagi, mythical co-creator of Japan, who was given a precious lance from high heaven above with which he stirred the primal sea below, a drop of which dripping from the lance coagulated into an island.

infesting the spring fields. Those who attempt heroic endeavors are broken by this; it's something to be extremely cautious about.

Having a whole lot of utensils, such as tea sets and bric-a-brac, is not worthwhile for warriors. As a knight, to spend money on these hobbies is on account of ignorance of warriorhood.

The only essential implements for warriors are weapons. Once you have equipped yourself, moreover, if you don't revise your arsenal from time to time, it won't be wholly effective. Establishing their functions, always adjust for their inadequacy. Test their advantages and disadvantages again and again, and see to becoming accustomed to them, never slacking off.

For warriors the most important creatures are the falcon and the horse. Horses are admired for their ability, while falcons are prized for their character as well as their ability.

Horses are the feet of knights. To keep a swift steed, therefore, is a priority of a knight, in appreciation of its ability.

Falcons are bold and always spirited; no living thing in the sky or on the earth can match them. This is the character of falcons, so they are invariably prized. Training for military purposes is an ability of falcons; that is why they are admired.

This is different from the custom of other countries where they consider jewels most valuable.

Unavoidable poverty is a misfortune for a knight. Poverty without good reason is not what a knight would want. This is an affliction from not having always taken the purity and simplicity of warriorhood to heart. Even if a warrior leader has the wealth of the whole world, he should still keep himself informed of overall expenses and income, appoint ethical and honest knights to that office, and have plenty of money for military preparedness.

4. Knowing People

The way to spread martial virtue through the land is first of all to know people. It is truly difficult to govern all the multifarious affairs and individuals in the world; the only basis is in knowing just three to five people to elect for employment. Then won't it be quite easy to govern the land, in spite of its difficulty? This matter is a profoundly serious concern for a warrior leader.

For a warrior leader, knowing people is considered the essence of intelligence. Even if you are well-read, smart, and memorize a lot of anecdotes old and new, if your knowledge of people today is not accurate you cannot be considered an intelligent leader.

Most things are easy to see when you look down on them from above; only human beings are the opposite. So it is hard for a lord to see subjects clearly, while the lord's right and wrong are easy to see. Why? Because a lord has a wide range of interaction, while a subject has a narrow range of interaction. The lord is one individual, while the subjects number in the millions. When millions of eyes look up to one man, he appears like a majestic mountain; when a lord uses his individual eyes to observe millions of people, he may apprehend or may miss accordingly.

So it is not easy for a leader to see subordinates.

Human character is generally good or bad. Good people are beneficial to others. Bad people are harmful to others. Those who are neither beneficial nor harmful are called neutral people.

Now then, there are five characteristics of goodness: courage, intelligence, benevolence, sincerity, and loyalty. There are also five characteristics of badness: selfish courage, deviant intelligence, weakness, indifference to justice, and perverse greed.

Of course, every one of these characteristics has major, middling, and minor versions, and there are also major, middling, and minor neutral people, so there are nine main types of human character, and thirty characteristics. It is not easy to know all their nuances. Their outward manifestations, moreover—good, neutral, and bad—each have formal and informal aspects, while the formal and informal can each be superficial or serious.

Formality means that usage is taken to be the main concern, with effect considered secondary. Informality means the opposite.

It's all a matter of individual endowment. Competently cultivating virtue with the formal and informal, each in appropriate measure to improve character, is top-class talent.

Local repute is a robber of virtue—this is a maxim of an ancient sage. What seems to be so but is actually not will eventually deceive the ears and eyes of a leader. This is ultimately disastrous to the state.

Most people are unsophisticated, so there is little difference between their external manifestations and their inner states; that is why physiognomy is possible. When people are sophisticated, what they conceal inside does not show. They contrive to appear innocent, so it's hard to perceive. This is where the power of clear observation is most needed.

There are two main ways for a warrior leader to assess and know people by himself. First is knowing by seeing, second is knowing by calculation.

Knowing by seeing means getting to know what is within others by seeing what they manifest outwardly. What shows of them outwardly is speech and conduct. Speech and conduct are externalizations of what is within, so when they remain silent and say and do nothing, the wise and the foolish cannot be distinguished. Once they speak or act, they produce differences great as sky from earth.

If you want to know people, first of all ask them about things to get them to talk. When subjects speak in the presence of lords, they take caution seriously, so it's impossible to plumb their depths by asking questions once. It is necessary to ask them questions again and again. Sometimes initial replies are detailed while subsequent answers are imprecise, or they are clear at first but afterwards cloudy—in such cases you should know they're hiding something inside. If they gradually go into details as they are questioned, this should be noted as consistent, without hiding anything. If there is contradiction between what they say before and after, they may have spoken in confusion out of fear of the authority of the lord, so don't blame them but ask again and again in different terms. Then if there is still inconsistency, note that this is not consistent and they are hiding something inside.

To be talkative from the start and tell everything is something found in straightforward knights as well as disrespectful knights;

to distinguish them is a matter of knowing by calculation. Those who are talkative with a lot of literary ornamentation but speak of superficialities at the expense of essentials seem to be intellectuals but really are not.

This is how to know words; don't think people are necessarily right or wrong on this basis. Note that so-and-so says this, so-and-so says that, and then afterwards observe their actions. Action is the substance of speech, where evidence of ability and intelligence is found. Listen to what people say, watch what they do, then compare the two. Those whose speech and action are in mutual accord are consistent. If their words are alright but their actions are not, either they are hiding something inside or they are overly artful and insufficiently substantial. Those who speak improperly but act acceptably are either artless and excessively simple, or else uncultivated in verbal communication.

At this point note should be made of the main idea of the three levels of human character. Those whose speech and action accord and are correct are of the highest caliber. Those who are insufficient in speech and inappropriate in action are of middling caliber. Those who speak well enough but act improperly are of the lowest caliber.

The characteristics of good people are of five classes. Those who have all five are the finest of knights. They are most difficult to find. Those who have two or three are of a middling category, while those with only one are inferior. But even those of the inferior type, where their achievements are great, may surpass those who have two or three good characteristics but have only achieved minor accomplishments.

These judgments are extremely subtle matters, and it is most difficult to grasp the measure of others' character accurately. Generally you pick out their words and deeds like this, and then assess their intentions. If you decide right and wrong solely by overt words and deeds, you cannot get the real substance. The second kind of knowledge, knowing by calculation, means recognizing underlying intentions and actual aims that are not overtly evident but concealed inwardly. Even if you know the outward by knowledge through seeing, if you do not make certain of the inward by knowledge through calculation you will inevitably mistake right and wrong. Therefore the method of knowing by calculating is most recondite and subtle.

Knowing by calculation also has two main meanings. One is to observe their ordinary household management. First, if there is no discord or strife with parents, siblings, or spouses; second, if there is little misconduct among servants; third, if there is no sexual misbehavior; fourth, if they are selective in their social relations and not inclined to indulge in amusement; fifth, if they are unchanged by poverty or wealth and are not obsessed with money; sixth, if they work unremittingly on warriors' tasks, even in their leisure—those in whom all six are found are essentially top-class knights.

There are, however, those who sell their names for profit, acting out of contrivance. And there are those who personally don't want anything to do with militarism or military affairs but still unavoidably strive at them in conformity to the times. When you always examine them in the course of oversight, eventually their reality cannot be covered up. Even if it is contrived action to sell repute, you shouldn't blame them; but not to praise them either is correct. On the other hand, to reward them is a prerogative of the leader.

The second meaning of knowing by calculation is to know people through the way they react to how they are treated. That means after you know how they manage their households you take the initiative in the way you treat them to figure out their strengths and weaknesses. For example, you push them down to see if they pop up; you elevate them to find out if they'll keep their integrity; you entrust urgent matters to them to see how they strive, you turn over troubles to them to assess their courage and warriorhood; you provide them with wine and women to observe their chastity and fidelity; you give them money to see if they're honest; you give them leisure to see if they slack off or stay focused.

When a warrior leader exercises his intelligence to the utmost to test, there are infinite adaptations of application of this method. One should definitely not do anything, however, that seems like an ad hoc ploy. When a warrior leader rules millions of people by stratagem, this invariably reduces moral influence. Whatever is done by way of testing appears to be strategic; when it is done only in cases of absolute necessity where appropriate, this is what is called an expedient. When it is forced in its application, it is in fact strategy.

Whenever you apprehend the outward in its entirety by seeing and hearing, and determine the inward by calculation, in the end people's real aims cannot be concealed.

While the way to know people is in knowing by seeing and knowing by calculation, the ways of seeing and calculating have essential keys. Generally speaking, to be biased by one's own likes and dislikes is a common human flaw; therefore one should not consider one's own perception and calculation to be necessarily so. To judge right and wrong by one's individual sense is subjective decision. So when you know good and bad by the ears and eyes of the world, approving and disapproving as does the world by your own perception and calculation, then right and wrong are settled here, not to be doubted. If everyone calls something good that you perceive or consider unacceptable, or if everyone calls something unacceptable that you perceive or consider to be good, you must reflect on whether what everyone says is wrong, or whether you're mistaken in your perception or calculation, so you can decide right and wrong.

This having been said, "the ears and eyes of the world" does not mean popular conventions or popular opinions—*the ears and eyes of the world* means what has always been considered good and bad everywhere. When everyone praises one good deed or one fine word, that is not the ears and eyes of the world. When universal blame and praise of persistent patterns of speech and action are established, that is called the ears and eyes of the world.

When feelings are the same through time, it is an immutable law. If a warrior leader wants to know this, he must be the first to discern the feelings of the world. When you know the feelings of the world, you know the ears and eyes of the world without going out your door. Getting to know those ears and eyes, not anticipating that knowledge but actively seeking the ears and eyes of the world, is getting to know the feelings of the world.

The general principles of knowing people are fulfilled at this point.

If the way for a warrior leader to know people were a matter of personally knowing every individual by seeing and calculating, it would be impossible even if you spent all your time at it. You should just carefully and thoroughly observe and figure out those whom you want to give important offices. When you know them accurately, then it's easy to appoint the others.

The basis of this is in extending your ears and eyes. Extending your ears and eyes is a matter of employing inspectors and officials to observe and examine. When they are unsuitable, their discernment is narrow and dogmatic; so when appointment to offices of observation and examination is inappropriate, that can increase confusion.

The function of officials who observe and examine is to connect their ears and eyes to the ears and eyes of the warrior leader. If the warrior leader lacks clear ears and eyes of his own, and decides right and wrong by the ears and eyes of inspectors alone, that is a mistake. There are eyeglasses for seeing the small, and there are telescopes for seeing afar. Inspectors are the eyeglasses of the warrior leader—if the eyeglasses are bad, then what is straight appears to be crooked, what is bright seems to be dark. But even if the eyeglasses are good, if the person's eyes are dim they'll miss the remote and the minute. It is the same of inspectors vis-à-vis the leader. Therefore people who are honest and faithful are to be employed as inspectors. They neither contrive nor embellish, and do not interpret right or wrong by their own opinions. Noting whatever they see and hear just as it is, and reporting it as such, is the main function of inspectors.

There are two types of inspectors, overt and covert. There are also three types of covert inspectors. One type is those who live in the provincial villages like other inhabitants, always communicating the affairs of the locality. Another type moves repeatedly and reports on what he sees and hears. Another type is sent to a certain locale to report on a specific person or affair. Whether in peace or in wartime, these three kinds of inspectors must always be active. When investigated through these three kinds of inspectors, truth and falsehood of affairs and people cannot be covered up anymore.

A warrior leader's ways of knowing people are actually in order not to overlook people. Most people in the world are less than mediocre, few are better. When you know people clearly, you can employ them according to their capacities. When they are selected carefully, people will aspire to cultivate their virtues. This is the way to civilize manners; it is the tolerance and benevolence of the warrior leader. As for those of the most inferior quality who can never be civilized and are a menace to the state, the essence of martial order is to let them go among foreigners, not assimilating to mainstream society.

In a state at war, it is important for a warrior leader to use spies. It requires clear knowledge to discern double agents among them. In an era of peace, people's mental states are not kept deeply hidden, so it is comparatively easy to discern them; even if you make a mistake in your perception or calculation, you can still correct it. Double agents are subtle and artful in their concealment; once you make a mistake, there's no correcting it. This is a matter of life and death, essential to survival or destruction. Clear discernment in this context is a matter of intuitive sense and silent perception.

5. Promoting People

Promoting people means raising them from lower positions to higher responsibilities. When appropriate, the benefits are very many; when inappropriate, the harm is very much. Neither lord nor minister can be effective if they are negligent by nature. There are many precedents.

When there has been peace and order for a long time, there are a lot of people eligible for hereditary rank. To keep their genealogies accurate and perform their offices generation after generation is one example of keeping the peace. Even if his probity is somewhat less, if you promote a person with proper lineage people will accept that more easily than if you promote a functionary of low status whose probity is slightly more. This is how people feel in a time of peace. When there is a lasting peace, moreover, there are no domains bereft of rulers that require major appointments all at once, so offices are mostly hereditary.

If appointments are made for homosexual favoritism, or through misperception of opportunistic flattery as intelligence, even if no major harm is done these are still mistakes for a military leader. Generally speaking, it is hard to know people, and promoting people is even harder than knowing them. You have to consider carefully and analyze intelligently.

When the world is peaceful, mores are upright and habits are wholesome, the country is prosperous and the people have plenty, regulations are based on the classics, and there are no external troubles with rival nations, then it's all right to employ mediocre people of proper lineage according to a normal course. Once society deteriorates and the state has a lot of troubles, when official order is also in confusion and chaos is not far off absent immediate restoration, so skilled commanders emerge to renew martial virtue and achieve extraordinary accomplishments, then it is necessary to appoint people of outstanding capacities, otherwise they can't succeed in the endeavor.

It's like eating a normal diet to maintain your health while you're well, but seeking good doctors everywhere for medicine to take when you're sick. It's all a matter of acting on ineluctable realities, according to the conditions of the time.

Knowing people is the beginning; this is knowledge. Promoting people is the end; this is action. To know clearly and promote appropriately is maturity in a leader.

Once you know people are good, it is not proper to neglect to have them transferred to appropriate posts. In particular, if you know people to be exceptionally excellent and yet do not promote and employ them, there is no use in knowing them. Is this because of stinginess with salaries as a leader, or because there might be a basis for malicious gossip? Neither of these is authoritative exercise of government. For this reason, promoting an extraordinary knight of low office who proves capable of the charge is the epitome of intelligence on the part of a ruler. No government promotes greater good than this.

6. Ordering Offices

Everything needs focus for its function to be fulfilled. Therefore establishing heads for everything is the origin of offices. When what they oversee is organized and orderly, this is called ordering.

If an office is established without a precise aim, perhaps on account of lordly leisure, it is really an empty office, an unreal occupation. Not only is it a waste of a salary, it is an obstacle to the extension of intelligence. This is a matter requiring conscious effort to ascertain accurately.

There are many kinds of office, but basically they are either civil or military. Why? Because sky and earth and people and things are all governed by yin and yang. However multifarious human feelings may be, none are beyond like and dislike; that is because they are manifestation of the two energies of yin and yang. When feelings of like and dislike emerge appropriately, they are called benevolence and righteousness. The concrete representations of benevolence and righteousness are the civil and the military.

Therefore the ministers who head the civil and the military administrations are the most important. Two people should be appointed, a civil head and a military head, to be ministers of the left and right. Thus administrative affairs dealing with myriad events will be coordinated. By extension, this ultimately produces tens and hundreds of categories, whose classifications are a matter of figuring out actual conditions and acting in accord with the inevitable. When you figure accurately and carry through considerately, you wind up with nothing more to do. This is the key task among the myriad affairs of military science.

Two people may be appointed to one office, or three to five, or even dozens of people, more or less according to the major and minor divisions of affairs overseen by that office. So it is an essential task to make the relationship among the people and positions in the same office clear. It is most rare for people in this world to be complete in all qualities, so you should find out what they're best at and team them together so that their efficacy approaches completeness.

When military offices are undertaken only in terms of current conditions, the assignment of warriors is imperfect. When that is imperfect, military method is accordingly also imperfect. Generally speaking, the assignment of warriors is the basis of establishing formal preparedness. So formal preparedness is established after warriors have been given assignments, and military method is also made firm once formal preparedness is established. The rule for deciding warriors' assignments is in knowing the conditions of preparedness; knowing the conditions of preparedness is in knowing what leads to victory and what to defeat; knowing what leads to victory and defeat is in carrying this out to the full.

To know people and promote people are still relatively easy, and so is setting up offices and their functions, compared to the supreme difficulty of matching their capacities to their offices. When they do not match, then things don't get done. This is the error of the leader.

This is even more serious under the conditions of war. It is like the example of Shingen having Kosaka[1] pin down Kenshin.[2] If he'd had the likes of Hiitomi[3] or Itagaki[4] pin him down, they'd have been beaten in a contest of strength. Kenshin was much bigger than Hiitomi and Itagaki, so even if they opposed him fiercely, because they were smaller they'd have simply been slaughtered by Kenshin. If the likes of Atobe[5] had taken the lead to put him down, he'd have been overwhelmed at once. Kosaka was neither weak nor strong by nature, and Kenshin couldn't beat him. Such is the matching of ally to opponent.

For this reason official posts in peacetime are a matter of capacity and office, while posts in a state of war include consideration of the opponent. Therefore selection is even harder.

There is no special method for knowing the correspondence of capacity and office. When you know people thoroughly, understand the affairs of office clearly, and combine the two, comparing the great

---

[1] Kosaka Masanobu (d. 1578) vassal of the warlord Takeda Shingen.
[2] Uesugi Kenshin (1530-1578), a major warlord, was the arch rival of Takeda Shingen.
[3] Hiitomi Torasaka, a vassal of Takeda Shingen.
[4] Itagaki Nobukata, a vassal (d. 1548) of Takeda Shingen.
[5] Atobe Katsusuke (1547-1582), a vassal of Takeda Shingen.

and small, slight and serious, strengths and weaknesses, expertise and crudeness, then guidelines cannot be concealed.

7. Understanding Affairs and Objects

What is still and has form is an object, what is active and performs functions is an affair. So every country in the world has its own affairs and objects. All that we deal with in day-to-day life are affairs and objects. When their order is unclear, official duties and legal edicts are all neglected. Understanding is a matter of striving to make them clear.

Heaven and earth are separate and yet they interact, producing infinite affairs and objects. Human lives are also separate yet interact, creating countless affairs and objects. If their order is unclear, affairs and objects cannot find their proper places. When they are not in their proper places, there is conflict.

Preemptive victory without opposition, defeating formations with formlessness, arresting subtle impulses before they sprout, all implicate clarity versus confusion about affairs and objects. The main affairs and objects of everyday human life are familial and social interactions, and food, clothing, and shelter. Countless variations evolve from these.

The affairs and objects of warriors' duties require further qualification. If these are not understood in a time of peace, then it will be impossible to win before fighting. Things like personnel, machinery, fortresses, battle formations, and encampments are objects. Things like offense and defense, military strategy, and rules of war, are all affairs. Each of these has its order, which is not to be confused.

The way to understand affairs and objects is first to strive to know their means and ends. Means and ends are the main indicators of order. You can clarify the order once the main indicators are established. If, however, this is done without guidelines, then you can't distinguish the means from the ends. When you take the means for the end or the end for the means, the main indicators are confused.

Therefore the rule for analyzing order is a secret of military science. Once you find this rule, it's easy to distinguish the order of all things, and ultimately to approach attainment of clear analysis.

8. Establishing Regulations

When guidelines and regulations for each affair and object are not established, then above and below, noble and base, change their positions, diminishing martial dignity and damaging martial virtue more than anything else.

Establishment refers to what is to be enforced permanently. What is not to be continued permanently is not a real regulation.

Heaven and earth each has its natural laws which they never transgress. This is why they are eternal. When a state is in disarray and renegade ministers and rebels ruin the people, this originally arises from neglect of guidelines and regulations.

Of the sages abroad who comprehended all affairs and objects in the world and made detailed regulations, I have never seen anything surpassing the *Manners of Zhou*. Our own central civilization's ancient legal codes have been lost in the fires of war, or are scattered throughout society in secret archives; in any case, I have never seen any complete texts. Now, over the last hundred years, regulations going all the way back to the sacred reign of Emperor Jimmu[1] have been revealed, to the joy of people of all classes. This is the supreme benevolence of the state.

A warrior leader must make law strict. The bases of law are in the civil and the military. In times of peace, most law is mainly civil, whereas in times of disorder most law is mainly martial. The civil is the way to harmonize the inside, the military is the way to control the outside. The meaning of that is deep.

The root of regulation is in the clear analysis of affairs and objects. When you attain expertise in clear analysis of affairs and objects, then the affairs and objects spontaneously reveal rules and regulations. This is the supreme rule of law. If you take this for the rule of law, it can never change in a hundred generations. If you concoct them without that objective revelation, those regulations cannot be considered guidelines for all time everywhere.

---

[1] Jimmu: The first human emperor of Japan according to Shinto myth. His name means Divine Warrior, like the epithet of the god Izanagi, Divine Warrior of the Precious Lance

Regulations include unwritten laws and informal rules. Here if you do not adapt you cannot command the three armies. When officers and infantry do not fear the enemy but fear their own commander, when they know advance but not retreat, when their minds and guts are steady and their eyes and ears are alert, only then should you speak of battle.

Ceremonies such as seeing off the armies and welcoming back the victorious should not be neglected, for they are ways of fighting, winning, and growing stronger.

9. Civil Administration

Civil administration consists of two things only, benevolence and governance. Benefits are bestowed by virtue of benevolence, regulations are established by governance. Then government is right.

Civil administration abroad in ancient times offers little of practical use for our state in the present day. The four classes were not correctly designated and differentiated, and there is a lot about the state of nature and agriculture, or a lot of admonitions about oppressive regimes of violent rulers. Therefore most of the teachings are too benevolent.

When the way people are ruled is too benevolent, the decadence that ensues is that they invariably act extravagant and ignore the law. Therefore the general idea of martial government is to establish precise regulations of affairs and objects, refrain from giving out unearned favors, have no luxury in years of abundance and no famine in years of crop failures—this is the epitome of benevolent care. To speak of every family within the four seas prospering so abundantly as to eliminate all poverty and pain, is the empty elocution of common Confucians, and cannot be considered the real work of governing the people.

The civil administration in our state has followed on old traditions over the ages, so it is very detailed. There have only been some minor adjustments in standard measurements of distance and size, taxes and corvee.

Generally speaking, government is in charge of finance, so it is essential to choose scrupulous and honest men for the task. There are not many such men, however, so promote one or two honest men out of ten and place them in the role of supervisor; as he keeps careful accounts, the others, mediocre people, will be influenced by this.

It is also essential for government to admonish idleness, for when there are many idle hands among the people this is wasteful for the state. Even boys and girls should be given suitable jobs.

Belief in Buddhism in our country has fluctuated over the ages, but it is foremost in idle people, with little benefit for anything. Buddhists originally aim for chaste poverty, with a single robe and bowl, so there is some harm in becoming wealthy. It seems to me that to have Buddhism all over the land is also a function of the warrior's rule—in military science this is called the use of the useless.

As for regulations concerning mountains and forests, rivers and seas, cities and citadels, borders and passes, streets, levees, towns, markets, Shinto shrines and Buddhist temples, as well as birds and beasts, fish and turtles, grain and salt, vegetables and fruits, lumber, kindling, and straw, all of these are tasks of government. There are regulations for each, whether to rectify the people's desires and not let them waste natural resources, or to get them to pay taxes to requite their debt to the state. These are all unavoidable measures, whose details are a matter of policy.

Famine, epidemic, flood, and the like are emergencies for government. If there are no preparations established beforehand, the damage these cause will greatly diminish martial virtue. If a warrior leader is not normally frugal in daily life, in such an event disaster will be unavoidable.

In the manners and morals of merchants, falsehood is traditionally the norm. This is an unavoidable condition, and while there are good ones, this is an impossible position. To speak of making them all honest and sincere is the empty rhetoric of corrupt Confucians. Nowadays everyone knows that their product is falsehood and no one is deceived, while they for their part normally feel no shame. That is why they are confined to the lowest of the four classes, and are not noble even if they are rich. For those who skew their scales or misappropriate money, there are heavy penalties. So what is the harm even if falsehood is their norm? Wherever sun and moon shine and frost and dew fall, the four classes can never be more correctly defined than they are now.

When there are people among the three civilian classes who are filial, brotherly, and honest, to praise and distinguish them as a way of refining popular mores is good government by the warriors' rule. Refinement in popular mores means simplicity and rusticity in all things, without perverse principles or false cults. To clarify the law of group responsibility to rectify mores is greatness of benevolent government.

When people believe false religions and form cults, or become brigands and kill others, or mistreat their parents and siblings, or violate public laws, there have to be punishments corresponding to each crime.

Peasant girls getting married without their parents' permission, and poor women prostituting themselves to sons of rich families, are leftover customs of Zheng and Wei;[1] when examined from the point of view of sages, they are inescapably criminal. Even so, there are crimes which at times should not necessarily be considered so, depending on conditions. That is because in such cases there has to be some inner meaning to the choice of what to enforce and what to let go.

The existence of actors and entertainers all over the land is like dust in the house—to try to eliminate it absolutely is counterproductive. When mores are upright and martial virtues are actively exercised even among the lower orders, would a man of integrity get addicted to these things? Nevertheless, they should be regulated and not allowed to assume an air of importance.

---

[1] Zheng and Wei were ancient states of pre-imperial China. Wei was the birthplace of the infamous Lord of Shang of China's Warring States era, to whom is attributed the *Shangjunshu*, a classic of Legalism, the original form of Fascism in Asia. He is also called Wei Yang because he came from Wei. While the earlier Legalist classic *Guanzi* speaks of segregation of the sexes, Wei Yang wrote in a vein as if to suggest that this kind of moralistic social control was not actually essential: "As for righteousness, loyalty as a subject, obedience as a son, courtesy between juniors and seniors, and segregation of men and women—these are not righteousness. Righteousness means not eating opportunistically even though starving, not living opportunistically even though facing death. This is the constancy of lawfulness."

When people pay bribes to pervert lawsuits, that is not the fault of those below but entirely the error of those above. Careful inspection should be carried out to make certain of the real facts of the case. Bribery is considered very destructive to morals.

Tax and trial are the mainstays of government of the people. Taxation corrects them materially, trial and prison correct them mentally. With this people come to find their proper place.

The basis for determining the amount of tax is that the people have sufficient food, clothing, and shelter, even if they have no surplus wealth. As for judgment at trial, the ultimate achievement is when the people are themselves aware the truth is not to be distorted.

The way to accomplish this is a question of the enlightenment or ignorance of the supervisors and overseers. Therefore the root of government is in finding the right personnel. When you find the right people, the details of order emerge inevitably from affairs and objects themselves, and are not to be contrived.

Money and goods are produced by the farmers, and turned over to the warriors. From the warriors it goes to the artisans and merchants, circulating throughout the land. When there is no unhealthy hoarding and yet the storehouses everywhere are well-stocked, it is good fortune for the world; this is the warrior leader's virtue of frugality. It is imperative to understand the method by precise accounting of expenditures and income.

Money and goods mainly mean gold, silver, rice, and copper cash. Things like cotton thread, mulberry bark, lacquer, and oil are next. Foreign trade ships are always coming and going, and we trade our native gold for goods. The only useful products of those countries, though, are medicines; I've never heard of anything else of use to warriors. But who knows how much gold is expended on luxury items for show. And I've never heard of gold being offered from abroad. I don't know how much the mountains and seas produce either. So expenditures always outstrip income. I only fear that our country's main resources will run out after a thousand years.

This is not something for common fools to pronounce upon, but it's not that there is no reason to fear the sky may fall.

10. Review and Perceptivity

Review and perceptivity are pivotal to the spread of martial virtue, involving warriors' administrative orders and legal codes relating to all situations. When review of the past is not precise, perception of the future can hardly be accurate. Therefore review of the past is for the purpose of perceiving the future.

There are some who only employ review, and others who focus on perception. Although this depends on the affair or the object, unless one remains in between review and perception, pursuing the course of the past to the present and future, true warrior rule cannot be achieved.

"Seeing the present of the future is like seeing the past of the present"—this is the expression of a calligrapher, but when you actually apply its truth, it is an admonition about keeping the peace. As time passes and fortunes change, human likes and dislikes have no past or present. But what is past leaves evident traces, so right and wrong are easy to see. There are as yet no traces of the future, however, so gain and loss are hard to figure out. This is where the diligent exercise of review and perception comes in.

When a state is founded it is pure and simple and orderly, but after long conservation of its achievements, pure and simple mores gradually deteriorate. The populace wearies and people become resentful, eventually creating major problems within the four seas. When value judgments change and black suddenly becomes white, even though people are aware of this they don't know what gradually causes prosperity to shift to decline. This comes from neglect of review and perception.

So when warrior rule of a state follows ancient rites and classics unchanged, it seems as if there should be no unrest or disorder, but the simple rites and regulations of the founding phase are not necessarily to be preferred for the conditions of an era of peace. On this account rulers and ministers get to dressing up and ultimately become extravagant to the point where state finances are exhausted. Once the damage has been done, even if you suddenly realize it and try to revert to pure simplicity, it is impossible to return all at once.

This has been so without exception in both Japan and China.

So to propose to apply pristine customs directly in a decadent age is a course that may have its reason but can hardly be put into action. Therefore as long as you take lessons from every era by review and perception, you should not go too far wrong.

The way to tailor regulations and laws is to unfailingly review and perceive every single thing involved in an affair, however minute it may be. When the practice of review and perception is not meticulous, that habit will be inherited and become trouble for your descendants, with many misfortunes attending the diminution of martial dignity.

11. Studying Military Science

Not neglecting to study military science even in times of peace is a specialty of a warrior leader. In this there are three main lines: one is studying military formations, second is studying military tasks, third is studying the conditions of military expeditions. These three studies have two aspects, men and materiel. When tasks are carried out properly, formations are established, and the men and materiel are ready, this is one achievement of the study of military science. Having accomplished this, you study further, and with further study you accomplish another achievement. The sole concern of studying military science is that a man stop only on death.

As for military formations, one is the castle, second is the camp, third is equipment. Of military tasks, first is the battle formation, second is the march, third is the wielding of five weapons.[1] The conditions of military expeditions are, first, the surprise and the straightforward, empty and full; second, the offensive and defensive, with many and with few; third, battles that can be survived and battles that will lead to death.

Dealing with personnel means choosing someone older and more aware as a teacher from whom to study military science, or

---

[1] Five weapons: The traditional Chinese reckoning of what the five weapons are is hard to translate into English, because it includes several kinds of spear and lance that cannot be easily distinguished simply by naming. Here it is employed in a general sense, as noted in the text, for the uses of weapons.

strategizing with experts to determine what is best and what will win, or lining people up and testing their methods.

Dealing with materials means, for example, explaining their significance according to classic texts, circulating the information in manuals, making maps and diagrams to check formations, or stabilizing construction with earth, wood, and stone, and disseminating accurate information.

As for military formation, the first, the castle, involves not only learning the methods of constructing citadels, but also personally making rounds of inspection, having damaged walls and turrets repaired, perhaps making ramparts higher or moats wider, examining the strongholds of branch castles and border castles, always understanding their advantages and disadvantages. Second, for the camp, diagrams are used to define the method of encampment. Third, equipment, is a matter of never neglecting to have appropriate weapons and armor in your arsenal.

The first among military tasks, the battle formation, refers to settling preparations. Settling has a very subtle meaning, profoundly important. The general idea is that the personnel be settled, the materiel be settled, and the tasks be settled, their regulations decided once and for all, immutable. Once a state of immutability is attained, only then is it possible to produce endless adaptations.

Second, the march, means making lines of movement orderly. One line is normal, five lines is the limit, mixed lines are the end. The principle of controlling energy is most important on the march.

Castle, camp, battle formation, and march are what are called the four laws in military science.

Third, wielding five weapons, refers to the uses of weaponry. For a warrior leader to practice these himself, and cause the knights all over the land to immerse themselves therein, that is martial culture.

As for the conditions of military expeditions, the first, surprise and straightforward, empty and full, are the father and mother of unfailing victory. Second, offense and defense, many and few, summarize power formations. Third, battles that can be survived and battles that will lead to death, are outlines of victory.

This completes all the categories of the study of military science.

Ancient study of military science in this country seems to have been based mainly on horsemanship and archery, and the practices of shooting dummy arrows at running dogs and stationary target shooting have been conserved in later generations. Although they are not much use nowadays in the art of war, they are still called ancient traditions of warriors. They are sufficient to stir up emotions. Whether to use them or not ought to be a matter of the leader's judgment.

Falconry and hunting are the main exercises employed in martial training. Therefore good generals past and present have all made them obligatory.

Going out into the fields yourself to experience the toil of the chase, or entering mountain forests yourself, crossing ravines and fording streams, knowing both hardship and ease of hand and foot, or shooting with a bow yourself, or firing guns, testing out their advantages and disadvantages, or personally directing test maneuvers—these are functions of a warrior leader.

What is essential in military training is to be resolutely realistic. When you are unrealistic, merely making a magnificent sight and sound, you excite vulgar habits, and can hardly fulfill the function of suppressing brigandage and rebellion.

When you soak your mind in the situation, as the enemy and as yourself, intensively checking gain and loss, better and worse, the principles should become clear.

In times of peace, even though the issue is external security, even in defensive military matters achieving effective order capable of concentrating and dispersing, dividing and combining, is realism in military training.

So in military science there are rules for inner and outer eight battle formations. When the inner and outer eight battle formations are accomplished, even if enemies arise inside the fence there is no reason for fear. The function of military training is complete at this point.

12. Reward and Punishment

What induce human feelings to act or refrain, to be suppressed or inspired, are reward and punishment. What can be used to induce the feelings of thousands of people to act and refrain equally as one, all together? Without such command and control, how can you impel the troops of the three armies to overcome enemies?

So reward and punishment are the warrior leader's means of control. If you don't keep this control at all times, you will lose the authority of leadership. When that is lost, organization of the armies will not be possible. For this reason reward and punishment are regarded as grave responsibilities of a leader.

The principles of reward and punishment are principally two: clarity and certainty. When merit is not overlooked even if people try to hide it, and it is also impossible to cover up fault, this is called clarity. When law and order keep their contracts unaltered, this is called certainty. When a warrior leader has the virtues of clarity and certainty, then martial authority covers the four seas. This is the norm for the leader of an army; to go easy on wrongdoing and make rich rewards sometimes, or to smooth over faults and lighten penalties, are standard strategies of warrior wisdom.

As the warrior leader commands the three armies, there are three things that should be rewarded, and three that shall be punished. Loyalty, duty, and bravery should be rewarded. Disloyalty, dereliction of duty, and lack of bravery should be punished. Each of these three has three grades, furthermore, higher, middling, and lower, so there are altogether eighteen categories of reward and punishment.

Even a superior achievement, if of inferior quality, may not be as good as an inferior achievement of superior quality, or may be comparable to one of mediocre quality. It is a matter of apprehending the actual realities. If even once a single reward is not appropriate to the achievement, people will resent it; and if even once a punishment does not fit the crime, people will be angry over it. When people are resentful and angry, in an emergency they won't obey orders. This is a source of serious defeat. If you don't consider it day and night, you can't win the feelings of the masses.

The saying that a subject must be a subject, even if the ruler isn't a ruler, is a principle sages taught people, not an expression of shallow human sentiment. The saying that when rulers look upon subjects as so much dust, subjects see their rulers as enemies, is an explanation by Mencius of the conditions of the Warring States. In the context of the customs of a warrior nation, these sayings should certainly be considered.

Making rewards and punishments strict and severe is like taking a powerful medicine; it is very effective if accurately prescribed, but very injurious otherwise. Therefore you should not contrive strictness and severity based on the leavings of others without having any grasp of your own. Nevertheless, in a nation at war it is impossible to expand the state, strengthen the army, and preserve the territory intact without strictness and severity. Herein lies the work of the warrior leader.

There are also three grades of reward: reward with words, reward with things, and reward with land. Each grade also has superior, middling, and inferior, so there are nine grades of rewards in all. Reward with land is highest, reward with things is next, and then reward with words.

Generally speaking, the warrior leader's words of praise and blame for courage and cowardice, as everyday administrative orders, are the basis of influencing martial customs. Their connection is extremely important. As people's preferences and inclinations are not the same, criticism with blame and praise is never the same. Deciding this is up to the judgment of the warrior leader. If there is nothing controversial in the judgment of the warrior leader, the judgment of the nation is decided accordingly. To be decided means that all the knights envy the strong and everyone wants to gain the praise of the nation. This is administration that influences martial manners.

Any battlefield is a ground where you go to face death, so why would any conscious creature willingly walk into a hail of missiles and a crossfire of cannon without an adequate reason? It is because beforehand there is the promise of praise and reward, while there is the potential shame of disgrace and ridicule in the aftermath.

So when a warrior leader's judgment leaves a lot of room for criticism, and the realities of courage and cowardice are contradictory, everyone knows there's no benefit in going forth into a dangerous situation. When they know it's of no benefit, they just follow along fraudulently, using worldly wit to try to win praises and prizes. This is one reason why martial authority deteriorates, the root of ruination of the nation.

So what enables a warrior leader to evaluate courage and cowardice accurately is his own knowledge of military affairs and strategies of combat. When the warrior leader is himself expert in the realities of military affairs and the arts of war, then the guidelines for evaluation of courage and cowardice, the facts to be rewarded or punished, cannot be concealed.

For the categories of select achievement to be accurate in a time of extended peace, the administrative orders must be made known to all the knights. This not only encourages brave warriors, it is critical to the influence of warrior rule.

In ruling, to make rewards rich and penalties slight is magnanimity and humanity on the part of a warrior leader. In times of disturbance, to make both rewards and punishments strict and severe is the military authority of the warrior leader. But to enforce strict and severe rule in times of order while governing with magnanimity and benevolence during disturbances is strategy on the part of a warrior leader.

Generally speaking, when those who go forth effectively are unfailingly rewarded while those who retreat in cowardice are unfailingly punished, when facing enemies there is no way of predicting death in battle, but there is reward for merit, punishment more than half the time, and never any reward for cowardly retreat. As long as the three armies understand these things they will all advance according to orders. The efficacy of reward and punishment is most evident here.

The use of reward and punishment to encourage the good and discourage the bad is the current policy of warrior rule. To give out rewards and punishments without any specific purpose was the policy of kings of antiquity. What had neither reward nor punishment was the pure and simple government of most ancient times. To ignore the inevitability of contemporary mores in the present day, admiring antiquities instead, is a doctrine of Confucians that military men need not regard as necessary.

13. Acculturation

When the customs of any country in the world are not acculturated to martial virtue, it is impossible to attain ultimate success in warrior rule. This cannot be done in a day and a night; development must come about by long-term character building. Generally speaking, though knights may strive to follow orders at first, when they eventually get used to them and they become everyday customs, because of this it is considered easy. Eventually they arrive at the point where they perform without needing orders. The actuality of education is therefore extremely important. Herein lies the aim of a warrior leader's government.

If a warrior leader lacks magnanimous humanity and great capacity, he cannot accomplish acculturation. When you want quick success, or are repeatedly influenced by gain and loss, you cannot attain great success. When you are magnanimous and humane, you are glad at gradual success and do not consider rapidity necessary. Therefore you strive unflaggingly yourself.

When you have great capacity, you have no mind to take minor gains and avoid minor losses. This is how acculturation is ultimately to be done. So-called minor gains and minor losses do not refer to the magnitude of things in terms of individual effort or ease. Even a small matter, if it affects the security of the state, is a major gain or a major loss. Clarifying this is a matter of lucid observation with warrior wisdom.

Acculturation to warrior rule means reaching the point where, order and education having gone on for a long time, the younger generations are influenced by the older generations, children and grandchildren are steeped in the ways of their parents and grandparents, so that even without orders the knights everywhere esteem justice and hate injustice, desire courage and strength and disdain softness and weakness, approve of plainness in all things and avoid ostentation.

The fulfillment of both the basic and the beautiful, as a ruler's manifestation of virtue, may be considered a sage era abroad, but not everyone can have everything. If orders were issued in the interests of having everything, then everyone would get into the habit of ostentation. Ordinarily, solid simplicity with somewhat unsophisticated manners is the custom of warriors in a martial nation. To set this aside in favor of fastidious manners and fancy things is the start of neglect of martial virtue. It is imperative to be careful.

14. Great Government

When the three mainstays[1] and five norms[2] disappear from states everywhere, there is an era of disorder, but it is rare in our central civilization. China's Spring and Autumn era [722-484 BCE] was not far removed from the age of sages, but such extremes of violence and barbarity are unheard of in our own history. The nobility of a martial nation may be seen in this. Therefore, referring to the establishment of the three mainstays and clarification of the five norms as great government is, it seems, a foreign expression.

As for a martial state, even if a leader lacking virtue is at the top, it is worth striving for. In general, supreme success for warriors is to subdue the enemy without bloodying their blades. To win by fighting is inferior to that. Thus war is fought only when unavoidable. By virtue of fighting only when unavoidable, there is military readiness certain to prevail.

Now that there are no opponents anywhere and there is invincible military readiness, it is kept close to the vest and not used all the time. This is what warriors call great government. If you have no adversaries anywhere but lack military readiness, having no adversaries is not really being unopposable, but merely a matter of luck.

---

[1] Three mainstays: A Confucian term referring to the duties proper to a ruler, father, and husband.

[2] Five norms: A Confucian term referring to the relationships between ruler and subject, father and son, older and younger brothers, husband and wife, and colleagues and peers.

The root of great government is a matter of invincible military readiness. Invincible military readiness, even after the passing of a hundred years, is as fresh as a fine sword just come from the whetstone. Violet lightning splits the clouds, pure frost chills the flesh; inviolable, unmatchable, all knights in the world accept. So even old enemies fold their hands and mentally submit. The consummation of acculturation has its ultimate achievement in great government. The meaning of this is very profound and very fine.

15. Transmission of Authority

Transmission of authority is the conclusion of great government by a warrior leader. Even if one spreads martial virtue in one generation, if this should be lost by later leaders, it means virtue is still imperfect. Holding back from this, for ancestral rites to be transmitted for a hundred generations is an earth that human effort cannot create, a mate for heaven, epitome of virtue. Its profound importance cannot be fully told.

Yao's promotion of Shun, and Shun's promotion of Yu, as examples of the perfect virtue of sages, were entirely ordained by Nature, the Mandate of Heaven.[1] Their cases cannot be made models for later ages. Just to pass the great treasure on to the appropriate person according to the blood line is the norm of virtue. In the customs of our country, we do not wish to make common men of other clans into lords, even if they are people of superior virtue; when the sentiments of the multitude is not to trust them, the Mandate of Heaven will not rest with them. Within the lineage of the same clan, however, even if one is somewhat lacking in virtue, the hearts of the multitude must submit; and when they submit, the Mandate of Heaven will be vested. The realities of transmission of authority all become mandates of heaven, part of the natural order, impossible

---

[1] The Mandate of Heaven, or Order of Nature, is a Chinese concept referring to fitness for rule. According to Mencius (q.v.), whose work is one of the Four Books of Confucianism studied in standard Japanese schools, the loss of popular support through inhumane government was an indication of the loss of the Mandate of Heaven, after which a ruler was not a ruler but an "isolated individual" who could therefore be opposed in good conscience.

to affect by contrivance. In particular, to pass on the great treasure to a beloved bastard son on account of affection is extreme confusion. It is not even worth discussing.

A warrior leader of a whole land oversees the death and life of millions. There is nothing that can compare to the weight of that mandate from Heaven. However, most people Heaven makes are of average abilities. Those of highest intelligence and lowest ignorance are quite rare. Men of average abilities may become top quality by education, and even the inferior and ignorant may become average in ability by education and training. Much of the difference in people's quality comes from learning. Why would Heaven put seeds of violence and evil in wombs, allowing hardship and pain to be inflicted on the people all over the land? When the recipient of the transmission of authority is violent and evil, for the most part that is not due to his basic nature, but comes from negligence in education and upbringing.

If education and upbringing are principled and not negligent, and yet the recipient of the transmission of authority is violent, and of such a character as will eventually lose the land, this is because of the Mandate of Heaven. For this reason, to substitute a concubine's son for the heir apparent is done as a matter of necessity, according to the feelings of the multitude, sensitive to the reason why the Mandate of Heaven is so.

The basis of transmission of authority is principally education and upbringing, as a norm of virtue. Those who are utterly ignorant in spite of education are that way by the order of Nature, not by human effort. Therefore human effort must be deliberately cultivated.

The main roots of education and upbringing are choosing the virtues of the mother and carefully observing the routines of fetal education.[1] This is an ancient practice, to be careful of what the human heart feels. Even so, the main part of education and upbringing takes place between the age when children can look, listen, and

---

[1] Fetal education is a practice from ancient Chinese medicine. It means that a pregnant woman regulates her surroundings and environmental intake according to the impressions they make on her, and thus on the fetus. It is based on the idea that the formulation of character and emotional structure begin in the womb.

speak, and when they pass the age of twenty—this is the time to educate and admonish them carefully.

Now then, though there may be differences according to their natural strength and intelligence, normally the time from three or four years of age to ten years old is considered one phase, while the time from ten to twenty years of age is considered another phase. There is education and training suitable to each phase. As for the education of young leaders, the mainstays are but three—knowledge, virtue, and bravery. They should be taught to cultivate these three things according to the phase they're in.

When you set up "education" as something separate, a young leader invariably gets bored. When he's bored, his heart won't be in it, and it will not be effective. Therefore the first key is to associate the actualities of education with the affairs and objects of everyday life. When people are young, they find amusement easy, so you may entertain them with pictures to teach them the names and forms of nature and creatures; this is a way to produce knowledge. You may make a sport of chasing on bamboo horses, or practice dueling with reed swords; this is a way for them to become imbued with bravery. Observing their inclinations, you may practice manners and bearing, or tell stories of the sternness of generals of old; this is a way to guide them to virtue.

On the whole, when you use one item or one object, young people will get bored, so it's a matter of always using new things to develop their vigor. When their tutors understand the essentials, observe the conditions of young leaders, and devote themselves deeply to education and upbringing, then there should be no failure.

Though the excellent examples of each family might not be the same, when boys reach the age of eleven the great ceremony of the first donning of armor is carried out. Posting on their first battle formation between the ages of fourteen and eighteen, according to their strength, is standard for military families.

When boys reach the age of eleven, their intelligence is already beginning to stir. At this point education and upbringing are no longer as before. The way to develop them is based on two main elements, people and things.

What we mean by people here is a matter of selecting close retainers. First, people who are honest, sincere, and trustworthy are adequate to develop a young leader's virtue. Second, people who know the classics and legends of the warrior clans should develop the young leader's knowledge. Third, people who have mastered military science and martial arts should develop the young leader's courage. When the proper people are chosen for these three things, they will be adequate to instill martial virtues. As for the office of attendant, one who is imbued with all three is considered fit for the responsibility. If he talks about sex on the side, speaking and acting soft and lazy, this is an affectation injurious to bravery.

As for "things," this refers to housing, clothing, food, and everyday articles. Household organization keeps the proprieties of rank clear, so as not to allow any approach to the ladies' chambers. Don't build a hideaway. Set up a space for practicing martial arts next to your home.

Clothing should not be ostentatious in stitching, dying, or design, but appropriate to the seasonal cold and heat. On ceremonial occasions dress is to be correct, admitting of no casualness. Food and drink should be at regular times, not permitting extremes of hunger or fullness. Make the spleen and stomach strong, so sickness will not develop.

These are ways to promote courage and develop virtue. Knowledge is to be cultivated by defining other issues and objects, their comprehensive and summary distinctions, making the principles of simplicity and economy clear guides.

What spoils a young leader is basically doing as he likes. The root of indulgence in doing as he likes is twofold: his father getting carried away by love for his son, and attendants and personal retainers determined to please him for the time being.

Mistakes in the path of knighthood all originate from insufficiency of courage. Therefore attendants and personal retainers should each make courage and warriorhood their aim, and take every event and every object as an occasion to foster the constancy of a champion.

It is a standard norm of society to consider literary learning necessary to education. While this is a good doctrine, yet when it is done without the warrior's teaching that makes it effective, it is invariably harmful. As a young leader's intelligence gradually develops, the main essential is first to guide him to the duty of the warrior and the courage of the warrior. After this is done, to assist it with literary learning is very beneficial.

Prose and poetry are an element of literature, but one should not become immersed in their enjoyment. There are two major benefits in literature: one is to know the ideas of sages and the conditions of past and present. Second is to know a lot about the world.

There are distinctions in this knowledge of things. Most scholars know about things abroad but not about things of our own country. This is a common ailment of the age. A warrior leader should strive first to know about his own country. Knowing even popular culture is what should be called broad learning on the part of a warrior leader. When one has no will for warrior rule, one will invariably neglect this.

Therefore it is very beneficial to let the young leader know about vulgarities even from childhood, taking opportunities to talk over tea about even common low-class matters, so that they can understand the conditions and attitudes of the lower classes. Unfamiliarity with the coarse diet of the peasants, for example, is most common among provincial commanders—this verges on ignorance on the part of the warrior leader.

After a young leader reaches adolescence, he should be kept occupied with military duties and military tasks. Especially when his sexuality begins to stir he should not be allowed leisure or ease. It is a matter of controlling his sexual desire and correcting it. This is an extremely obscure area, which is hard even for attendants to deal with. The choice of personal retainers hinges particularly on this concern. In ancient times it was said that the father is the carpenter's square. The father leader is invariably the guide of the young leader; if the father leader does not behave in an easygoing and lax manner, his successor in leadership will naturally be inclined to circumspection and conscience himself, and not take to weak behavior.

After the successor in leadership is established, it is most urgent to instruct him properly on feminine virtues in a wife, as well as bedroom arts. No human relationship is closer than man and wife. When a wife is proper, this is most beneficial in inspiring her husband's conduct. It is a reality past and present that a man without a firm moral fiber may act right or wrong depending on the probity or otherwise of his woman's character. It is imperative to be careful.

Once the successor leader has the capacity, it is essential to plan the state's military administration together, enabling him to develop martial character. It sometimes happens that successor leaders know nothing of politics until they're grown up, when rulership is passed on to them all at once and they are unfamiliar with the duties of state. This is the fault of the father leader.

When a father-leader gets too old to take up administrative affairs and so transmits martial potency to his successor in leadership, or appoints his successor for after his death, this is to be done in a manner inevitable in view of the great duty of the path of knighthood. The rules should not be altered at all by personal intentions involving human wishes.

Death's relationship to people is very easy but also very hard. To leave one's work half done for lack of foresight, or to try to devise a legacy all at once in face of death, is not the diligence of a real man. Dying in the arms of wives and daughters instead of dying in state in the audience hall, or believing heavily in Buddhism and hoping for a hearty funeral, are both conditions where martial courage is slight, arising from lack of clarity of warrior wisdom. At this point a hundred years of warrior work will finally cease. So it cannot be disregarded.

BOOK THREE

Essentials of
Military Matters

Compiled by Yamaga Takatsune

1. The Origin of Military Education

The superiors of the three civilian classes, knights are called warriors. If the words and actions of knights are not good, the civilian classes become bandits. So the education of knights is the basis for preserving all four classes. One who governs the four classes is called the warrior leader.

Detailed Discussion

It seems to me that what is to be taught to men who are warriors is nothing else but as knights to be leaders of the three civilian classes. To have them be leaders of the three civilian classes without doing any work in agriculture, crafts, or commerce, is basically because they govern the three civilian classes and employ the three civilian classes. Because of this, if their governance and employment are negligent, the needs of the nation will not be met. So the three civilian classes are the great treasures of the nation: employ them well, and their value is sufficient; misuse them, and they become plunderers of the nation.

Of course, when there are people among the three civilian classes who commit violent, antisocial, and illegal acts, then it is the job of warriors to control them, restrain them, and put them to work. So the knights of a district quell rebellion and disorder in the district, the knights of a prefecture quell rebellion and disorder in the prefecture, the knights of a state quell rebellion and disorder in the state, the knights of the world quell rebellion and disorder in the world. Thus a knight's job is to keep down rebellion and disorder; so if a knight's speech and conduct are inappropriate, he is not a knight.

In an era of peace, when knights devote themselves to duty with diligence, conscious of the imperative to correct injustice justly, without being violated by the three civilian classes, then the three civilian classes will always be orderly, and knights too will be cordial and agreeable.

This means that a knight without education should not be called a knight, much less be considered a warrior. To establish education in an era of peace is called being a warrior-knight. This is of course a fundamental idea that should always be perpetuated.

2. Transmission of the System

This system is called the system of Yamamoto Kansuke, because he established the tradition as a warrior, he put it to use in the world, and he actually held the secret of certain victory.

The order of the transmission is as follows:
> Suzuki Hyuga
> Yamamoto Kansuke (retainer of Takeda Harunobu)
> Hayakawa Misazaemon
> Obata Kanbei (retainer of Tokugawa Ieyasu)
> Hojo Awa-no-kami (teacher of Tokugawa Iemitsu)
> Yamaga Jingozaemon [Soko]
> Thus it was transmitted in succession.

Detailed Discussion

This is the order of succession of the tradition:
> Suzuki Hyuga Shigetoki
> Yamamoto Kansuke Haruyuki [1501-1561]
> Hayakawa Yasazaemon Yukitoyo
> Obata Kanbei Kagenori [1570-1644]
> Hojo Awa-no-kami Ujinaga [1609-1670]
> Yamaga Jingozaemon Takasuke [1622-1685]

Here are some rough notes about these individuals:

Suzuki Shigetoki

A retainer of Imagawa Yoshimoto (1519-1560), he was the master of the castle of Terabe in Mikawa province.

Yamamoto Haruyuki

Haruyuki was ordained as a lay monk named Doki, *Demon of the Way*. His forebears lived in Ushikubo in Mikawa province. He was also called Yamamoto Tosa, and had a fief with an income of two thousand strings of cash, according to the tales of elders. Having learned military science from Shigetoki, he concentrated on establishing the teaching; thenceforth the school of Kansuke became known in the world. His name became prominent in the provinces of Suruga, Totomi, and Mikawa. Subsequently Takeda Shingen[1] of Kai province hired him. This was in 1543.

At first his contract was for one hundred strings of cash, but the day he first met the warlord, his standing was increased to two hundred strings of cash. Later he was given charge of fifty foot soldiers, and made teacher of arms. Gradually he was given more. After the battle of Toishi in 1546, he was given eight hundred strings of cash, and the number of his foot soldiers was increased to a total of seventy-five men. In the Takeda establishment he was called the Quintuple Infantry Commander.

Hayakawa Yukitoyo

His father was Hayakawa Bungo. At first he was an ally of Baba Mino of the Takeda establishment. Later he became a retainer of Ii Naomasa. Details are in the *Koyo Mirror of the Military*.

In 1583, at the time of the battle of Nagakute in Owari province, Hayakawa Yukitoyo, comparing the battle formation of Lord Hideyoshi, privately told Naomasa, "The enemy has a huge army. It's time to divide the troops and go inside Okazaki in Mikawa province. (This means avoiding the well-prepared, a military term from the Kyoto area) Lord Hideyoshi has an immense army of over 120,000 men."

When Tokugawa Ieyasu thought of withdrawing to Kiyosu in Owari province, he probably had about that many men too, but it seems that when facing a tremendous opposition one should not fly the flag of preparedness. If you're going to strike a larger force with a smaller one, the advantage is in striking unexpectedly. To attack

---

[1] Takeda Shingen (1521-1573) was a renowned warlord of Japan's Warring States era. He deposed his own father in 1541 to take over as head of his family, then built up a power base by military actions and strategic alliances. In 1567 he forced his eldest son to commit suicide after rebelling. Subsequently he turned on his allies. He defeated the great warlord Oda Nobunaga and his protégé Tokugawa Ieyasu (who was later to unify Japan under the Third Shogunate), but Shingen died before he could capitalize on these victories. Takeda Shingen is also known for achievement in administration, public works, and industrial enterprise.

unexpectedly, you shouldn't let opponents know your movements. On this account, he had judged it appropriate to furl his banner and return to headquarters, and Naomasa too told him so. That is, when Naomasa suggested this urgently to Ieyasu, the supreme commander considered Hayakawa's suggestion quite reasonable and gave orders to that effect, actually returning to his headquarters. Mr. Hayakawa used to relate this story to Obata Kagenori; Kagenori related it to Takasuke.

Obata Kagenori

Kagenori was a direct vassal of the ruling house [of Tokugawa] with a salary of fifteen hundred *koku*.[1] His forebears were masters of Katsumata in Toyomi province. Therefore his original name was Katsumata, but later was changed to Obata.

In 1410, Obata Moritsugu, also known as Lay Monk Nichijo, turned against the Imagawa establishment and became an officer of Takeda Nobutsuna, governor of Mutsu. As a commander of foot soldiers, he served as an officer for two generations of Takedas, Nobutsuna and Nobutora.

His son, Obata Yamashiro Toramori, accompanied his father at the age of ten when he came to the capital of Kai province to work for Takeda Nobutsuna, and eventually inherited his father's commission and clan leadership. Thus he was given the character *tora* (tiger) for his name. He also served two generations of Takedas, Nobutora and Shingen himself.

His son, Obata Bungo Masamori, served both Takeda Shingen and Takeda Katsuyori in his father's position. At Shingen's command, he inherited the name and clan affairs of Obata Nobusada of Kazusa province, changing the written characters of the name Obata.

His son, Obata Kanbei Kagenori, was hired by the establishment of Tokugawa Ieyasu after the fall of Kai province, when he was eleven years old, in 1572. When he was twenty-four, he became an independent (*ronin*) by his own wish. After that, in 1614, he went

---

[1] *Koku:* a dry measure used for grain, slightly more than 5 U.S. bushels; Japanese feudal incomes were typically expressed in terms of so many *koku* of rice.

into Osaka Castle as a spy, and because of his loyalty he was called back into the service of the Shogun.

Kagenori transmitted the Yamamoto system in his nine-volume *Minor Book* and his nine-volume *Summary of Essentials*, which set forth traditions from olden times. The three-volume *Three Types of Dragon, Tiger, and Leopard* is all Kagenori's composition.

Kagenori's dedication to warriorhood was well-known. Though he was simple by nature, and bold and violent, without him this tradition would have passed away from the world. This system is widely appreciated in the world because of Kagenori's inspiration. He was also peerless in his dedication to instruction and training.

Later on he wrote *Earlier Anthology* and *Later Anthology*, *The Cold Comes* and *The Heat's Here*, *That Scroll* and *This Scroll*, *Military Preparedness* and *Essentials of Warfare*. At the request of Lord Yorinobu, Councilor of Kii, moreover, it is said he wrote how he made Tokugawa Ieyasu's arms comparable to Takeda Shingen's, setting this forth in *Record of the Source of Renaissance*.

Hojo Ujinaga

Ujinaga was a direct retainer of the ruling Tokugawa house, with a salary of two thousand *koku*. Ujinaga inherited everything in Kagenori's tradition, and to spread the teaching in the world he wrote *Models of Defeat* in a total of forty-two volumes, and *Models of Victory* in a total of fifty-two volumes. He also wrote *A Scroll on the Subtle Ultimate Good* in two volumes, and after this wrote *Mirror for Knights: Practical Rules* in one volume. This is the extent of the writings Ujinaga transmitted to his students.

Yamaga Takasuke [Soko]

Takasuke was of the Yamaga family of the Fujiwara clan. His ancestor was the master of the castle of Yamaga in Chikuzen, Yamaga Hyotoji Hideto. Takasuke was born in Aizu in eastern Mutsu, on the Eastern Mountain Circuit. From the age of six he steeped his mind in literature; by ten he surpassed others in both poetry and prose. He obtained transmission of the way of Japanese verse and Shinto.

When he was seventeen he read the Four Books and Six Classics, taking only Hayashi Razan, Doshun, as his teacher, and wrote fifty volumes of colloquial interpretations of the Four Books.

At eighteen he set his mind on military science, which he learned from Obata Kagenori. When he finished, he received a license and seal of approval. During this time he also learned from Hojo Uji-naga and received a comprehensive license from him. With that background, when he was twenty-one he wrote *The Art of War—The Divine Warrior's Preparations for Victory* in fifty-one volumes, all about the traditions of the two masters Obata and Hojo, exhaustively setting forth the secrets of the system, so concerned was he that the tradition he'd inherited would die out.

Books he wrote on military matters:

Questions on the Art of War
Record of Essentials of Military Education
Record of Essentials of Self-Reflection
Record of Three Ranks
Military Education: Primer and Complete Works
Military Education: Basic Discourses
Notes on Military Matters
Ancient and Modern Battle Strategies
Colloquial Interpretations of the Seven Books
Further Discussion of Military Education

Books he wrote on civil matters:

Teachings on Government: Record of Essentials
Teachings on Cultivation: Record of Essentials
Classified Sayings of Yamaga
Record of Essentials of Sage Teachings
Complete Punctuation of the Four Books
A Hundred Types of Compound Characters
Facts about the Central Court
Children's Questions in Exile

In this way he devoted his attention to both civic affairs and military preparedness, always thinking and striving to be helpful to humanity, devoting his entire attention to the end of his life. His great vow was no more than to clarify and correct the doubt and confusion of people with aspirations for the nation.

Takasuke was an independent (*ronin*) all his life. For six or seven years he received a small stipend from the Asano Clan while remaining independent, but he resigned and became even more independent. Concentrating on scholarship and military science, he wrote *Record of Essentials of Sage Teachings*, a book intended to analyze and explain the doubts and confusion of scholarship for people, but he was censured by the government and remanded to the custody of Asano Naonaga of yesteryear. After ten years he was pardoned, and went back to his residence in Edo as before, as a teacher of military science, meeting with knights of all ranks, sometimes training, sometimes teaching. He died of illness at the age of 64.

The family tradition was continued by two sons of Takasuke, Yamaga Shoran Takatsune, and Yamaga Tosuke Takamoto.

3. The Law of the Warrior

The law of the warrior starts with rectitude and ends with victory. This basis is found in the deified ruler's establishment of law on the basis of warfare.

Detailed Discussion

Rectitude means staying on one line without deviation, victory means winning, not being overcome by others. It began with Yamamoto Haruyuki as the teacher of military science who passed it on to Takeda Shingen of Kai province, determining Shingen's system of warfare. In his lifetime Shingen fought thirty-nine battles without a single defeat. This is a teaching of certain invincibility, a comprehensive tradition including defense, offense, siege, security, massive combat, minimal combat, mountains and rivers, sea and land, night combat, night security, ambush, and all other military matters, involving nothing risky at all.

Shingen's operations impressed Tokugawa Ieyasu with the teaching and training of [Yamamoto Kansuke] Haruyuki. Thinking he should dictate that everything be like Shingen's preparations for the practicalities of combat, and his rules and procedures, Tokugawa Ieyasu ordered a search for all the families of the Yamamoto clan in Hamamatsu. (Ieyasu occupied Hamamatsu castle in 1568; the events here seem to have occurred later.) But there was no one comparable at that time. Then Ieyasu heard of the military science of an uncle of Yamamoto Haruyuki named Yamamoto Tatewakizaemon Shigeuji, in the establishment of Makino Umanojo Yasunari of Ushikubo in Mikawa province. He was hired as a direct retainer and given a salary of three thousand *koku*. In those days, even Sakai Kawachi-no-kami Shigetada was getting five thousand *koku*. Kuze Sanshiro Hironori of the Yokosuka contingent and Sakabe Sanjuro Hirokatsu both performed bravely time and again, but up until that period they'd each been given one hundred *koku*. As for [Yamamoto] Tatewaki, he was given the aforementioned amount because of his heritage of military science. He accompanied the lord at the campaign of Odawara in 1590. It repeatedly occurred to the lord that the teacher of military science should not be of low rank, so it was determined that he should thenceforth be patronized and favored, particularly in his status, according to the will of the lord; but being an elderly man, he died of illness.

Tatewaki had neither a biological son nor an adopted son, so his lineage died out and no longer exists.

4. The Basic Aim of Leadership

The basic idea of leadership is in knowing how important the military is to the country. Next, a leader is a standard for the group, so he determines to establish his own personal intelligence and uprightness, preserving humaneness from the beginning all the way through to the end, making justice his watchword.

Detailed Discussion

The basic aim of leadership is rooted in knowing the need of the state, directed toward establishing clarity and correctness in oneself to be a model for the multitude, and preserving humaneness from the beginning throughout to the end, guided by right.

As for the need of the state, all nations must have knights, and the supervisor of those knights is the warrior leader. If he employs these knights well, he is a helper; if he employs them badly, he does harm.

To employ well means first to consider their route and have them go by the way that is suitable, to figure out where to station troops and locate them there, getting both officers and soldiers to abide by the will of the commander; to get rid of harm and remove difficulty, stable in both normalcy and emergency, thus reaching the point where there is no one who does not obey the orders of the lord.

Next, to establish clarity and correctness in oneself to be a model for the multitude means that as the person of the military commander is the model for myriad people, everyone imitates his every word, his every act, considering him exemplary. Clarity means making the mind clear, perfecting one's own knowledge to be able to comprehend things. When a wise ruler is called an enlightened ruler, and an ignorant ruler is called a benighted ruler, this too refers to clarity or obscurity of mind.

There is a way to clarify the mind. The human mind necessarily has cognitive consciousness, which is called thought. This is also what is conventionally called consideration. So even in minor matters, things should not be done without thought. First think to yourself whether it's right or wrong this way. This is the foundation of clarifying the mind.

Even if you think in this way, if you act just as you think, this is called taking your mind as master, which ancient sages and saints warned against. So you call those with ability and merit in the avenue concerned and check your thinking with them, to see whether it is suitable or not beforehand, or have critical discussion afterwards and implement whatever seems appropriate, making it a lesson for later. This is called learning. Even if you study the books of sages and savants and find something that seems to be a traditional maxim or virtue, if you don't think about it first and question others, it's hard to attain clarity.

Next, to preserve humaneness from beginning to end means that for a ruler of men to dwell with humaneness is something that should be maintained. It means to accept the masses and love the masses. It is also like saying the ruler is the father and mother of the people. The ruler of the whole land considers the people of the whole land his children; the ruler of a province considers the people of the province his children; the same goes for the ruler of a prefecture and the ruler of a house.

Next, to be guided by right means that people should carefully maintain circumspection even where others don't see or hear, being guarded when at home or alone, invariably being upright even when nobody's there. Since ancient times the teaching of caution and apprehension has been in this.

5. The Main Bases of Teaching and Training

Planning, intelligence, and strategy are the three main bases of military science, teaching how to govern internal and external emergencies with appropriate response.

Detailed Discussion

Teaching planning means first seeing to internal order, regardless of what's going on outside. In the context of arms, it begins with ability to command allies before the enemy. This is considered the first main basis of teaching and training.

Intelligence means knowing the outside. It means that once you've got yourself in order and your alliances are lined up, you get to know the people, things, and concerns you are facing and then you figure out what to do to deal with those people, things, and concerns. In the context of arms, it means knowing your enemies and calculating what to do according to the condition your enemies are in. This is considered the second main basis of teaching and training.

Strategy refers to figuring out how to win easily according to changes. Even though you may have established internal order and have information about the outside, unexpected events are the beginning of defeat, so think of all possible changes in your opponents, consider changes in your allies, and also consider changes in the sky and changes in the earth, so you don't get bogged down and don't go wrong. In the context of arms, this means not letting enemies figure you out, but catching enemies in your own strategies. Stationing men in military houses and having weapons on hand, taking every possible precaution against emergencies, is the beginning for warriors. This is considered the third main basis of teaching and training.

6. The Main Aims of Military Training

When it comes to arms, practice means making officers and soldiers strong and robust. It is based on the men following the leader's instructions. For the officers and soldiers to follow instructions, three things are essential for coordination.

First is to know people and assign posts to people who can do the job.

Second is always to reward good and punish wrongdoing, so that the good and the bad of both high and low are clear. With this clarity, officers and solders will be enthusiastic, without hesitation.

Third is to train officers and soldiers even in ordinary things, so that their manners at home become training, meaning that they have no trouble getting ready and mustering.

These are traditionally called the three official signals. The secret transmission from Mr. Yamamoto to Shingen too was this. This tradition is called the main purposes of military training.

Detailed Discussion

The main aims in leading a large army are the three signs. There are three signs in the secret transmission from Mr. Yamamoto to Takeda Shingen. The first is to know people.

There are good and bad, substantial and superficial people, there are majorities and minorities, there are sophisticates and rustics, there are insiders and outsiders, familiars and strangers.

In the world there are people of the world; in a state there are people of the state; in a province there are people of the province; in a house there are people of the house. Land is far or near, large or small; depending on the land, state, province, and house, there are people and things; based on people and things, they have their rules.

There are people of lesser and greater importance, old and young people, canny and stupid people. People of greater importance are the chiefs, those of lesser importance are the ordinary samurai. A chief who cannot distinguish good from bad is not a chief; the job of a chief in times of peace requires testing the ordinary samurai.

Knowing people means selecting people. Knowledgeable selection means recognizing people who can be chiefs, and appointing people suitable for selection. This is the great carpenter's square of warfare, the beginning of predetermined victory.

Second is to make rewards and penalties clear.

For a ruler of men to reward the good and punish the bad may be normal, but attention is focused solely on promoting the good and demoting the bad. If there is negligence at this stage, the officers and soldiers slack off. When they slack off, you have to watch out for an outbreak of war.

It seems to me that the world and the state should both make reward their priority. This is something that must constantly be given consideration. Constant consideration means good ones from among the various commanders and myriad knights should be picked out and rewarded, according to the individual, with offices, seats of honor, favors, or prizes.

For example, there are good officers in every rank—summon them to their command, or a mansion in the preeminent citadel, and present them with a declaration to this effect:

> *You have been upright in public service, and considerate of your parents, relatives, and offspring; your words and deeds have both excelled others, and good report of you has been heard on high. In particular, the lord's pleasure is considerable. Because of this, you are to be appointed to such-and-such a rank, given such-and-such a command, presented with such-and-such a prize; if you continue to be careful and diligent, it will certainly be taken into consideration.*

When news and rumor of special excellence surpassing anything hitherto is heard by others outside, then the circumspection of the world regarding the character of the people of the world becomes the individual's clarity and correctness. The nation will conform, and evil people will desist. When punishment is inescapable for anyone who violates the law, but there is no selection of good people, then those of good character are ultimately not encouraged, while the corrupt remain concealed. Moreover, since it is hard to improve and easy to become corrupt, focus on promoting good is therefore considered basic. Then the bad don't have to be repelled, but spontaneously withdraw and turn to good.

Even among those of great status there couldn't be more than five to seven good men. Among those of middling estate, there can be no more than ten or twenty men. Among those of lesser estate, there are no more than two or three good men per group. If there are more good men than this, credit should be given their leader. This is the actualization of encouragement of good; if this is continued over the years, the best of the good people emerge. Therefore since time immemorial the essence of rulership is to make it a matter of daily business to select the best people. As for people who are supremely good, there might be one or two in all the land.

When you go on doing as described above, this is the foundation for the emergence of savants and sages, so you deserve credit as an enlightened ruler or intelligent minister.

Here there is something further to be understood. With the passing of the generations and the way people are, the aforementioned idea has weakened over time, so it is only relatives or family friends of clan elders or administrative bosses who become officials and get established, at the pleasure of the boss. Even good men may live in the shadows if they have no connections, with no hope of success or fulfillment all their lives. There are also many cases where something unexpected happens and the names of good people don't get out; instead they run into trouble and get hurt all their lives.

Even if they are in the shadows of trees deep in the mountains, promote good people. And even among the distinguished families, or among relatives, there are those who are not good and who are unworthy, so there should be appropriate discretion in dismissing them.

For example, there are plants and trees that do not belong in a carefully tended private garden, while there are many vistas of extraordinary plants and trees in deep valleys and high mountains, in places unknown and unseen by society. Some might simply say these are all natural happenings, but that is failure to discern the truth of what ought to be. This does not apply only to plants and trees; in terms of people too, such a thing should not occur to the best of savants. There should be proper measure.

Next, there must be a way to choose the good. Selecting the good based on the wrong premises is not worthy of mention; even if everyone says someone is good, you still can't be sure this means he's good. There are fine qualities that everyone admires, but fine qualities are not useful to others. If wise people praise someone, then you can know he's good. It's like the ancient tradition that goodness in one locality is not good—what the good of the whole locality praise is called good. This means that the standard is what is said by the experts in a discipline, those who are successful at it, those who have the talent and the knowledge.

Next, getting rid of the bad must also have its varieties. There are ways of dealing with this. Even the bad often turn good. To contrive to get them to turn good, somehow or other getting lots of people to become good, should be considered meritorious on the part of a magistrate.

But even when this is done, there are still those who persist in doing wrong for the wrong reasons. Sometimes they are put to work in a secure place. Those who become even worse when sent to work are not offenders against one individual—everyone points at them. This means that even if one fell into crime, one is an offender against the whole world. Of course, people don't suddenly turn bad and become criminals all at once; on the whole, to be able to influence people to change, meanwhile preventing them from acting on their evil, could be called the mercy of the commander.

Third, training should be concentrated. In a time of peace, the training of officers and soldiers is a specialized function. As such, it is a matter of training in a concentrated manner. The substance of training is to convey the will of the ruler to subordinates, causing the leader to reflect on the importance of the chief officer, while impressing subordinates too. It is a matter of informing the warriors what to do, both in ordinary circumstances and in emergencies.

Even if personnel are posted and preparations are set in front and back, left and right, as long as training is superficial people will be uncertain, so their functionality is inhibited. The point is to see to it that all ranks work together freely.

When there is enthusiasm in training and all ranks thoroughly absorb it, drilling and exercising repeatedly, the men become strong and robust. It's like glossing fabric—the texture tightens, the color stands out, the luster appears, and it is strengthened. So it is with personnel. Therefore the third signal, as it is called, is the fundamental concern of developing strength for combat.

7. Questions and Answers on Military Education

There are various questions and various answers regarding education for warriors. If you understand these well, you will know that the way of warriors is nothing more than this education, and will realize the depth of meaning of the education of warriors. Therefore I set forth twenty-one questions herein.

Question One: This system should be called the system of Yamamoto Kansuke, but it is commonly referred to as the Koshu Tradition, or the Takeda System. Is this mistaken?

Answer: This system is the system of Kansuke. Because he passed it on to Takeda Shingen, and Shingen's successes were based entirely on that teaching, it is called the Takeda System on account of Shingen's fame. Because his homeland was Koshu, or Kai Province, it is called the Koshu tradition. The teaching did not originate in Kai, and Shingen was not the first to teach it. As the teaching came from Kansuke, it should not be referred to by any other name.

Question Two: In this tradition, is the teaching based on ethics and morals, or is it a teaching employing artifice and deception?

Answer: In this system both are used, and also not used. Ultimately what must be used is used, what should be left out is left out; it's not a matter of bias toward one or dependence on one. The reality is based on concentrating on peacetime arms, keeping the mind upright and cultivating the mood in peacetime, so there is no impediment to military functions. Its essence is in perpetuating the order and peace of the whole nation. In the context of warfare, artifice and deception are also employed to gain victory. Of course, real actions are also used. Ultimately the idea is to change according to the enemy—if the enemy thinks you're using surprise, you win by being straightforward; if the enemy thinks you're being straightforward, you win by surprise. This is a system that teaches how to bring enemies to you and not be brought by enemies to them; how to get others to take on form without having any form yourself.

Question Three: If someone doesn't know this system, or even knowing it doesn't use it, can it still be effective if there is a sudden call for it?

Answer: If officers and soldiers are both well trained through experience over the years, it will certainly be effective when dealing with events. If the rules of the system are handed over to a group of men all at once without proper preparation, then it has little efficacy.

Take the example of papering a screen as an analogy. If you have an expert make the frame and also have an expert apply the papering to it, it will look good and also be strong and sturdy. Then again, if you have an amateur make the frame and also have an amateur paper it, it will be extremely unsightly and insubstantial too. If the frame is bad but the papering is skillfully done, it won't be good wherever the basic framing is bad, but it will be better than if there were no expert overlay. This principle applies to everything—in arms too there is a difference between doing things all at once and doing things well from the foundation up.

Question Four: Is the practice of this system different when accomplished over years from when it is learned all at once?

Answer: This is the same thing as the foregoing rule. To steep in something for years is not the same as doing something all at once. This difference applies to everything, as previously stated.

Question Five: Unless one devotes all one's efforts, the real character of the system will be hard to see. But those serving in office, without free time, and those who are old, don't have years to devote all their effort. Then there are cases such as nobles of high rank with no convenient opportunity to pursue inquiries. Is there a way to convey the teaching quickly to such people to enable them to master it readily?

Answer: This too is the same rule as the foregoing. The results of devoted endeavor and receiving instruction without diligent practice are quite different things, though easy understanding and ready attainment do exist to some degree.

Question Six: This system is praised in the world because of its understanding of how to win. Is practice of its winning ways acquired from others, or is it in ourselves?

Answer: This system teaches us not to be one-sided, so it takes in what the other is doing, and is also produced from oneself. Even if it is in the action of the other, something suitable is adopted and put to use. Whatever is suitable for adoption, be it from events of long ago, or events of the present, and of course the methods of distinguished generals and brave knights, that is taken and put to use, even things from elsewhere or other schools. So anything useful in one's own school, as well as whatever comes from one's own effort and understanding, is all put to use if it should be used.

Even if someone memorizes things of past and present and constantly reads the writings of sages and savants so as to be ignorant of nothing, if one is ignorant of immediate actuality this is not learning, it is no more than memorization of things of the past. It should be understood as only having books of ancient matters and dictionaries by your side, looking up what you need, and saying it aloud. Real learning applies to the job at hand, to the matter at hand, such that things are easily accomplished. In unexpected emergencies and national government as well, even in matters we ultimately don't know, when the reasoning is sufficient, the form is appropriate, and the application excels, this is called practical experience, and should be thought of as the essence of learning.

Accordingly, in arms as well, it should be understood that whatever comports with a way to victory, and can be passed on to personnel such that they can carry it out gladly without suffering, may be adopted and put to use.

Question Seven: It is said that adopting something for use is not in the other yet does not disregard the other, is not in the self yet does not disregard the self. If so, what is the aim toward which one strives?

Answer: Our aim is for ease of application and enduring perpetuation. Therefore in this system we avoid using what is hard to accomplish, and what is risky. We behave the way normal people behave, we do what everyone should do. We do not use unusual forms or unusual phenomena at all.

To continue to work at the business of arms even in peacetime is the safeguard of the warrior, the discipline of the warrior. As such, it could even be the household prayer. For those born in warrior clans, those called warrior leaders, those called knights, always understanding this and never being negligent is the work of the warrior.

Since ancient times it has been said that dredging canals in hot weather and acquiring armaments in peacetime are jobs of a good commander. This is because in the hot weather of summer there is rarely so much rain as to cause flooding, and if this time is taken to prepare water channels, then when autumn comes the water doesn't fail to drain when there's been several days of rain. Similarly, when the world is at peace and there's not a single rebel, if you inspect the troops, parcel out preparations, organize squads, and test the bows, guns, spears, swords, and other weaponry and riding gear, then even if an emergency should occur at any moment, it won't take trouble to handle.

In sum, men of old warned against insistence on giving up arms in peacetime, forgetting warriorhood when you race to prosperity.

Question Eight: What is the way of the warrior? Is there anything to it from which one cannot depart?
Answer: The way of the warrior is to correct those who go wrong and set them straight, to make those who disrupt social order conform—this is all in the way of the warrior. As this is called controlling disturbance and aberration, military men of all ranks should understand this as their job, calculate likely disruptions, and act so as to prevent them. This is called the right way of the warrior.

> An ancient poem says,
> *When a knight is born, a bow is hung;*
> *Things are happening in the four quarters.*

This verse means that when a boy is born in a warrior's house, a bow is hung in the birthing room, so whistling arrows can be shot, informing all of events occurring in the four quarters, announcing the taking on of all emergencies without hesitation.

So carry long and short swords at all times, set out spear and halberd, array bow, gun, and lance, post foot soldiers as gate guards and street-corner sentries, and set out the three criminal-catching weapons [stick, fork, sleeve-catcher] along with lamps, torches, and rope for making arrests. Seen from outside, this shows it's a military house, while its functionality is unhindered, from the entrance to the interior.

To establish guard posts and sentries in various places so there is no negligence whatsoever is all in the manners of a military house. Especially on the road you bring along men and horses according to status, having men with free hands in front of you and behind you, the kind you can have wield spear and halberd, considering all emergencies that could arise, planning and preparing ahead to set things in order according to the emergency. This too is all to prevent hitches in these matters. This is proof that this is not something from which you can depart.

Question Nine: Since olden times it has been said that the way of culture and the way of the warrior are both necessary; how is this to be understood in actuality?

Answer: The way of culture is the human path, meaning teachings on how people can make an honest living. These are the teachings of sages, the warp and woof employed both past and present. Once something has happened, to bring disturbance under control is what is called the way of the warrior. Therefore since ancient times culture and arms, as yin and yang, have been likened to the two wheels of a chariot. That means it won't stand up if one side is missing.

Question Ten: This system of military science is named after Mr. Yamamoto. What is it about Mr. Yamamoto's story that this has come to be so?

Answer: Yamamoto Doki became famous in the world because he had the art of certain victory. Its forms lack nothing, and its methods enable you to avoid being controlled by others. First the process of warfare is taught using the three fundamentals (of strategy, intelligence, and planning). The three signs are presented as the beginning of the education of commanders, then step by step order is taught to ultimately enable attainment of certain victory and invincibility. As it is a teaching that lacks nothing and also keeps officers and soldiers from danger, society honors it and people admire it.

Question Eleven: Mr. Yamamoto was originally a wanderer, and though he was subsequently hired by the Takeda clan, he was not of great status. Is it proper or customary for someone of minor status to teacher a major science?

Answer: Even if one is of minor estate, or indeed a lone individual, in establishing a teaching after mastering the training the transmission is suitable for the accomplishment of great deeds, even for the success of military operations all over the land.

The training does not involve a lot of talk, and the basics are not that many. Establishing laws and acting on principle is the same thing for great and small clans alike. There are carpenters who don't even own their own houses, yet they construct palaces, towers, shrines, and temples, building the homes of great personages as they see fit. With only plumb line and square, provided their use is well practiced, projects are completed without being onerous.

Similarly, in all endeavors, it's not a matter of personal estate but depends whether or not someone has acquired the appropriate tradition and training.

Question Twelve: Since olden times, Minamoto Yoshitsune[1] and Kusunoki Masashige have been considered model warriors. Now if you consider Kansuke's system the quintessence of guidance, does that mean he was better than Yoshitsune and Masashige?

Answer: Although Yoshitsune surpassed others in wit and bravery, his strategy wasn't as good as Masashige's. While Masashige's strategy was peerless, his preparatory instruction method was imperfect. The Yamamoto system first teaches principles, then teaches about castles, battle formations, preparations, and operations, and finally teaches arts of war and certain victory. The traditional teaching methods are still taken for guides. The power of arms and the usages of arms in this system are incomparable.

Question Thirteen: Do the teachings of this system consist only of the Yamamoto system, not using other systems?

Answer: Although there are many different systems in the world, they lean toward operation of energy and are insufficiently realistic, they are short on strategy on account of planning, or they attend to mental states and don't apply physical forms, or they have the core but stumble at the outgrowths. This system develops presence and

1 Minamoto Yoshitsune (1159-1189) was a half brother of Minamoto Yoritomo who collaborated with him in the destruction of the rival Taira clan in the famous Genpei war that consumed the 1180's and paved the way for the establishment of the military government in Kamakura. Yoshitsune is noted for winning brilliant victories by employing novel methods quite different from the conventions of his time. He fell out with Yoritomo over an appointment, and was kept out of Kamakura. He obtained a warrant from the emperor to attack Yoritomo, who was a usurper from the imperial perspective, but was assassinated in the process of plotting against him.

form from the root, teaching perfection of the outgrowths as well, so nothing else can compare.

Question Fourteen: Is this system the armament of the way of kings, or the armament of the way of overlords?
Answer: I'm not learned or literate enough to discuss the difference between kings and overlords. It's just a matter of justly striking the unjust. Rooted in perpetuation of the populace, it only consists of things people can readily do.

Question Fifteen: So you don't have a doctrine for governing the country?
Answer: Cultivating the person, ordering the home, and governing the country constitute the everyday path of the science of sages. The chapter in Mencius on using mind fully says, "Sages are teachers of a hundred generations." Also, "The world has three wishes: ordinary people wish to be obeyed, conscientious people wish to be upright, sages wish to be guided." It is imperative to discourse on this to people who aspire to the Way without asserting themselves, and it also requires thorough inquiry.

The science of sages is in everyday activities, not the laws of arms. Military science is the teaching of arms, not a philosophy of everyday life. If you discuss them together, this is essentially disorganized information and is of no use. If the laws of war and everyday life are compared in terms of ultimate logic, how could they be separate? Nevertheless, when their significance is distinct, their doctrines are also different.

Question Sixteen: Is there a difference depending on the place even if one studies with determination? If one works in an isolated area or remote region, is there a difference in quality?
Answer: Wherever the particular profession is concentrated, famous experts may be found there. For literary and artistic pursuits, Kyoto is the place. While those with the ambition can also learn the work of warriors there, in that place there are few warriors and lots

of writers and artists. As the works of these latter are seen and heard, warriorhood weakens while culture is enriched.

For boats, it's best to ask people of Kyushu and Shikoku, and other seaboard regions. In such places, the existence of that profession is a matter of course, and expert craftsmen will be there. Otherwise, without boats, a lot of operations are not feasible.

Among people of the eastern provinces there are distinguished experts in land maneuvers. This again is also due to matters of physical possibility and constant familiarization.

Nagasaki is the place where great merchants foreign and native interact, so they are knowledgeable about business there, and because that is the ordinary habit, people's mentalities tend to be influenced by it.

As for the ways of warriors, they are concentrated in the capital city Edo (Tokyo), where they all practice martial activities and military offices as their everyday occupation, so military science can't be mastered effectively anywhere but Edo. Especially as teachers of military science, even those of outstanding talent and intelligence in isolated and remote provinces are in a different class from the teachers to be found in Edo. Within Edo as well, the same would be so of those who associate with the great personages as their teachers.

Question Seventeen: Not only military science—in other endeavors as well, those in isolated and rustic areas who are famed as experts find their skills cannot match up when they come to Edo. With no one to acknowledge them, they become like ordinary people. What about that?

Answer: Even if there are people in remote and isolated regions who have aspirations, since all professions are underdeveloped there, there are few who are better than they, so people praise them, and they think no one is better or more expert than they. When they show up in the capital, however, and are put to the test in a major arena, their faults, failures, and inadequacies all become evident. Because of this their aspirations are thwarted, and they even fade away physically.

Analogously, the same principle applies to mastery of calligraphy and writing. When you have someone write a crude inscription on poor paper or scrap paper with a coarse brush, the words of the inscription sound fine and the calligraphy too appears to be all right, but when you give him good paper and a good brush and have him rewrite, the flaws in the words and the irregularities in the characters become clear, so his mistakes and his faults become evident.

Even practices such as meditation, copying and memorizing, and internal dialogue seem quite all right when noted in private, but when it is set out in the open, what you had originally been certain was good turns out to be unacceptable.

These examples all show that when presented in public it becomes clear whether or not one has mastered an activity. Be it siege, preparation, march, and so on, the reality is not known through crude diagrams on rough paper with a coarse brush. Therefore even those who are battle-seasoned and have accomplished great feats of heroism in remote and isolated regions may be famed thereabouts, yet people of the capital city never talk about them. Combat means civil war, and the proof of the arms of distinguished commanders and good generals. This is how different art and arms in the countryside are from the way things are in the center of events.

Question Eighteen: Is there proof that rustics are not employed even if they are acknowledged commanders and brave warriors?
Answer: The standard of arms of the generalissimo who rules the whole land serves as proof. Next are the distinguished generals and excellent leaders, next the warriors of major campaigns.

In olden times too, Kusunoki Masashige exercised military authority on receiving imperial command, and his feats and fame resounded through the imperial capital. As for Takeda Shingen, though he lived in Kai province, he fought a number of battles with famous military leaders; on this account his achievements filled the eastern seaboard. Kiso Yoshinaka and Shibata Katsuie were unrivaled in bravery, but their usages were the customs of remote mountains, so their presence was thoroughly humble and therefore no one is interested in them. This is the proof. In the case of a lone individual of low status, in particular, even if he has worked diligently in remote regions, why employ him?

Question Nineteen: Is the region to work in also to be selectively chosen in the case of sages and savants as well?

Answer: In *Discourses and Sayings* it says, "When the hometown is humane, that is excellent. If your choice does not situate you in a humane context, how can you attain knowledge?" This means that when you select the right place to live you acquire knowledge.

Sages were glad to visit emperors and contribute their virtues to the cause of governing the empire, so their discourses to great men and princes were exhaustive. Even so, ignorant and base people call their consummate courtesy flattery.

The mother of Mencius moving three times was also an example of choosing location. Choosing a location, considering the people one can mix with, planning a practical course, if all is good one's achievement will be told throughout the land.

For a knight, aiming to become a man of mettle is called happiness, and also a great aspiration. The state of a man of mettle is the main basis of knighthood, a vessel of magnanimous humanity and greatness of heart. It means focusing on this, unconcerned with petty things or trivial works, admitting multitudes and maintaining greatness, unwearied even by the labor of campaigning on a national scale, confident that there is no hardship and no crisis you cannot work through. Even if a major emergency arises your thinking does not change—you do not abandon people, do not abandon things, but consider and apply relevant rules, comprehending past and present, self and other, clearly distinguishing justice from profit, good from bad, thus bringing everything to completeness. Of course, stability of temperament is fundamental; this should be acknowledged as the capacity of a man of mettle.

A person of such a character as this is no different from an ordinary man in peacetime, cordial and accommodating, someone people tend to be attracted to. Then when it comes to major operations, critical planning, and emergencies, he is not shaken, and his standards don't change.

A detailed evaluation of what a man of mettle is would take forever, so I abbreviate it.

> *The emptiness of the sky lets the birds fly,*
> *The breadth of the sea sets the fish free—*
> *A man of mettle cannot be*
> *Without this greatness of heart.*

I set out this ancient saying here for considering the capacity of the man of mettle. The ultimate attainment of a knight is to be able to do things freely even when undertaking major enterprises and critical planning on a national scale, with greatness of heart, magnanimous and humane. His heart takes in the myriad concerns of the whole world without weariness. This may be appreciated as being like a mighty river whose end cannot be found, or an immense mountain lodging plants and trees and birds and beasts without being crowded.

Question Twenty: Is the judgment of the countryside also inapplicable in matters of morality and character, humanity and justice? Are sages and savants also nonexistent in the countryside?

Answer: The conditions and efficacy of morality and character, humanity and justice, are not different in city and country, near or far, but when it comes to lectures, classes, and debates, the customs of the marginal and remote areas should be observed. This is because the branches and leaves differ even though roots are the same.

As an analogy, plants and trees that flower and fruit become entirely different according to their nourishment and care, or the manner and mode in which they are groomed. Similarly, even the painting of a master or the calligraphy of an expert will not be attractive if the mounting, framing, or hanging is bad. Even for sages and savants the manners of sophistication are inappropriate when they live in the countryside; because of this knights with aspirations, men of humanity, like to go from the countryside to the city to work.

Question Twenty One: I am not extremely stupid by nature, my homeland is martial and active, and I even live in Edo, the capital city. I aspire to military science and am a follower of this system. I mix with distinguished men of great estate and have sat in attendance on men with ambitions. As for books, I struggle over the writings of sages, savants, and military leaders, steeping mind and body in this lore for years. In spite of this my disposition hasn't changed, and I haven't qualified as a teacher. Is there a reason?

Answer:

If you have received the transmitted tradition but have not reached its reality, there is a flaw there. To begin with there are five points to focus on. First, the method of instruction makes form basic and begins with this. Correctness of form is considered the rule and the key. Four forms of warfare are the beginning of the teaching. The form of a military commander includes both the sophistication and substantiality of a military commander. There are rules governing the capacities of military commanders and the implements of military commanders. Without the appropriate forms, without the appropriate rules, what merits the name of warriorhood?

Second, though you've received the transmission of the tradition from olden times, you haven't effectively practiced it to the point of mastery, so the reality is not right.

Third, though you've received the tradition, you prefer your own rhetoric and rationalization, with but slight interest in the tradition, so you don't match up to the time-honored principles.

Fourth, the instruction of a teacher is military education, but what he does is not military education. Everything in military teaching and training is application of what great generals make their officers and soldiers do in order to train them. It is because you don't act on precedents that you haven't penetrated the basic mentality of warriorhood, the ways of warriors, or the deeds of warriors.

Fifth, after acquiring competence in the forms and the principles, then the arts of combat, the requirements of emergencies, and principles of total invincibility and certain victory are settled. You do not know the traditional principle of the importance of surprise in the art of certain victory.

Using these parameters to consider the question of one's success or lack thereof, it may be that while you have gotten the traditions for each task you haven't mastered their application; your ambition is warriorhood but your efforts have been slight. Or it may be that you've fallen into theoretical discussion of arms and are ineffective in dealing with the tasks of the day, failing to "think in the morning and practice in the evening." Or it may be that you can understand but not explain, or you can talk but can't understand. It may be that you're inclined to theoretical inquiry and have no heart for real action. It may be that you are unaware of your own faults and only notice others' faults and errors. It may be that you know yourself but don't know others.

The steps of this inquiry are not the same, having a thousand differences and myriad distinctions. Ultimately, if you have your will, develop your form, take to what is good in others, see what is bad in others as a warning to yourself, practice principles fully in respect to self and others, accumulating years of experience within the guidelines of your job and status, eventually you may become famous for courageous achievements, lauded as a man of will, a conscientious knight, a distinguished commander, a fine general, or a good man, a wise man, a princely man, or even a sage.

But our practice must be well-informed and thoroughly considered, followed up with corrective introspection, personal practice, and testing on others without confusion or danger. This is the basic intent of the warrior leader, the mastery of perpetual survival by arms.

BOOK FOUR

The Education of
Warriors

By Yamaga Soko

Author's Preface

Why was this treatise composed? It is for a young reader to educate his posterity. There are more than a hundred writers on military science, ancient and modern, but their books and their prose are either prolix or excessively abbreviated, and they only discuss combat and arts of deception, very far from the Divine Warrior. Therefore martial arts have degenerated into schools of strategy and technique. Ah, the doctrine of the supreme penalty surely has a reason![1]

In this country, the government of the nation emerges from the military caste, but warriorhood includes cultural education, so the martial element naturally has its own doctrine.

I. The Universal Sources

1. The Source of Humanity

There are many things between heaven and earth that derive their forms and produce their functions by combinations of structure and energy, but it seems logical to consider humans the most intelligent of beings. Humans are imbued with the essences of heaven and earth, imbued with soundness of reason and spirit; so we observe heaven above, examine the earth below, and depend on people in between.

So when we use the unchanging nature of the Way, we comprehend the great and the small, the fine and the crude; we find out everything past and present. That wonder is immense; it is why humanity forms a triad with heaven and earth.

Physically there are male and female, functionally there are poor and rich, noble and base; there is no deviating from the Way. Even if there are differences in willpower, when you don't follow the Way as a human being, the way of humanity comes to an end. Then even

---

[1] This refers to Mencius' statement, "Those who enriched lands that did not exercise humane government were repudiated by Confucius; how much the more those who aggressively warred for them—fighting for territory, they killed so many people they filled the fields; contending for cities, they killed so many people they filled the cities. This is what is called leading the land to eat human flesh. Death is not enough for this crime. Therefore those who make war out to be good deserve the supreme penalty."

riches and rank, longevity and health, are all out of place—how are they worth grasping? The function of the Way of humanity is very important indeed.

When there are exceptional complete sages whose knowledge comprehends heaven, earth, and humanity, whose virtue nurtures all beings, and whose action is informed by the whole world, they become lords and masters of millions, lawmakers for myriad generations. Their Way is the Way of heaven and earth, their virtues are the virtues of heaven and earth, their conduct is the action of heaven and earth, their laws are the laws of heaven and earth, upon which sage after sage has successively established the central pillar[1] of leadership.

2. The Source of the Way
The Way involves no fabrication; wherever it appears is natural truth. All events and objects have inevitable natural laws. When you deduce them truthfully, you have actualities and principles. The ignorant do not attain this, and do not understand, while intellectuals analyze excessively; thus there is the difference between going too far and not far enough.

Sages establish education and institute teaching, to enable younger minds to find out the roots of heaven and earth with the help of mature minds. When there is truthfulness inside, it naturally shows its form and function outwardly. The way is not accomplished just by thinking about it, but must be put into practice before it can be accomplished.

3. The Source of Phenomena
Nature circulates inevitably through the interdependence of yin and yang and the natural suppression and mutual production of the five

---

[1] Central Pillar: an epithet of leadership, is a very ancient constitutional concept outlined in the Hong Fan, or Universal Guidelines, a text contained in the Shang Shu or Ancient Documents allegedly compiled in the Zhou Dynasty (1122-255 BCE), to which culture Confucians typically looked for their concepts of social ideals. The image of the Central Pillar derives from the concept of the ruler as bearing the burden of responsibility for social welfare and political order.

elements. Even the functions of water and fire alone among them, it appears, never cease regeneration. Imbued with these, earth produces warmth, heat, cool, cold, rain, dew, frost, snow, wind, thunder, flood, and drought. By their means humans produce plenty and scarcity, disaster and fortune, flourishing and decline, emergence and disappearance. Sages systematize them to define the four seasons, arrange the years, months, days, and hours, determine the four directions, distinguish the eight trigrams,[1] consider past and present to recognize what to reduce or increase, guard and rest by day and by night, make changes by supersession. They judge success and failure according to the time. The function of natural time is very important indeed.

Earth is still and level, with natural forms and natural conditions. Its forms include high and low, dangerous and safe, broad and narrow, long and short. Its conditions are created by wood and stone, mud and water. Individually, there are natural forms and conditions, and there are artificial forms and conditions. Sages examine the patterns of the earth, create provinces and prefectures, set boundaries at mountains and rivers, determine border lines, organize agricultural land, consider customs far and near, correct conduct indirectly and directly, and establish laws coordinating heaven, earth, and humanity.

Humans and other beings belong to heaven and earth; heaven and earth are the father and mother of all beings. Among humans there are higher and lower, intelligent and ignorant; among other beings there are animals and plants, things that exist by nature and things that are manufactured.

As long as there are high and low and intelligent and ignorant humans, their functions come to fruition when their types are distinguished, offices are established, classes are defined, education is provided, high and low communicate, and the intelligent and the ignorant assist each other.

---

[1]   Eight trigrams: the elemental symbols of the I Ching or Book of Changes, the most ancient Chinese classic, studied by both Confucians and Taoists. They also represent natural forces and phenomena, and are used to construct all sorts of symbolic systems.

As long as there are animals and plants, and natural and artificial objects, people profit from birds and beasts, fish and turtles, plants and trees, grains, salt, minerals, metals, jades, and the manufacture of implements. There are natural laws governing them, of which humans make systems from time to time. For every single thing there is also a principle; its function is very important indeed.

II. Essentials of Leadership

1. The Office of the Lord

Humans are the most intelligent of beings, and leaders are chief in intelligence among humans. They eat without tilling, dress without weaving, and reside without building. Those who are able to stand over the multitude do nothing else.

The people are too involved in their work to have time to get to know the Way; their behavior when uneducated is like that of birds and beasts. Therefore the central pillar of sovereignty is set up in their midst to cause the manners of people to return to the rule of heaven and earth and embrace the order of natural norms.

The office of leadership involves first knowing the trouble of being a lord. Mediocre leaders are conceited on account of their country, and take wealth and status for ease. Therefore they have a lot of leisure, and can hardly fill up a whole day. Hosting parties, hunting for sport, pursuing whatever is pleasant, they know nothing of the peasants' hardships. They don't ask about the toil of the common people.

Obsequious ministers also do the leader's job, becoming shadow rulers by connecting with the sympathies of subordinates. This is the meaning of the saying of the Duke of Zhou,[1] "Ah, the right position for a lord to take is in not being negligent." Thus is one capable of exerting an edifying influence.

In golden ages of the past, education was based on ethics, order was based on family structure, and each class of people was settled

---

[1]   Dan Shao, one of the co-founders of the Zhou dynasty in the 12th century B.C.E, a major contributor to the crafting of the cultural and legal system of Zhou, a classical Confucian ideal.

in its own occupation. So they harmonized with heaven and earth, responded to the gods, profited from the mountains and rivers, cultivated fields, spread civilization, and were cordial in their manners.

2. Three Tasks

The office of lordship has three essentials: learning, knowledge, and action.

Learning means familiarization with the realities of things past and present. It's not just a matter of reading books.

Knowledge means clarifying your knowledge and information. If you study but your knowledge is unclear, you'll be confused. When you're confused, you don't know what to do, and can't get through.

Action means acting on what you learn and know. If you don't put it into practice, there's no use to learning or knowledge.

If you want to fulfill these three tasks, there are also three assistants: mentors, friends,[1] and retainers. With mentors you can correct deviations, with friends you can discuss details, with retainers you can observe effects.

3. Admonition

Negligence when not admonished is natural. It is like the opposition of yin and yang, the mutual suppression and mutual fostering of water and fire, metal and water, cyclically producing one another. This is true even of the eternity of heaven and earth; how much more of human affairs! How much more of the family, the nation, the world!

In general, admonition refers to mind, body, home, country, and the world, all in terms of principle, form, object, function, time, and place. It is on this that civil and military authority rely.

4. Establishing Offices

When there are superiors, there are subordinates; when there are rulers, there are ministers. This is a material law of heaven and earth.

---

[1]   Confucius said, "Three friends are beneficial, three friends are harmful. Friendship with the honest, the truthful, and the learned is beneficial; friendship with the ingratiating, the hypocritical, and the obsequious is harmful."

When ministers do not divide their offices, their functions are inadequate. Therefore when the hundred offices are indefinite, each is uncertain of its role, so the court is not correct. When the court is not correct, ruler and minister are confused. This is why the origin of established offices is inevitable.

Essential among the hundred offices are civil and military affairs. Overall, one man is made an exemplar, a model of conduct for the whole country, directly serving the virtue of the lord, deciding affairs in myriad situations, a prime minister for civil affairs and a general for military affairs.

Society is especially decadent these days, and talented people are hard to find, or they pursue different occupations. The selection of a prime minister and a general is very serious. But character, knowledge, and courage constitute a sequence. Character means mental balance and personal cultivation. It is simple and uncomplicated, harmonious and not harsh. Knowledge means skillful strategy, intelligence, knowing self and others, knowing heaven and earth, familiarity with past and present, and distinction of black and white. Courage is effort in action, it is boldness and daring, it is being imperturbable and indomitable, it is awe-inspiring gravity, it is straightforward simplicity. Someone who has all three of these qualities is called a great minister or a great general.

The prime minister and the general each has his own responsibilities of office. When the ruler chooses them correctly, he can entrust everything to them without hesitation. When the selection of department chiefs and officials is inappropriate, they cause clogs, unaware, so the conditions of subjects are not communicated. So their selection should not be done casually. Take into account, in that context, intelligence, trustworthiness, humaneness, courage, and loyalty.

5. Selection and Training

The *Strategies of Gao Yao*[1] says, "Don't leave offices empty; humans stand in for the forces of Nature." Generally speaking, the way to

---

[1]   Strategies of Gao Yao: a text contained in the Chinese classic *Shang Shu* or *Ancient Documents*

accomplish order is in finding people. The way to find people is all in selection and training.

When the Zhou Dynasty was flourishing, it used a method of local nomination and hometown selection to get men. This is how earnest the interest in finding people was in ancient times.

Even the sages consider it hard to know people. That is because human subjectivity fabricates falsehood every day, acting so selfish as to dare deceive one another, forming factions to overshadow each other, while claiming it to be in the public interest.

If you unsuspectingly appoint people without merit to office, and trust words without wondering, then subjective artifice will grow day by day, until you can no longer distinguish who is worthy or not. This is why even the method of local nomination and hometown selection is inapt for later ages.

The method of testing men is by their words and conduct. Each has three essentials. To examine them, eight methods and eight indicators are employed. Without at least having methods of testing, administration of security and observation, and principles of examination and appointment, true and false will not be clear.

When people are uneducated, they are prone to prejudice and false conceit. If they are incorrectly educated, they fall into unorthodox eccentricities. People all have an inclination for good, but because they're uneducated they are ignorant of social principles. When they are not educated and trained, they don't fully comprehend these matters. If they are not slowly steeped and developed, efficiency is unclear.

Therefore the decadence in education without training is clever talk and eloquent insincerity. Education and training must sustain one another for things to be clear.

In ancient times the method of selection and promotion through the school system began in hometowns and ended in the capital city. They taught virtuous conduct and arts of the Way, then promoted the intelligent and able. This is where election and education were interdependent.

When education and training are unknown, there are no diligent and earnest people among the lower classes, so the process of selection and promotion doesn't work. When there is selection and promotion but no education and training, there are no knights of any service to their superiors.

Generally speaking, when superiors employ subordinates, they do not merely seek utility, but have them educate and train others. This is the virtue of the leader, so even when he appoints a prime minister and a general he still establishes rules: cultivate yourself, rectify external defects, be dignified in appearance, be loyal and diligent, develop and educate subordinates.

There are, moreover, methods of development and education to teach knights. Development means improvement, capable cultivation. Education means learning and practice. There is physical cultivation and there is psychological cultivation. Education has knights establish their will, study literature and arts, master etiquette and harmony, speak correctly, regulate their appearance, and make their manners cordial.

Unless the people are adequately educated, they will be indolent in their work and have no normal production. With many idlers in a state, the state finances will be inadequate as expenditures go out day by day; the people cannot help having no constancy. When this is widespread, the country falls into chaos. Therefore when you teach these occupations, define their status, establish education, correct their customs, and make rewards and punishments clear, the people will have enough to eat, and a civilian militia will also be effective.

6. Military Preparedness

Military preparedness is the basis of being alert. The sacred warrior of the *Book of Change*, Kings Wen and Wu in the *Documents*[1]—all the sages discuss this. All beings created by Nature, even animals and plants, have their own means of preserving their lives—how much the more so human beings! How much the more so human leaders!

Being careful of your attitude, guarding your speech and facial expression, being careful as you walk, stand, sit, and recline, observ-

---

[1] *Documents*: the Chinese classic *Shang Shu* or *Ancient Documents*, one of the main source books of Confucianism.

ing the proprieties of the four seasons and the daytime and nighttime, being careful in court courtesies, regulation of city construction, palace security, castle administration, encampments outside the citadel, safeguarding suburbs and countryside, preparations of nearby states, imperial organization—in peace or in chaos, be serious about all this, be prepared for all this. This is the basis of alertness and military preparedness.

Formation is settling, in that people quietly settle down. It means setting people out in lines to instruct them. A standard court ceremony as well as an ad-hoc administrative method, in military affairs it is called formation. In reality they're the same thing.

Generally speaking, for superiors and subordinates to face each other, rulers and subjects to protect each other, is a natural formation. It is the way of sky and earth, the norm of the individual. Subordinates gather facing the superiors; the ruler commands the center, in charge of orders. This is what is meant by the presence of stillness within motion.

When superiors and subordinates protect each other, they naturally create a form, circling four sides, organized to be readily deployable far or near. Relative number and strength, advance and retreat, and strategic projection of appearances, each produce specific forms, depending on time and terrain. It's a matter of deducing the realities of the situation to form the structure.

Considering the composition of teams, the advantages of equipment, the interdependent use of movement and stillness, yin and yang, surprise and convention, appearance and intention, internal and external, there are natural measures in calculating manpower and materiel, timing and terrain. In later times, names have been affixed according to those formations.

Stillness is the root of movement. The formation of movement is called a march. A march has its own structure; the rule is for movement and stillness to protect each other, such that it is easy to set up a battle formation. Generally speaking, on a march the commander, officers, and soldiers protect each other, equipment and transport vehicles are properly placed. Safeguarding their deployment in all conditions, following regulations, advancing and withdrawing in an orderly fashion, signals agreed upon so as to be prepared for the unexpected—these are the rules of the march. When it comes to deployment of troops according to terrain, timing, and change, these must of course be taught and practiced.

Encampment is when people stop, form a circle, and keep each other on the alert. When squads are set out in battle formations for a long time, not a matter of days, people tire and gaps occur. Therefore equipment is used to replace human power; wood, bamboo, and earth constructions are built for temporary barriers. Their structures should be such as to provide for shelter from rain and for rest, in addition to stationing squadrons.

So make the equipment in a battle formation light and the walls of the encampment crude. Consider how to call the inside and outside guards; consider curved and straight and square and round forms; consider measures of relative breadth and density; consider construction of cabins, walls, and moats. Consideration of roads and open space, establishment of alerts and signals; setting up observers and keeping out spies; making rules strict, figuring distances and setting up temporary barriers; discerning the weather patterns; and warding off cold and heat—this is the general outline.

The distinction of commander, officers, and soldiers; differences in numbers; where to set up equipment and store baggage; quantities of water, food, wood, and bamboo; calculations of danger and ease, where to go and what to avoid—these are organized according to the time.

Land regulation refers to the admonition of kings and lords to build barriers. The land has natural formations, human labor makes constructions, and there are substitutes for human labor. Whenever rulers establish cities according to the terrain, there are distant establishments of prefectures and provinces, and regulation of rural districts. At hand, there is the construction of the suburbs and the citadel.

Now a camp is not for the long term, so the citadel is where formation is perfected. Battle formations and encampments are regulated entirely according to the terrain. The principle is based on the battle front, the form is made for security. The people and the ground are interdependent, danger and ease are relative; all that matters is inner and outer security. Now when deployment is the first concern, occupy easy terrain; when defense is the foremost concern, stay on inaccessible ground.

To make the easy inaccessible, set up impediments high and low. Walls, moats, barriers, shields, bamboo and wooden fences, all have their functions. Use them according to how light or heavy they are, depending on whether they're to be used inside or outside.

To make the inaccessible easy, set up facilities for free passage. Roads, boats, bridges, stairs, and doors have their functions; observe the terrain to consider their uses in order to organize them. When they are organized in accord with both the terrain and the time, then they complement one another.

Generally speaking, formation is formulation of reason, while reason is rationalization of formation. Formation is rooted in reason, rationale is rooted in form. Where there are form and reason, there is actually a corresponding phenomenon. When you discourse on reason without comprehending formation, that doctrine is aberrant and has no use. If you speak of formation without clarifying reason, the application is alienated and obsessive.

7. Rules and Regulations

Rules are rules to be followed; orders issue rules, enjoining them on the multitude. Rules and orders give verbal forms to the guidelines of heaven and earth, setting up limits so people won't go beyond them.

There are instructional orders, seasonal orders, and situational orders. Human feelings always change according to time, place, and events. A commander must observe those occasions at the outset, secretly take precautions against what they conceal, consider them in light of natural laws, and induce people to take to what's good. This is what rules and orders come from and relate to.

Rules are rooted in loyalty, respect, care, and conscientiousness. Orders distinguish manners according to hierarchy, relationship, precedence, and comparative refinement. Regulations facilitate functions and fulfill needs by implements and objects. Agreements use formal terms to communicate commitments and eliminate uncertainties. In civil life there are implements and objects for utility, ritual, and music. In military affairs there are implements and objects for essential preparedness and communication of commitments. So if the regulation isn't according to agreement, the actual objects won't be appropriate.

Forms are the means by which the eyes are enabled to sense things, while names are the means by which the ears and mouth are enabled to refer to things. Forms and names being what ear, eye, and mouth experience, they are what affect feelings. So they have a great many uses, in communicating far and near, uniting the inaccessible and the easy, engaging the feelings of the multitude, advising them of the ordinary and the abnormal.

The use of sounds such as of gongs and drums, as well as flags, fires, and various signs, depends on the time, according to the place.

8. Internalization and Examination

Internalization and examination mean effectively educating internally and examining its development externally. If you educate without examination, principles will not be actualized, and suffocation will ensue. Therefore when what may seem suitable in private testing is not examined thoroughly, it surely will not be perfected. There will invariably be something concealed, and one should not make assumptions about the whole of affairs or objects based on but a part.

There is refinement of atmosphere, refinement of speech, refinement of ears and eyes, refinement of face, hand, and foot. If these are not internalized and examined, it will, it seems, be quite mistaken to wonder why they are not ready when needed one day in an emergency.

When the Zhou Dynasty was flourishing, ritual hunts were conducted four times a year, with a major expedition every three years. They'd call the excursion a peacetime war, refer to the conclusion as lining up the troops, toast their return at the ancestral shrine, and count the spoils of war. They called it a peacetime war instead of peacetime hunting, and referred to spoils of war instead of the catch of the hunt, in order to use this to teach military matters and cultivate awe-inspiring conduct.

9. Reward and Punishment

Good doesn't happen without encouragement, and evil doesn't stop without chastisement. Reward and punishment are used to educate people to each resort to what is good for them. They are the means by which the ruler controls subordinates, lessons for teaching and training. Words and acts of loyalty, duty, and bravery are weighed according to their efficacy, as they apply to the time and place. When rewards and punishments are out of order, people will invariably become negligent.

III. War Strategy

1. Military Education

What is basic and essential all depends on military education. Therefore, when a leader can capably comprehend the means and ends, educate subjects and cultivate the people, thoroughly training inside and out, examining actualities to consider their success or otherwise, and make this clear by means of reward and punishment, then military education has been successful. Only then should arms be employed.

2. Planning and Intelligence

The principles of planning and intelligence are to plan ahead and always be informed, broadening seeing and hearing. When you search inside and out by watching, observing, and examining, nothing is concealed.

Planning is keeping strategy secret within; intelligence is knowing by seeing and hearing outside. When you plan and know inside and outside, it is clear who will win and lose even without fighting.

Generally speaking, in matters of the commander's principles, intelligence, and methodology, the development of officers and troops, the amount of supplies and equipment, and the advantages of weather and terrain, with skillful planning and intelligence there is no confusion.

Planning requires the employment of people of superior intellect. Intelligence requires three kinds of spying—remote, nearby, and anticipatory. These won't work without the right methods.

Strategic spying on the harmony of a ruler and ministers, or superior and subordinates, may be done by using officials, or compatriots, or secret agents, or interlopers' arts. When strategic spying is successful and you find out their condition, rival states will submit.

The method of employing spies requires selection of personnel. There are times when it is necessary, and there are places where it is imperative. There are ways of using secret agents. There is a restriction that when you are doing detailed planning, outside agents are not to watch inside. When information and observation are lacking, external affairs are not watched. When strategic spying isn't done, plans do not succeed. How can military affairs succeed if there are no men of superior intellect inside, and no one to look and listen carefully outside?

3. Principles of Warfare

Train repeatedly before warring, making the principles clear. Give your pledge to the knights, making commitments firm. Be careful about internal and external investigation and observation. On the eve of battle, be on high alert, and be strict about rules. Considering proper measure, be circumspect after battle, sharing the spoils to reward merit. These are principles of warfare.

4. Battlegrounds

To go to another's territory to fight is called invasion. Invaders always go by way of difficult terrain, overcoming perils and crossing defiles, becoming most acquainted with those methods. Those who go do so with security, so they lose none of their momentum or force. They do not look down upon the other, and do not covet small gains. Taking advantage of the food and water, making signals clear, facilitating their way back, reassuring the populace but seizing their wives and daughters, cutting off their supply routes, burning their stores, taking over the places where they'd seek security, thus forcing them to have no choice but to come and fight—this is turning invasion into occupation.

Waiting to fight on your own territory is called being on the defensive. Harmonize the citizens, keep wives and children for security, make food and water accessible, be careful of supplies, occupy narrows and defiles. Make the enemy keep their troops exposed for a long time, cutting off their food and water, occupying the roads, blocking their way back, threatening their rear, breaking their spirit, exhausting the strength of their troops. When you take advantage of this, you'll benefit without fail.

Generally speaking, there are grounds for defense, support, and battle; there are times when it is necessary to fight and times when it is necessary to defend; there are fake troops and false surrender, which can be used in many ways to deceive opponents.

These are battles of aggression and defense.

Going to besiege a citadel is called attack. Besieging a citadel is an inferior strategy, used only when unavoidable; unless you have five or ten times the opponent's strength you don't surround and besiege. On the other side there are fundamentals and outgrowths, material and mental factors, and differences in distance, accessibility, order, and urgency.

There are differences in encircling and besieging a citadel.

When encircling, you set up a battle formation on critical ground, and occupy the strategic positions of the situation. Once you are not in danger, then you observe the opponent's condition. Cut off food and water supplies, take over the places they need. Reassure the local people, respect boundaries, and when your opponents leave then you become the defender.

When besieging, encamp securely on critical ground, prepare shields against arrows and missiles, sharpen your weapons and secure your battle formation, with fore and rear in communication, supporting each other in movement and at rest, with a strict system of signals. To take over without attacking and conquer a citadel without a siege, is considered foremost. It is essential to attack where there are no people. There are methods of withdrawing without conquering, and also methods of putting in troops after conquering.

As for methods of defending a citadel, the formation to be used is whatever is necessary. First the commander settles his resolve and then fortifies the feelings of the multitude, getting rid of doubt and hesitation. Food and water are supplied sufficiently, all tools and implements are stored in abundance, troops are distributed and battle formations practiced. Castle walls, ramparts, gates, and doors are prepared for defensive battle, signals and orders are strictly systematized.

Observing outside, examining conditions, you weary opponents and induce them to err. Guarding and going out as appropriate, each has its function. When others surround you, you must fight; when others attack, you just defend—this how to battle on the attack and on the defense. Defense and attack are one rule, but aggression and defense are interdependent, and their functions are fulfilled when defense and attack are properly timed.

In a battle on level, accessible ground, there is advantage in forming a battle front with a mass of troops. On high ground, observe the enemy's condition. Hide in the woods, set up barriers, conceal troops, divide into groups, tire the enemy out, watch over front and rear, facilitate food supply routes.

In mountaintop fighting, conceal your forms; send your soldiers on circuitous routes, coordinating advance and withdrawal, light and heavy troops supporting each other, not losing any momentum.

In fighting at the foot of a mountain, hold out long enough to make the opponent stay put, waiting until they're tired out, then lure them down with the prospect of gain. Set your signals skillfully, and be careful of the road behind.

This is mountain combat.

A ravine is no place for a battle. If you come to one, search for enemies hiding there and get out right away, without halting. If you are in a bind, just use strategy.

When you are waiting to battle, there is advantage in cutting off the front and rear, blocking supply routes, and closing in like a scissors to strike. On territory where the roads are narrow and the paths are steep, the ones on the move and the ones awaiting are all in the same straits.

On densely wooded ground, there is advantage in deploying a small number and setting up an ambush. The ones on the move must be alert on the lookout, find ambushers and burn them out, according to the wind. The ones who await stay put, tire the enemy with diversions, and fight with fire and ambushers. This is valley forest combat.

Cover for ambush is entirely dependent on the lay of the land. It is a matter of concealing troops physically to assail enemies on the move, acting unexpectedly to confuse them.

When there are a lot of soldiers, there are many uncertainties in the use of signals. The appropriate timing for ambushers to rise up is all a matter of observing the energy of the moment.

To find ambushers, consider the lay of the land and look for indications, or figure out where they are strategically, or find out by searching. When you are alert to the unexpected, there's nothing ambushers can do.

These are the principles of ambush fighting.

To control a river, you have to have strategies for defense and combat. When defending, carefully consider the advantages of the land, calculate the force of the water, set up barriers and stick by them, causing opponents to get tired out and grow weary. Set up spies and lookouts to observe their condition, apportion troops to form battle lines, set out ambushers and spoilers, send light troops to attack those half across; those who maintain the follow-up fight, occupying the barriers in defense, are reinforcement troops. When you don't keep to your battle plan, once they have crossed over you'll be at a loss for a strategy.

Crossing is only done in the interests of advantage. The rule for crossing is to observe the lay of the land and the conditions. However, it is done by strategic division and combination. It is imperative to be careful about configuration on the verge of crossing and after having crossed.

This is river combat.

Boat battle means methods of land-to-boat combat and boat-to-boat combat. There are large and small vessels, military and service vessels, designs for river and for sea. There are considerations of tides, currents, wind and rain, places for mooring and stationing. In applying these, moreover, there are principles of forming battle fronts, operating vessels, making naval stations, agreeing on signals, fighting and defending. And there are also matters of setting up facilities for supplying equipment and machinery, food and water.

In battle between land and boat, on land it is comparable to occupying a river; scouting far afield, observing from on high, finding out conditions. As enemies are about to land their boats, sink them and attack them right away. If they manage to debark onto land, seize their boats and cut off their rear; employ ambushers and light troops, with emphasis on subsequent security.

As for the boats, it's like crossing a river; wear opponents out while at ease yourself, agitate opponents while staying calm yourself. Attack unexpectedly, strike the unwary. Defend and rest at appropriate times, stay or leave according to the terrain. Let those on sea and land support each other, use shielded scaffolds to shelter from arrows and shot, take down tents and conceal the troops. There is even a ruse of burning boats and sinking supplies.

Boat-to-boat battle is done only when unavoidable. Sometimes momentum is maximized by taking advantage of wind and tide, or machinery is used to assist in battle. There are methods of offense and defense that are employed in boat-to-boat battle.

As for a naval station, consider the land, figure out the opponent, go out and in at appropriate times, and tie down the boats in conformity with the current. Determining signals and gathering kindling and water each involve practical principles.

This is boat battle.

Fighting with water means using water to help your battle. Taking away their spirit and cutting off their retreat, you flood and drown them.

Therefore to refrain from camping or making a battle formation on observing the lay of the land is to keep the troops useful. Wetlands and mud flats are no place for battle—double your march, keeping yourself away from them while luring opponents toward them, with you facing them while opponents have their backs to them. When they try to cross over, to defend with pitfalls and bamboo spikes, or battling by cutting off the rear and setting up ambushes, each has its uses. When you yourself have no choice but to cross, first send someone to find a way over. Make a separate path, call on combat strategy—the direction and distance depend on the relative positions of you and your opponents.

5. The Time to Fight

Generally speaking, there are morning, afternoon, and evening battles. The mood of morning is keen, the mood of afternoon is lazy, the mood of evening is to head back home. These are natural tendencies.

In the year there are differences of cold and heat; in the day there are distinctions of day and night, dark and light. Times may tend to survival or destruction, fortune or disaster. For combat, timing is uniquely important.

To fight by night, consider the enemy's mood, take advantage of their gaps by the dark of night to create confusion and take away their energy. Select the soldiers, keep equipment light, agree on signals, use tactics to tire opponents out. Startle them with fires and drums, have your defense and offense support each other, make your strategy according to your aim, go out and in at opportune junctures, with emphasis on rapidity of advance and withdrawal.

For night defense, there is strictness of formation, encampment, and signaling. When enemies come, hold out to tire them, eventually eroding their discipline. Then either attack their rear or occupy their return route.

When there is violent wind and rain, that is a time not to fight. Avoid it, but if you can't help it, then make your battle front solid, station your equipment, and wait for the storm to stop. When enemies get caught out, take advantage of the opportunity to startle them left and right, cut off their rear, send out ambushes, and strike while they're in disarray. The use of the timing of the weather is very great indeed!

6. Practicalities of Combat

When commanding a multitude in battle, it is especially important to divide up your numbers in formation and encampment. The way this is done requires barriers and signals to be clear. As for the lay of the land, this depends on even ground. Battle strategy is kept carefully, configurations are made complete. The mood is made spirited, work and leisure is balanced, guard duty and rest are timely. If you depend on large numbers and forget about practicalities, acting impulsively in eagerness for gain, you will eventually fall into an enemy's trap.

When commanding a small number in battle, select your soldiers and solidify your lines; consider the timing, go by the lay of the land, conceal your forms and arouse your spirits, causing opponents to weary and lose their coherence, cutting off their rear and striking in the center. There is particular advantage in night ambush fighting, taking advantage of conditions to advance softly, using the element of surprise when you see an opportunity.

This is how to deploy large and small forces.

Deploying infantry and cavalry together is a practicality of the battle formation. Deploying cavalry or infantry alone is an adaptation according to the time.

Mounted combat requires level ground. Going in from left and right, you startle them from front and rear; swiftness is uniquely important.

In infantry combat there are officers and soldiers. When infantry encounters cavalry, there is benefit in setting up temporary barriers and waiting and watching for an opening.

As for the deployment of foot soldiers, let them concentrate on training with their equipment, getting their formations and principles straight, advancing and withdrawing in an orderly manner, making their signals clear, calculating distances, preparing for security and safety.

In combat there are times to rush and times to relax. There are uses for surprise and straightforward tactics, there are structures for lines and squads, there are methods of mixing infantry and cavalry in battle formations, and there are methods for deploying foot soldiers alone. The orders of chief officers are most exacting; when cavalry and infantry are each unable to regroup, then their deployment is not entirely effective.

These are the uses of cavalry and infantry.

In fighting with fire, accelerants are employed depending on wind and dryness, according to the ground cover. Generally speaking, fire is alarming and burns quickly, so fire is used as an auxiliary weapon. Burning forests, villages, and stockpiles, raising smoke, each has its uses. Just be careful to keep watching the direction of the wind.

In defensive combat, strategic mutual reinforcement of fire and arms is advantageous.

In order to utilize fire, first tear down houses and cut down trees, being careful of your own supplies and preparing water buckets, having troops at the ready once fire breaks out, guarding all gaps, calmly awaiting developments. This is the use of fire fighting.

When you go forth in pursuit, there's no thought of stopping; lines and squads scatter, moving and resting at different times, so on the advance you use signals to alert and advise, units and squads each on guard, keeping infantry and cavalry in unison, lining up the equipment, the brave inspiring the timid.

Chasing the fleeing, when you overtake them and fight, be bold, not looking for ambushers, not keeping up sustained battle. Limiting the range, therefore, and determining the time, keeping the troops whole and uniting their minds, there are arts of hasty and unhurried pacing, light and heavy arms.

When you withdraw troops, they'll be scared; so practice your formations and make sure of your signals, help each other defend and fight, know the lay of the land precisely and consider the timing to withdraw; then the enemy will not be able to overtake you.

When you retreat in defeat, your soldiers' spirits will all be down. So set up impasses and consider timing, contriving ruses to confuse the enemy, settling the troops with the thought of death in combat. Their configuration shouldn't be considered essential.

These are the practicalities of combat, on the advance and in retreat.

7. Essentials of Combat

Those who fight well plan well. A superior army wins without fighting. One who plans well is conversant with conditions, opportunities, configurations, and functions. The enemy is always kept off guard and unprepared; your defense and attack are elsewhere than he anticipates. Therefore officers and soldiers are united, as warriors to the death. Unfailingly firm in defense, they invariably seize what they attack.

Generally speaking, the form of a militia is like water dripping down and fire flaming up, its momentum like the way water tends to flow downward and fire takes to what's dry. Making firm the roots of their actions—surprise and straightforward, circulating, movement and stillness—when they defend each other and fight together vertically and horizontally with the fore guard responding to the rear guard, the way to run a battle is all in strategy, and that is a matter of actually understanding heaven, earth, and human beings.

BOOK FIVE

Primer of
Martial Education

By Yamaga Soko

1. Rising Early, Retiring at Night

The general rule for knighthood is first to rise early, wash and groom, dress properly, including accessories; cultivate the mood of dawn, acknowledge gratitude to your lord and your father, think about the household tasks of the day, reflect that you receive your physical body from your parents, so the beginning of filial piety is not to cause it harm, while the end of filial piety is to establish yourself, put principles into practice, and elevate your name for future generations to distinguish your parents.

After that, give instructions for household tasks, and meet with visitors and guests. If you are in the service of a lord, turn out promptly for duty. In serving your parents, go look in on them to see how they are. When on duty outside, your planning should not go beyond your position. In attendance on elders, respect them as you would your father and elder brothers, being deferential and not arguing.

Associate with friends in civilized ways, foster humaneness by friendships. When you have beneficial friends, ask them about things. Be truthful, not deceptive. Always think of the duties of knighthood, never being negligent. This is the way to perfect your social relations.

In public service, the way to go is to show up before others in the morning and leave after others at night. After returning home, first look in on your parents, with a gentle mood and a cheerful expression. On taking your seat, inquire about household matters, assess their order of urgency, and see to those tasks.

If you are free, review the day's activities and events. If there is time, do some reading to reflect on the right way for knights and recognize just and unjust actions.

Once the sun has gone down, see to precautions for nighttime. Going to bed, rest your mind and relax your body. Allow your soldiers physical repose.

2. Living at Ease

A tradition says, "In public life, forty is the age of strong service." Consider the capacities of your children and grandchildren, and even at the age of twenty have them experience public service.

Even when knights serve a lord they have a lot of free time. If they have unfortunately not entered the service of a lord—perhaps because of the early death of their parents, or because they're too far away for duty morning and night—so they live at ease with a lot of time on their hands, if they become negligent and don't maintain the family profession, they're almost like birds and beasts.

The *Great Learning*[1] says, "When immature people live at ease and act immorally, there is nothing they won't do."

Therefore knights living in leisure need instruction and admonition.

Rise early, wash and groom yourself, go out and meet your men, greet your guests, inspect the horses in the yard, and take a horseback ride. Eat breakfast promptly, then after washing your hands and cleaning your teeth practice swordsmanship, archery, shooting, or spear fighting. All of these are methods of improving the physique and developing coordination.

So betake yourself to a teacher, or invite a teacher over, without further delay. If you slack off for long, your hands and feet won't do as you will, you'll be uncoordinated, sluggish, and out of condition, inevitably compromising the work proper to a knight.

If you still have free time, read and reflect on the duties of warriors, study military science, and inspect your weapons and armor.

When a knight's will is like this, he is single-minded and undistracted; no wayward or distorted ideas occur to him. So Mencius said, "When people have no consistent occupation, they have no consistent mind."

3. Speech and Interaction

Speech and interaction are outcomes of intention. This is why it is

---

1 Great Learning: *Daxue*, a Confucian work, one of the so-called Four Books taught in Japanese primary schools in the Tokugawa period. The other three are the *Lunyu* or *Discourses and Sayings* of Confucius, the book of Mencius, and *The Mean*.

said that even a joke comes from thought. When a knight's speech is not correct, his conduct is invariably loose. One should be particularly wary of weak words and contemptible talk.

The technical terms for combat methods, military maneuvers, weaponry, and cavalry each have their proper usage. Speeches for ambassadors and for guests, for funerals and for feasts, for shrine and for court, each have their models. When speech is inconsiderate and interaction is inappropriate, this is impolite. It is sure to bring on trouble.

Topics that knights should typically talk about are issues of justice and injustice, tales of ancient battles, acts of bravery and righteousness past and present, the flourishing and decline of righteousness among warriors over the ages. All of these ought to be discussed in order to become alert to present-day errors. When you carp on other's errors, or criticize the government of the time, or chat about amusements, or talk about sex, your mind will inevitably get carried away, and your conduct will surely sink. The human heart is very interested in this, so don't say anything improper.

4. Walking, Standing, Sitting, Reclining

When you walk, don't take shortcuts, don't get in other people's way, don't act impolitely, don't say anything unnecessary. Once you've gone outside your own gate, be as if you were facing enemies. When you go out, you should forget home.

When sitting, keep your bearing correct; have your equipment at hand, and never forget to be on the alert for the unexpected.

When reclining, don't lie like a corpse. Keep your swords by your side, make sure security is strict by night.

You should do all your work in advance of others.

Generally speaking, in the way of knighthood, if you let your mind wander for even a while, you'll surely lose constancy in an emergency, and your whole life's labor will be lost in a single incident.

Since we can't know when an emergency may arise, how could we be lax? The *Records of Manners* says, "What makes people human is courtesy. The beginning of courtesy is in presenting a proper appearance, regulating your facial expression, and harmonizing your speech. Once your appearance is proper, your expression is regulated, and your speech is harmonious, then courtesy is there."

5. Clothing, Food, and Housing

If you are ashamed of poor clothing and poor food, and want a comfortable dwelling, you are not a man of will.

Clothing, food, and housing all have class distinctions. When excessive, they are immoderate and expensive, exhausting finances and making military preparedness impossible. When they are substandard, the motive is invariably stinginess, which isn't right either. To keep the correct moderation is the rule of knights.

Generally speaking, there are limitations to the attire of knights. In practice, it always has to be suitable for military readiness. There are norms for dimension and design.

Unpolished rice should be the staple of the diet, to share the same fare as the soldiers. Knights who are sickly and have digestive disorders should nourish themselves physically for the rest of their lives, while having the courage to be constant to death all along.

Housing should be given little thought. When your house is comfortable and your rooms are beautiful, your mind is on your home—this is not the mentality of a man of will. The dimensions and functional layout of your house should of course conform to military style.

Legend says that when Emperor Yao reigned over the land, he didn't wear brocade or finery; his palace walls and residence were not plastered, the beams, rafters, and pillars were not planed. Reeds grew all over the grounds and yet he didn't have them cut. He kept out the cold with deerskin. His clothes were only enough to cover him. He ate unpolished grain, with spinach soup. Because of their labor, he didn't infringe upon the people's time when they were tilling and spinning. Humbling his heart and minimizing his ambition, he pursued a course avoiding artificial contrivance in anything.

6. Money and Material Things

Money is customarily used for providing for the impoverished, helping out the destitute, eliminating shortages, inviting savants, and gathering knights. Material things are for fulfilling present needs.

The way for a knight to be is to devote yourself to your lord, constant to death all along the path. This is a maxim of men of old. If you are stingy with money and take an interest in material things, martial duty will be missing and you'll hardly be able to forget home in an emergency.

Those who are intensely concerned with their homes abandon duty, flee death, bring censure on themselves and disgrace their fathers and grandfathers. What is there to enjoy about having a human face but an animal mind?

Throughout history there have been countless wealthy people who lost their nations and destroyed their families, or traded themselves for money; how can we be casual about this?

The money that circulates in society is society's wealth, not the wealth of one man. Profitably exchanged, it makes myriad things available. That is why it is called wealth.

People with money all speak of avoiding expense and don't know how to spend. When gold and jewels fill the halls and there are money and goods in the storerooms, yet one doesn't know how to use it, the wealth of the world stagnates in one place and does not work for society. What is more costly than that?

When people like money, they usually hoard it, so sages don't consider gold and silver themselves to constitute wealth, and they don't value hard-to-get goods. How much more confused it is to store pottery, paintings, bronze and iron vessels, considering this to be wealth, trading a thousand pieces of gold for this!

7. Food, Drink, and Sexual Desire

Food, drink, and sex are humans' main desires. Food and drink are for nourishing the physical body, to act with courtesy and morality. Sexual desire is to produce heirs, and appease lust.

Everyone has natural measures. Knights are chiefs over the three civilian classes, with even more burdensome business, their professional responsibilities being extremely serious—how can we fail to be careful?

Eating too much causes illness, and drinking too much starts arguments. Or else you get sleepy and feel heavy, so you're lazy about a lot of things, you neglect your occupation, and your work piles up. So the cost is very great.

When sexual promiscuity leads to domestic arguments, clandestine engagements, and loss of vital energy, then plans do not succeed. The responsibility is heavy and the road is long, so this is considered an important admonition.

8. Falconry and Hunting

Falconry and hunting are ancient institutions.

Birds and beasts that ravage fields and gardens should be killed as a matter of course. The way to be a knight involves knowing the lay of the land, the defiles and dangers, distances, mountains and rivers; surveying the varieties of customs, popular songs, and local opinion; personally going into the marshes and forests wielding bow and arrow, gun, sword, and spear, becoming nimble of hand and foot, training your body; considering the abilities of your knights and soldiers, and reviewing the warriors' exercises.

Knights must not fail to work diligently at these things, but there are proper times for them, appropriate seasons. If you disregard the time and ignore the season, you ravage the fields and gardens and waste the people's work even worse than birds and beasts.

Everything a knight does, even be it entertainment, always has a reason. When you don't assess relative importance, you're always liable to be destructive.

9. Giving and Receiving

Giving and receiving include the duties of ruler and subject, superior and subordinate, and the courtesies of social relations, about which knights must be circumspect.

In the laws it says, "When the army has no money, warriors do not enlist. When the army gives no rewards, warriors do not go. A fish is found hooked where there's tasty bait; there will always be men willing to risk death where there are serious rewards."

When fish take the bait, they get hooked; when people receive salaries, they obey their superiors. Enlisting people by rewarding salaries is an ancient system. Even if you have the wherewithal, if you don't distribute it soldiers won't come follow you. You'll just be an ordinary man, an isolated individual.

If you pay too much, your resources will run dry and salaries will be stinting; then how can you arrange military readiness? Therefore the rule for knighthood is to calculate income and expenses, and consider proper measure in payment and prizes.

When prizes and payment are not made in a principled way, then men of principle will not enlist. A tradition says, "Employing moral men is not a matter of money. Offers of inducement aren't accepted even by beggars." Should we not be circumspect?

When acceptance is ethical, it's not a matter of the material value, but whether it's proper to accept. If there is anything unethical or unprincipled involved, even an enormous salary, or nationwide authority, should not be accepted.

As for knights serving in office who want to get more than their salaries, beyond their position, in excess of their measure, do they want extra spending money for extravagance? Or what about the vulgar who stint to save; do they want rooms full of gold? Both are unreasonable.

Giving and receiving are matters of which knights ought to be careful. Some say that for a knight, instead of stinting to save money, it's better to spend yet still have a surplus.

10. Instruction of Heirs

The gratitude of heirs is natural, produced by continuity of bloodline. No social relationship is closer. After we die, if our heirs are wayward, our families will die out and our people will perish. How can we withhold instruction and admonition out of excessive affection?

For knights, robust manhood means bravery. If you do not admonish those you love most and teach them faithfulness and courage, you are not a man of will, and not a humane man.

Generally speaking, children's disposition is simply natural; they do not as yet have a basis for autonomy. Their habits grow day by day and increase month after month; you should be very careful about the manifestations of good and bad impulses. Zhang Huangqu[1] said, "Males and females these days are already spoiled rotten from childhood; when they grow up, they become worse and worse." He also said, "Failing to instruct children on account of affection is called spoiling your children."

Knights' instruction of their heirs should see to it that their knowledge is accurate, their conduct is courageous, and they are trustworthy in their affairs. So as their intelligence emerges, consider wrong and right, admonish the wrong and praise the right, cultivate their courage so they can't be intimidated. Don't do anything by deceit, however minor it may be. For sport, have them practice the rituals of bow and arrow and hobby-horse. Conversation should all be about the ethics of warriorhood, courtesy and deference. To keep their vital energy complete, minimizing sexual desires, teach them literature. If they get into the habit of memorization, however, or amuse themselves with poetry and composition, they forget Japanese customs and want Chinese fashions.

Mingdao[2] said, "A hundred amusements rob you of will. If you become obsessed, even with books, you'll lose your will by yourself." Individuals have different temperaments, so they should be educated and trained according to their degree of seriousness and transparency. Once children can understand speech, choose tutors and consider companions; don't let their character become degraded.

---

1   Zhang Huangqu: Zhang Cai, a great neo-Confucian scholar of the Song dynasty, a contemporary of the famous Cheng brothers. Many of Zhang's sayings are cited along with those of the Cheng brothers in the neo-Confucian classic Jinsilu, in Japanese Kinshiroku, an annotated compilation of citations from the Song neo-Confucian masters made by Zhu Xi, whose work was the main authority for so-called Shushigaku, or Zhu Xi Studies, the state-sponsored school of neo-Confucianism espoused by Hayashi Razan, under whom Yamaga Soko once studied.

2   Mingdao: Cheng Hao, 1032-1085, one of the famous Cheng brothers associated with the development of neo-Confucian idealism in Song dynasty China.

The interaction between teacher and disciple should be most respectful. Military texts should not be placed on a dirty seat; they should only be opened after washing the hands and rinsing the mouth.

As for the education of girls, this requires extreme care. Most methods teach weakness, but that is a big mistake. The wife of a knight has to take care of household tasks in her husband's place, because he is always at court and doesn't know about domestic matters. Men don't know about domestic affairs, and women don't speak of public affairs; in making a home, they distinguish inside and outside. "Men and women don't use the same wardrobe; a wife doesn't presume to hang her clothes on her husband's hangers. She treats her parents-in-law properly."

From the Han through the Tang dynasties, there were women who died dutifully guarding their chastity; the wives of military leaders all over the country never altered their standards on account of prosperity or decline, never had a change of heart on account of survival or destruction. Some of them ran afoul of brigands, others died at the hands of enemies. How could such morality, such chastity, be accomplished by teaching weakness?

Women are mainly yin; their bodies are soft, their minds are submissive. This is their natural character, so in action they are pliant and obedient. They should be disciplined to be decisive, and their games and conversation should not be anything lewd. When you teach them the proper principles of duty, and show them the true meaning of warriorhood, then martial conduct is correct, so the main avenue of social morality is clear.

BIBLIOGRAPHY

Asayama Ensho, ed. *Rokujo Engi.* Tokyo, Sankibo Busshorin, 1935.

Bi Yuan, *Xu Zizhitongjian.* Shanghai Guji Chubanshe 1987.

Chen Shou, *San Guo Zhi.* Beijing, Zhonghua Shuju, 1959.

Doi Takeo, *Omote to Ura.* Tokyo, Kobundo, 1985.

Du Yu, *Chunqiujingzhuan Jijie.* Shanghai Guji Chubanshe, 1988.

Fan Shoukang, *Zhongguo Zhexueshi Gangyao.* Taibei Kaiming Shudian, 1964.

Fan Xuanling, ann. *Guanzi.* Shanghai Guji Chubanshe, 1987.

Fujimoto Tsuchishige, ed. *Bankei Zenji Hogoshu.* Tokyo, Shunjusha, 1971.

Funai Koyu, *Jinsei Gorin no Sho.* Kyoto, PHP Kenkyusho, 1985.

Gao You, ed. *Zhanguo Ce.* Shanghai Shedian, 1987.

Goto Mitsumura, ed. *Hakuin Osho Zenshu.* Tokyo, Ryuginsha, 1934.

Han Fei, *Han Fei zi.* Shanghai Guji Chubanshe, 1989.

Ha-u Ho-o (pseud.), *Gendai Sojizen Hyoron.* Tokyo, Mizuho Shoten, 1970.

Hirano Jinkei, *Nihon no Kamigami.* Tokyo, Kodansha, 1983.

Hong Liangji, ed. *Chunqiu Zuozhuangu.* Beijing, Zhonghua Shuju, 1987.

Hosaka Koji, ed. *Tsurezuregusa.* Tokyo, Gakutosha, n.d.

Hosaka Koji, ed. *Koji, Seigo, Kotowaza.* Tokyo, Gakutosha, 1973.

Ikebe Yoshinori, *Nihon Hosei-shi Shomoku Kaidai.* Tokyo, Daitokaku, 1918.

Imamichi Tomonobu, *Bi ni Tsuite.* Tokyo, Kodansha, 1973.

Inoue Tetsujiro, ed. *Bushido Shu.* Tokyo, Shunyodo, 1920.

Inoue Tetsujiro, ed. *Bushido Sosho.* Tokyo, Hakubunkan, 1905.

Itasaka Gen, *Nihonjin no Ronri Kozo.* Tokyo, Kodansha, 1991.

Ito Shunko, ed. *Eihei Koroku Chukai Zensho.* Tokyo, Komeisha, 1964.

Jiang Yinxiang, tr. *Shijing yaozhu.* Beijingshi Zhongguoshudian, 1982.

Jojima Masayoshi, ed. *Hagakure.* Tokyo, Shinjinbutsu-Orai Sha, 1976.

Kabutogi Shoko, ed. *Nichiren Bunshu.* Tokyo, Iwanami Shoten, 1968.

Kanatani Osamu, tr. *Lunyu.* Tokyo, Iwanami Shoten, 1963.

Kanatani Osamu, tr. *Sunzi.* Tokyo, Iwanami Shoten, 1963.

Kanatani Osamu, tr. *Zhuangzi.* Tokyo, Iwanami Shoten, 1983.

Kaneko Daiei, ed. *Kyogoshinsho.* Tokyo, Iwanami Shoten, 1947.

Kawasaki Yasuyuki, etc., ed. *Shukyoshi.* Tokyo, Sansen Shuppansha, 1965.

Kiriyama Yasuo, *Nenriki.* Tokyo, Tokuma Shoten, 1975.

Kobayashi Katsundo, tr. *Mengzi.* Tokyo, Iwanami Shoten, 1972.

Koda Rentaro, ed. *Shido Bunan Zenji shu.* Tokyo, Shunjusha, 1956.

Kubota Jun, ed. *Myoe Shonin Shu.* Tokyo, Iwanami Shoten, 1981.

Kusumoto Bunyu, *Sodai Jugaku no Zen Shiso Kenkyu.* Nagoya, Nisshindo Shoten, 1980.

Li Jiemin, tr. *Weiliaozi yaozhu.* Hebei Renmin Chubanshe, 1992.

Li Jiurui, *Xianqin Shizi Sixiang Gaishu.* Taibei Shudian, 1972.

Li Ling, *Simafa Yaozhu*. Hebei Peopleís Press, 1992.

Li Zhi, *Zangshu*. Taibei, Xuesheng Shuju, 1974.

Liu Ji, *Baizhan Qilue*. Hebei, Guangming Ribao Chubanshe, 1987.

Lu Zhan, *Song Sizi Shaoyao*. Taibei, Shijie Shuju, 1972.

Matsushita Konosuke, *Jissen Keiei Tetsugaku*. Kyoto, PHP Kenkyusho, 1978.

Matsushita Konosuke, *Keiei Kokorecho*. Kyoto, PHP Kenkyusho, 1974.

Mizunoue Tsutomu, *Ikkyu*. Tokyo, Chuokoronsha, 1978.

Mori Keizo, ed. *Kinsei Zenrin Genkoroku*. Tokyo, Nihon Tosho Senta, 1977.

Mori Senzo, ed. *Kinsei Kijin Den*. Tokyo, Iwanami Shoten, 1940.

Morita Shoma, *Meishin to Mozo*. Tokyo, Hakuyosha, 1983.

Muji Zenji, *Shasekishu*. Kyoto, Heiryakuji Shoten, 1933.

Nakahara Toju, *Nantenbo Angyaroku*. Tokyo, Hirakawa Shuppansha, 1984.

Odaka Kunio, *Nihonteki Keiei*. Kyoto, Chuokoronsha, 1984.

Ogawa Tamaki, etc., tr. *Shiki Retsuden*. Tokyo, Iwanami Shoten, 1975.

Nukariya Kaiten, *Wakan Meishi Sanzen Shu*. Tokyo, Shueisha, 1915.

Obashi Shunyu, ed. *Ippen Shonin Goroku*. Tokyo, Iwanami Shoten, 1985.

Ogiya Shozo, *Gendai Bijinesu Kingenshu*. Kyoto, PHP Kenkyusho, 1986.

Ogura Masahiko, *Chugoku Kodai Seiji Shiso Kenkyu*. Tokyo, Aoki Shoten, 1970.

Omori Sogen, *Ken to Zen*. Tokyo, Shunjusha, 1983.

Qiang Yiqing, ed. *Sima Bingfa*. Lian-A Chubanshe, 1981.

Sahashi Horyu, *Ningen Keizan*. Tokyo, Shunjusha, 1979.

Sakurai Yoshiro, *Chusei Nihon no Oken, Shukyo, Geino*. Kyoto, Jinbun Shoin, 1988.

Sato Taishun, ed. *Muchu Mondo*. Tokyo, Iwanami Shoten, 1935.

Sekiguchi Shindai, tr. *Makashikan*. Tokyo, Iwanami Shoten, 1966.

Shangshu Zhengyi, Taibei, Zhonghua Shudian, 1977.

Shibata Renzaburo, *Nemuri Kyoshiro Mujo Hikae*. Tokyo, Shunjusha, 1981.

Sueki Takehiro, *Toyo no Gori Shiso*. Tokyo, Kodansha, 1970.

Suzuki Daisetsu, *Imakita Kosen*. Tokyo, Shunjusha, 1975.

Suzuki Tesshin, ed. *Suzuki Shosan Dojin Zenshu*. Tokyo, Sankibo Busshorin, 1962.

Takahashi Junichi, ed. *Heike Monogatari*. Tokyo, Kodansha, 1972.

Takeda Shinji, tr., *Yijing*. Tokyo, Iwanami Shoten, 1969.

Takuan Zenji, *Roshi Kowa*. Tokyo, To-A-Do Shobo, 1910.

Tiannan Yisou (pseud.), *Zhouyi Qigong*. Changchun Chubanshe, 1990.

Tsukamoto Zenryu, ed. *Sekai no Rekishi. 4: To to Indo*. Tokyo, Chuokoronsha, 1975.

Ueyama Shunbei, etc., *Mikkyo no Sekai*. Osaka Shoseki, 1982.

Wang Yi, ed. *Huang Di Yinfujing Quanshu*. Xian, Xiaxi Liuyun Chubanshe, 1992.

Watsuji Tetsuro, ed. *Shobogenzo Zuimonki*. Tokyo, Iwanami Shoten, 1929.

Wei Xing, etc., ed. *Rujia Zhenyanlu*. Inner Mongolia People's Press, 1997.

Yamada Kodo, ed. *Zenmon Hogoshu*. Tokyo, Koyukan, 1895.

Yamazaki Ichisada, ed. *Sekai no Rekishi, 6: So to Gen*. Tokyo, Chuokoronsha, 1976.

INDEX